JOHN P. HOLLAND

JOHN P. HOLLAND

1841-1914

Inventor of the Modern Submarine

By Richard Knowles Morris

University of South Carolina Press

First cloth edition published in 1966 by the United States Naval Institute
Reprinted 1980 by the Arno Press
First University of South Carolina paperback edition published in 1998

01   00   99   98   5   4   3   2   1

Manufactured in the United States of America

Library of Congress Cataloging-in-Publication Data

Morris, Richard Knowles.
    John P. Holland, 1841–1914 : inventor of the modern submarine /
Richard K. Morris.—1st pbk. ed.
        p.   cm.
    Originally published: Annapolis, Md. : United States Naval
Institute, 1966.
    Includes bibliographical references and index.
    ISBN 1–57003–236–X
    1. Holland, John Philip, 1841?–1914.   2. Submarines (Ships)—
History.   3. Naval architects—United States—Biography.
4. Inventors—United States—Biography.   I. Title.
VM140.H6M57   1998
625.8'257'092—dc21
    [B]   97-24118

To the memory of
my father
Clifford R. Morris, Sr.

ACKNOWLEDGMENTS

In the preparation of this biography of John Philip Holland it was necessary for me to rely upon a wide circle of friends and acquaintances for information and assistance. I am not unmindful of the many unnamed individuals who each in his own way contributed to the final product. Yet I would be remiss if I failed to acknowledge my debt of gratitude to those whose specific acts of kindness and expert assistance far exceeded my expectations. If this book has successfully recounted the life and works of a great submarine pioneer, and related his accomplishments to the over-all history of submarine navigation, then the achievement in no small measure is to be attributed to those whose names appear below. I alone must be responsible for errors of commission or omission and for any other shortcomings which may become apparent to the reader.

I am particularly indebted to the officials of the Electric Boat Division of the General Dynamics Corporation, Groton, Connecticut, for their long-standing interest in the Morris Collection of Holland Memorabilia. This collection, I am happy to say, is housed in the unique and excellent Submarine Library originated by the Electric Boat Division and now established in Gilmore Hall at the U. S. Naval Submarine Base, New London. Without the co-operation of the staff of the Submarine Library, especially its former directors, Frank J. Anderson and Commander Edward R. Eberle, U. S. Navy (Retired), and the indefatigable librarian, Mrs. Emery E. Bassett, this book would not represent the authoritative account of submarine history that I believe it to be. Commander Eberle read the manuscript with great care and with attention to technical detail. Also, at Electric Boat, I wish to thank Carleton Shugg, former president, and S. J. Wornom, Jr., public relations manager, for the many courtesies which they have extended to me.

For his inestimable role in helping me to close the gaps in the hitherto scanty record of Holland's Irish years, I am sincerely grateful to Father Martin Coen, professor of history, St. Mary's College, Galway. A former curate in Holland's native village of Liscannor, Father Coen's enthusiasm for my subject has been most contagious.

From Ireland, also, came the amicable co-operation of William O'Brien, of Dublin, a co-editor of *Devoy's Post Bag,* without whose magnum opus the importance of the Fenian movement in Holland's career might well have remained confused and underestimated.

The opportunity afforded me to collaborate with Courtlandt Canby on an article for *American Heritage* marked the beginning of a genuine friendship on which I have leaned heavily for inspiration. Mr. Canby, one of the editors of *Dynamic America* and the editor of *Life's Epic of Man,* led me to new founts of information. He generously shared with me his extensive knowledge of the events with which I was concerned. To the late Dr. Frederick V. Zoref, curator of the Paterson Museum, Paterson, New Jersey, special tribute is due for his courtesy in providing me with access to the documents in the museum. I wish to thank Edward M. Graf of Paterson for his answers to my inquiries concerning Holland's residency in that city. Thanks go also to Earle Bailey, technician, Trinity College, Hartford, Connecticut, and to John F. Harris, teacher and former student of mine, for the care with which they handled, developed, and printed the crisp, sixty-year-old negatives in the Morris Collection.

The declaration of my indebtedness would be incomplete were I to fail to mention the hospitality of Floyd D. Houston and his wife, Ruth Tuthill Houston, on the occasion of a cruise to explore the Goldsmith and Tuthill Basin at New Suffolk, Long Island, the scene of Holland's activities at the close of the nineteenth century and the site of the first submarine base in the United States. We shared photographs and records of those early days, and we discussed the submarine models that have gained for Mr. Houston a national reputation.

The background for writing this book was greatly enhanced by the rare privilege granted a civilian to experience firsthand a training cruise on board a modern submarine. To Commander Howard E. Blum, U. S. Navy, and to the officers and crew of the USS *Sablefish* (SS-303), a fleet snorkel boat, I tender the warmest praise for their courtesy, their patience, and their meticulous instruction, not to mention the gallons of "Java" I consumed while on board. I wish also to acknowledge the interest and encouragement of the late Rear Admiral E. W. Sylvester, U. S. Navy (Retired), when he was director of The Mariners Museum, Newport News, Virginia; as well as the interest and encouragement of two veterans of submarine warfare, Rear Admiral Walter T. Griffith, U. S. Navy (Retired), and Admiral Lawrence R. Daspit, former Deputy Commander, Submarine Force, U. S. Atlantic Fleet.

It is highly probable that no book is brought to completion without the moral and material support of one's immediate family. This book is no exception. It really began in the family attic more than a dozen years ago when I rediscovered the diaries and voluminous papers of my grandfather, Charles A. Morris, which my father had the foresight to preserve. Then followed my mother's prodding, with liberal sprinklings of forgiveable confidence in my ability to put the papers into some meaningful order. But the successful culmination of this project would have been quite impossible without the tireless devotion of my wife, Anne, who typed the entire manuscript, served as my most constructive critic, and made innumerable concessions to my disruption of domestic routine—all at a personal sacrifice beyond the hope of recompense:

RICHARD K. MORRIS

Newington, Conn.
1 December 1965

TABLE OF CONTENTS

LIST OF ILLUSTRATIONS

15. A schematic drawing of the *Holland VI* by an artist of the *New York Herald*, 15 April 1898.
16. John P. Holland in the conning tower of his submarine, April, 1898, Perth Amboy, New Jersey. (*Submarine Library*)
17. The *Holland VI* prior to her trial before the U. S. Navy's Board of Inspection on 20 April 1898. (*Brown Brothers*)
18. The *Holland VI* and the *George P. Roe* off Old Orchard Shoal Light in Raritan Bay during the trial on 20 April 1898. (*Brown Brothers*)
19. Officials and guests of the John P. Holland Torpedo Boat Company on board a tug, with the *Holland VI* alongside, on 20 April 1898. (*Brown Brothers*)
20. The *Holland VI* before the trial dive on 20 April 1898. (*Brown Brothers*)
21. At the Raritan Dry Dock on the day of the trial, 20 April 1898, *left to right,* Walter Thompson, superintendent of the Raritan Dry Dock; Charles A. Morris, superintending engineer of the John P. Holland Torpedo Boat Company; John P. Holland, inventor of the *Holland VI;* and Mr. Matthews, a stockholder in the John P. Holland Torpedo Boat Company. (*Brown Brothers*)
22. The *Holland VI* surfacing after a dive of one hour's duration, 20 April 1898. (*Brown Brothers*)
23. Following the trial on 20 April 1898, the *Holland VI* is awaiting a tow back to Perth Amboy. (*Brown Brothers*)
24. The *Holland VI* in the Erie Basin Dry Dock, Brooklyn, New York, 26 May— 1 June 1898. The positioning of the propeller and rudder are clearly shown. (*Submarine Library*)
25. The little *Holland VI,* forerunner of the technological developments of the twentieth century, is dwarfed here by the towering masts of a brig whose era was waning. (*Submarine Library*)
26. The "cage," a torpedo loading device, at the Atlantic Yacht Basin, Brooklyn, New York, in the summer of 1898. *Left to right,* Frank T. Cable, John Wilson, and William F. C. Nindemann. (*Submarine Library*)
27. The *Holland VI* in the Morris Heights shipyard on the Harlem River in New York during the winter of 1898-99. William F. C. Nindemann, *in the foreground.* (*Submarine Library*)
28. Isaac L. Rice, founder and first president of the Electric Boat Company of which the Holland Torpedo Boat Company became the major subsidiary, 7 February 1899. (*Submarine Library*)
29. John P. Holland at the time of the acceptance of the *Holland VI* by the U. S. government, 1900. (*Brown Brothers*)

Theodore Bailey, chief engineer; Lewis Eckert, chief hull draftsman. *Back row:* George Duncan, office boy; Grant Edgar, electrical draftsman; Arthur Newman, chief engineering draftsman; Paul Andrine, mechanical draftsman; William Curtiss, mechanical draftsman; Hugo Grieshaber, hull draftsman; Walter Leonard, mechanical draftsman. (*Submarine Library*)

41. USS *Moccasin* (later *A-4*) during trials in Little Peconic Bay, Long Island, summer of 1902. (*Whitaker Memorial Collection. Courtesy: Floyd D. Houston*)

42. New Suffolk Basin, 1902. *At left:* USS *Shark* (later *A-7*) and tender *Kelpie*. *Background:* USS *Craven*, surface torpedo boat. *At right:* USS *Moccasin* and USS *Adder* (later *A-2*). (*Courtesy: Nat Hathaway*)

43. New Suffolk Basin, 1902. Outboard boats, *at left*, USS *Moccasin; at right*, USS *Shark*. (*Courtesy: Nat Hathaway*)

44. New Suffolk Basin, November, 1902. *In foreground, left to right:* USS *Fulton*, USS *Porpoise*, USS *Adder*. *In background:* USS *Shark* and USS *Moccasin*. (*Whitaker Memorial Collection. Courtesy: Floyd D. Houston*)

45. USS *Holland* at the U. S. Naval Academy, Annapolis, Maryland. Captain and crew, *left to right:* Harry Wahab, chief gunner's mate; Kane; Richard O. Williams, chief electrician; Chief Gunner Owen Hill, commanding; Igoe; Michael Malone; Barnett Bowie, chief machinist's mate; Simpson; Rhinelander. *In the background*, a monitor of the *Arkansas* class, *at left*, and the USS *Terror*, a pre-Spanish-American War monitor. (*Official U. S. Navy Photograph*)

46. John P. Holland, in 1912, when he retired from public life. This is his last known portrait. (*Brown Brothers*)

PREFACE TO THE 1998 PAPERBACK EDITION

Thirty-one years ago this biography was first published. It was reprinted in 1980 but has since become unavailable. Now the University of South Carolina Press offers this updated edition of what is recognized, here and abroad, as the standard biography of the noted Irish-American inventor of the modern submarine, John Philip Holland.

No written historical account can be definitive; the present work is not an exception. Revisionists always lurk in the wings of the play called "History." But facts are facts; what happened, happened. Proof to the contrary rests with those who object, in whole or in part, to the portrayal found in these pages.

The purpose of this reprint of Holland's biography is to remove any factual errors in the first edition, to supplement the account of his life with information not yet reported, to preserve more than fifteen years of scholarly research, and, further, to secure the subject's rightful place in submarine development.

New material has surfaced that was not at hand when the original work was undertaken. Specifically, the Graf Collection at the Paterson Museum (New Jersey)—a collection, now legally open to scholars, that enriches our understanding of Holland's early submarine experiments in this country and provides additional information about the man and his family. Also, several hitherto undisclosed monographs have reappeared that shed light on Holland as a teacher in the United States and in Ireland. This material is incorporated in a supplementary chapter found at the end of this volume.

I am most grateful to Fred Kameny, Editor in Chief of the University of South Carolina Press, and his staff, for recognizing Holland's historical importance and for their editorial expertise in bringing this biography back to the public's attention. Others deserve my thanks for their help and support in making this second edition possible: Giacomo de Stefano, Director of the Patterson Museum; Edward A. Smyk, Passaic County Historian; Stephen Finnigan, Curator, *Nautilus* Memorial, Submarine Force Library and Museum, Groton, Connecticut; James J. Gallagher, National Chairman of the Ancient Order of the Hibernians in America, and his cohorts Leo Shea and George Ryan. Thanks, too, to Thomas K. McGoonan for sharing with me his fine scale model of the *Holland VI*.

My first wife, Anne, who had so much to do with the first edition, has since died. To my present wife, Alice Getchell Morris, I owe a vote of thanks for her time and encouragement in the preparation of the present volume.

INTRODUCTION

On 26 May 1958, the USS *Skipjack* (SSN-585), the world's first submarine designed from the keel up for optimum underwater performance, was launched at the Electric Boat Company Yards after being christened by Mrs. George H. Mahon. As this submarine slid down the ways into the Thames River at Groton, Connecticut, it is doubtful that anyone thought of a similar launching more than sixty years before when John Philip Holland's little fifty-three-foot submersible, the *Holland VI*, was christened at Elizabethport, New Jersey. This craft was destined to become the first submarine of the U. S. Navy. Yet, if this Irish-born teacher-inventor could have seen the *Skipjack*, he would have recognized that some of his own theories for "the true submarine" had finally been achieved.[1]

Who was this quiet, unassuming man—John Philip Holland—who dreamed of undersea craft and of flying machines, as well? If we turn to the literature on submarines to find an answer, we will discover that this literature falls into three main categories: general histories, memoirs, and catalogues or inventories. While the general histories provide at least a cursory record of antecedents, they sometimes leave the reader with a false conception of the true history. The number of accounts beginning with the glass barrel of Alexander the Great exemplifies the confusion surrounding the subject, the lack of proper definition, and the temptation to report at length on the legion of paper schemes which are so fanciful as to be unworthy even of a writer of science fiction. The memoirs of submariners—unpretentious and basically chronicles—make excellent reading. They are set in great historical events and provide some technical understanding of the subject, but they contribute little to the over-all history of submarine development. The catalogues or inventories list significant data in current form, but devote no space to the saga of the brave men who built and operated the early underwater boats.

Beyond these sources, there is a surprising scarcity of printed material on submarines. No doubt the secrecy which often enshrouds military innovations accounts for the paucity of information and the inaccuracy of much that has been printed. Therefore, one must turn to forgotten monographs, private letters, diaries, and other documents, not readily accessible, in order to reconstruct the story of the submarine. To this end, the following pages devote attention to the evolution of underwater craft and to the men whose imaginative conception of submarines made these craft what they are today.

The task is clear: to focus, not to diffuse. The focus here will be on John Philip Holland—inventor, designer, and builder of the U. S. Navy's first practical submarine —the man who did so much to make the underwater boat a vital aspect of sea power. His labors earned for him the title of "father of the modern submarine." Yet, it must be clear from the outset that a machine as complicated as the submarine is not the creation of a single genius striving through one brief period of history. A man and his works may belong to his own generation, but both are molded by the achievements of previous generations and are judged by the generations which follow. So it must be with Holland.

JOHN P. HOLLAND

CHAPTER ONE

THE LAUNCHING
1897

On Monday, 17 May 1897, the late edition of *The New York Times* carried a masterpiece of cautious reporting in its account of a ship launching earlier that day:

... the *Holland,* the little cigar-shaped vessel owned by her inventor, which may or may not play an important part in the navies of the world in the years to come, was launched from Lewis Nixon's shipyard this morning.[1]

The "cigar-shaped vessel" was a submarine; the place, Lewis Nixon's Crescent Shipyard in Elizabethport, New Jersey. Early that morning workmen had stirred about the marine railway, hurriedly hammering together a scaffolding to serve as a platform for the coming ceremony.

By eight o'clock a crowd had gathered along the bulkheads on either side of the railway. At the foot of the launching platform stood those persons most directly concerned with the underwater craft. One was Lieutenant Lewis Nixon, U. S. Navy (Retired), owner of the Crescent Shipyard and designer of the battleships *Oregon, Indiana,* and *Massachusetts,* talking with Lt. Cmdr. William W. Kimball, U. S. Navy, and Arthur Busch, chief constructor at the yard. Kimball, a leading advocate of submarines, was a long-time friend of the inventor of the boat that stood on the ways. Assistant Naval Constructor George H. Rock, who represented the government, was nearby. Mrs. Nixon chatted with Mrs. Isaac Lawrence, a generous investor in the John P. Holland Torpedo Boat Company. The treasurer of that company, Elihu B. Frost, gave last-minute instructions to Superintending Engineer Charles A. Morris.

The launching had been scheduled for 8:30 A.M., but there was some delay. The flooding tide in the Arthur Kill threatened to cancel the event. Lewis Nixon, however, insisted that the christening could not take place until the inventor of the boat arrived. Finally, almost unobserved, a slender man of moderate stature, wearing a dark suit and a black bowler, with a large cravat bulging under his winged collar, slipped through the crowd to the railway and energetically scaled the ladder to the launching platform. There he paused beside Mrs. Nixon, who held a champagne bottle wrapped in red, white, and

3

blue bunting. The tense expression on the little man's face was almost hidden behind thick spectacles and a walrus mustache. Whatever thoughts the crowd may have entertained as to the fate or fortune of the strange craft, there was no doubt that this moment belonged to her inventor, John Philip Holland.

"Wedge up! Saw away!"

Heavy hammers thudded, and a saw bit into a key timber in the cradle. Mrs. Nixon swung the champagne bottle against the steel nose of the craft; the sparkling contents spattered her brown suit and a fragment of glass cut her hand. Above the sound of sliding, crushing timbers rose the shouts of the crowd, the clamor of ships' bells, and the screech of steam whistles. The fifty-three-foot, seventy-five-ton *Holland VI* stirred, slid down the ways, and splashed into the waters of Arthur Kill.

For an ominous moment the boat settled alarmingly low in the water. The crowd grew silent. Then she lifted to ride "trim and true to her estimated waterline," and a second tumult arose. A message chalked on the hull by a cynical workman, "This vessel when launched will never float," dissolved in her baptism.

A forty-five-star national ensign, donated by Lewis Nixon, unfolded on the *Holland VI*'s stern staff and spread proudly in the breeze that blew down from Newark Bay; and the staff safely cleared the long bowsprit of a steam yacht moored to an outer dock.[2]

It would have been difficult for anyone present at the launching of the *Holland VI* to have foreseen the full consequences of the event. No one there could have foretold that the strange looking craft would finally be commissioned into the United States Navy as its first submarine. No one could have envisioned the great submarine fleets of Great Britain and Japan for which the *Holland VI* would become the prototype, nor the assiduous care with which Germany and Russia would copy the *Holland VI*'s masterful mechanical innovations. Few people, anywhere, were capable that day of appraising the launching as the beginning of a revolution in naval warfare. It would have been completely in the realm of fantasy at that time for anyone to have predicted that some sixty years later the naval architects responsible for the incredible technical complications of the U. S. Navy's nuclear-attack *Skipjack*-class submarines would compare their hydrodynamic qualities with that progenitor of all submarines, the *Holland VI*.

On the day the *Holland VI* went into the water, John Philip Holland had already spent twenty-six years of his life trying to solve the problems of submarine construction and navigation.

Four other craft built by the Irish-born inventor had preceded the *Holland VI* down the ways of as many shipyards; and the *Plunger*, his fifth boat, was nearing completion at Baltimore. Other submarine inventors had gone before him, and more would follow; but Holland would take a unique place in the history of the submarine both for his technical improvements in design and for his persistence in developing the underwater craft.[3]

With the boat launched in May, 1897, Holland had nearly reached his goal. A letter to Lieutenant Commander Kimball revealed confidence seldom present in his earlier endeavors: "I don't think I can improve on the arrangements or general features of this design. It represents a powerful and effective boat."[4] Kimball, in turn, declared that Holland had "a wonderful nose for smelling out basic mechanical principles, with a capacity for practically applying those principles, and with a bulldog tenacity in hanging on and making things work under discouraging conditions."[5]

The high stage of advancement achieved by Holland in an invention as complicated as the submarine could only be accomplished with considerable knowledge of the successes and failures of his predecessors and with keen insight into the problems involved. Writing for the marine edition of *Cassier's Magazine* (London) a few months before launching his sixth boat, John Holland demonstrated both his familiarity with the history of submarine development and his understanding of the technical difficulties which had long plagued designers of underwater vessels.[6] He reviewed the efforts of Cornelius Van Drebbel, David Bushnell, Robert Fulton, Lodner Philips, Charles Brun and Siméon Bourgeois, James McClintock and Baxter Watson. He also gave fair treatment to his own contemporaries: O. S. Halstead (although not by name), Claude Goubet, and Thorsten Nordenfeldt. He seemed unaware, however, of the work of Wilhelm Bauer, an Austrian cavalry officer whose perseverance in submarine development rivaled his own.

Of all the early attempts at submarine development, Holland had the highest praise for the work of the American patriot David Bushnell who invented the *Turtle*, a one-man submersible used in the Revolutionary War. Holland wrote of Bushnell's accomplishments: "If some one of the large number of experimenters who endeavored to construct submarine boats since that time had contented himself with closely copying the valuable features of Bushnell's vessel, instead of starting out with radically new and untried plans, and without having any experience to guide him, we should have had success to record instead of an almost unbroken list of failures."[7]

Holland knew of the audacious attack which the diminutive *Turtle*, manned by Ezra Lee, had made on HMS *Eagle* in New York Harbor in August, 1776. The plan had been to attach a charge of gunpowder to the ship's bottom and to explode it with a time fuse, but copper sheathing on the hull of the *Eagle* presumably had prevented fastening the charge to the ship.

Unquestionably John Holland was impressed by the fact that Bushnell had incorporated in the *Turtle*, however crude the original materials, the essential elements of a submarine boat. Bushnell had made the submarine a potentially formidable weapon of marine warfare. He was the first to employ piston pumps to empty ballast tanks, to rig a safety device in the form of ballast that could be released in an emergency, to devise a depth indicator, to design a conning tower or its ancestor, to maintain a small reserve of positive buoyancy, to master longitudinal stability, and to use underwater explosives. Holland developed each of these elements in more sophisticated form. Yet to operate the *Turtle*, with all her paraphernalia crowded into a six-foot shell, was well-nigh beyond the skill of a single man. Her attack on the *Eagle* was a feat of daring the more incredible because of the complexity of the machine which Bushnell had designed. Recognizing the handicaps imposed upon Bushnell in terms of knowledge and machinery available to him in his day, Holland generously conceded that the American patriot deserved the epithet, "father of the submarine." Holland went even further, declaring: "Bushnell's remarkably complete vessel, by far the most effective submarine boat built before 1880, remained unappreciated in America, although his American Turtles might have prevented the capture of Washington and rendered America invulnerable to England in 1812 had they been in hands accustomed to their management."[8] The reference to the year 1880 was Holland's modest way of referring to his own *Fenian Ram*, his second boat, which, as we shall see, was a most remarkable craft.[9]

As for other submarine experimenters, Holland reviewed their contributions with care, discussing only those who had actually constructed and tested submarine boats. Paper schemes that were never turned into reality did not concern him. Unlike his younger contemporary and chief competitor in the United States, Simon Lake, Holland never claimed to have been influenced by fiction, although the first American edition of Jules Verne's *Twenty Thousand Leagues Under the Sea* was available in the bookstalls by the time that Holland arrived from Ireland.[10] However, his debt to an earlier *Nautilus*, that of Robert Fulton, was indeed substantial. Fulton, in 1801, had closely achieved the all-metal, porpoise-shaped hull which Holland favored. Fulton's innovations—the stern diving planes; a compressed air supply; and two modes of propulsion, one for the surface and one for submerged runs—were faithfully adopted by Holland.

The launching of the *Holland VI*, in 1897, set off arguments among naval architects and marine engineers as to whether she was a submarine, a submersible, or a semisubmersible. The use of these terms at the close of the nineteenth century raised more problems than it solved.

"Submarine" is a broad term. It is used loosely in reference to any vessel that operates submerged or partially submerged. The current use of the word commends the earlier, three-fold classification of underwater craft—a vessel designed to navigate totally submerged, to perform her operations under water, to remain independent of assistance from outside herself for extended periods of time. To move freely in the world of inner space, she must carry her own environment with her. A submarine's military function is to stay concealed and to attack from that favored position.

A submersible is a compromise submarine, constructed to perform her work with equal efficiency whether operating submerged or on the surface. To effect this compromise, the ratio of length to beam exceeds that of the submarine proper, enabling the submersible to compete with surface vessels in a seaway. Consequently, she boasts a larger reserve of positive buoyancy, increasing her freeboard when running on the surface. The result is a more limited performance submerged than that of the submarine. A submersible's military function is to "hit and run," acting as a surface raider that can strike and temporarily vanish, or as a submarine that can attack from beneath the waves and then blow her tanks to surface and finish the battle.

The semisubmersible is no longer built. She was a surface vessel designed so that her freeboard could be greatly reduced, making her a difficult target for the guns of a conventional warship. The semisubmersible was not created to operate beneath the surface of the sea. During the American Civil War, the Confederate States effectively employed these vessels, popularly known as "Davids." The Union Navy had its *Keokuk* and *Sputyen Duvyil*. Though interest in the semisubmersible is now largely historical, any account of the submarine should include mention of her, for all three types of vessels figure in the evolution of undersea boats.

In the nineteenth century, with the increase in attention given to those who favored the submersible as having greater safety and versatility, the development of the submarine proper was postponed. No one saw this issue more clearly, nor strove more energetically to counter the trend toward the submersible, than did John Holland. The *Holland VI* was still dependent upon the surface, though this was not to his liking. His goal had always been the submarine proper; but, he complained acidly, "The navy does not like submarines because there's no deck to strut on."

Sometime later, when it became evident that the capacity for submerged operation was being compromised in favor of superstructures cluttered with the accouterments of surface vessels—guns fore and aft and extensive stanchion-studded decks—Holland sent a memorandum to Lieutenant Commander W. Strother Smith, chairman of the Navy Department's Submarine Board. "Sweep out all interesting but useless devices that encumber the present boats. She [the submarine proper] cannot have a deck on which her men can enjoy sunlight."[11]

Holland searched unceasingly for the principles which would bring the submarine into her most perfect operational form. In the *Holland VI* he embodied those principles to a degree not previously attained by either his predecessors or contemporaries. This *Holland* was a diving or "porpoising" boat. Since she retained a small reserve of positive buoyancy even when submerged, it was necessary to use her power plant to drive her down in a dive and to give her sufficient submerged speed to ensure her positive control. Holland felt that the level-keel submergence technique, sponsored by Nordenfeldt, Lake, and others, was in large measure responsible for the developments which made of the submarine a submersible. He had handled the problem of longitudinal stability, which the level-keel boat was presumed to solve, by designing a low, fixed center of gravity. This center of gravity was ingeniously maintained by automatically compensating for weight loss owing to expenditure of fuel, torpedoes, or other materials by taking on board an equal weight of water in small trim tanks.

"The immovability of the water in large ballast tanks is arranged for by always filling the tanks chock-up; the small tanks that are used for securing the necessary delicate balance and trim are of such shape and so placed that the movement of water in them cannot practically alter the position of the centre of gravity of the boat as a whole."[12]

Holland was convinced that, by adhering to the diving principle, he could build boats capable of withstanding pressures at greater depths than could be attained in the level-keel boats built of the same materials. Hull sections would be nearly circular, producing a hull shape that would conform to optimum hydrodynamic flow lines. In fact, he was fond of comparing his boats to a porpoise, both in shape and agility. It became routine for the *Holland VI* to descend and rise at angles approaching fifteen degrees without at any time losing her stability. Skeptics and rivals thought that such angles were exceedingly dangerous. As surface observers, these critics erroneously concluded that the "wildly" porpoising craft operated at steep angles because of inherent defects in design.

When the *Holland VI* was launched, Holland's fifth boat, the *Plunger*, was nearing completion in Baltimore under government contract. The decision to build the *Holland VI* as a private venture was reached when it became evident that the Balti-

8

more boat was a clumsy monster. Much of the difficulty could be attributed to the huge, unrealistic steam plant installed for surface propulsion. In the building of the *Holland VI*, it was decided to return to the internal combustion engine which had served so well on the inventor's four earlier boats and which was now available in the improved Otto version. The cumbersome steam plant was therefore replaced with the compact Otto and combined with an electric motor for running submerged. This combination was to be successfully employed in all subsequent submarines of the United States Navy up to the introduction of diesel engines in the 1911 E-boats.

John Holland himself anticipated the application of diesel power to submarine boats. Had his 1899 negotiations succeeded with Adolphus Busch, American representative of the Diesel Motor Company, Holland would have added to his list of notable contributions the introduction of the diesel engine and thereby have set the major pattern of submarine propulsion down to the first run of the USS *Nautilus* (SSN-571) in 1955.[13] On 25 May 1899, only two years after the launching of the *Holland VI*, E. B. Frost wrote to Isaac L. Rice, president of the newly formed Electric Boat Company, requesting a "strong" letter of introduction to Mr. Busch. "If we have that," Frost asserted, "we think we can induce them to give us immediate attention on the ground that it would be an entering wedge for the introduction of their style engines in the Navy."[14] It is not altogether clear why this proposal collapsed, especially in view of Holland's assurance that economy and safety would be greatly enhanced by the use of diesel fuel.

Among the other features incorporated in the *Holland VI* was the position of the screw or propeller. The original plans showed the propeller aft of the vertical steering and horizontal diving planes, and it was so located in the completed boat. A hoop of steel guarded the blades. The propeller was similarly placed in all his previous boats and in all his early drawings, with the exception of the *Zalinski Boat* of 1885. In the *Fenian Ram* of 1881 the scheme had worked well. In the triple-screw *Plunger*, the main screw was abaft the rudders, though it appears to have been at the Navy Department's insistence that two propellers were added forward of the rudders. In 1898, W. H. Jaques, president of the Holland Torpedo Boat Company, told an audience of British naval architects and representatives from the Admiralty that Holland felt the Navy's proposal a totally unnecessary precaution. The single centerline screw, abaft the rudders, would be adequate for the propulsion of any Holland design.[15] In the sixth boat the inventor would test his belief.

The engineering principles which led Holland to mount the screw aft of the rudder and diving planes, and on the central axis of his spindle-shaped vessel, further testify to his intensive search for a submarine that would be highly maneuverable in her proper element beneath the waves. The story of his struggle to preserve this radical feature belongs to a later chapter.[16] The Navy returned to his principle in the initial design of the experimental submarine *Albacore* in 1953. The arrangement is now a central feature of the modern nuclear submarine.[17]

The machinery to be crowded into the fifty-three-foot hull of the *Holland VI* had grown both in amount and complexity. The plans called for a crew of five, but the inventor had not abandoned his determination that a submarine should require only a single operator. The final drawings prepared for future builders, and dated 1 August 1899, showed a one-man control system located in the turret. The controls included: on the port side, diving engine hand wheel, whistle cord, reducing valve, pressure depth gauge, bell pull, clinometer, jingles and indicator for the position of the diving planes; on the starboard side, steering indicator and steering engine hand stick; amidships, looking forward, two speaking tubes and a compass mount. In emergencies, hand steering and diving wheels were available in the bowels of the vessel, and were mounted on the port side aft of the electric motor.

For twenty years, from the time of his experiments in his first one-man boat to the early trial runs in the *Holland VI*, Holland undoubtedly spent more hours submerged than any other man in history prior to 1900. By his own courageous actions he demonstrated his faith in his creations. Always quiet and unpretentious, he refused to let others assume the grave responsibility for his submarines and their crews. With Holland, this was more than a matter of pride; it was a matter of conviction. A submarine's war potential lay in the intelligence of the pilot and in a control system that would respond fully and instantaneously to a single pilot's command.[18]

As the American submarine evolved in the twentieth century, the interior became so intricate that a serious division of labor took place in the control of the craft. Discipline and co-ordination were essential if the vessel and her crew were to act as one vast instrument. The culmination of this division was reached in the fleet submarines of World War II. Later, with the appearance of new and powerful sources of propulsion and the promise of increased underwater maneuverability, the focus returned to the problem of simplifying and centralizing control. The joy stick device employed by Holland was revived in experiments with the conventionally powered submarines *Albacore* (SS-569) and *Darter* (SS-576). In the *Skipjack* (SSN-585), this system provided full and almost instantaneous response through control by a one-man console.[19]

"American naval history," wrote Howard I. Chapelle in *The History of the American Sailing Navy*, "is far more than a running account of naval battles or a panegyric of naval officers." The "qualities and characteristics of the ships" and the men who design them are now accepted as part of that history. "This makes possible," continued Chapelle, "some examination, at least, of the official reasons for neglecting what now appear to have been obvious advantages."[20] Therefore, in order better to understand John Holland and the submarine which launched a new era in naval history, it is necessary to go into the background of this technological revolution; to meet the men who helped to make it possible; and, especially, to assess the motives of its leading proponent. For this last purpose, the focus of interest must shift to Ireland, before "the troubles," and to the desolate coast of County Clare where John Holland had his humble origin.

CHAPTER TWO

THE IRISH YEARS

1841-1873

Along the rugged coast of County Clare, from Galway Bay south to where the River Shannon meets the sea, there is but a single harbor of refuge from the stormy Atlantic. This is Liscannor Bay. On its north shore, the village of Liscannor nestles under Hags Head and the ruins of twelfth-century O'Connor Castle. In the village, the lime-coated cottage walls gleam white in the sunlight. Main Street is a brisk walk from the landing at Lower Quay; and, at the far end of Main Street, the road rolls northward over the undulating downs toward Lisdoonvara. A stone-lined lane to the left, called Castle Street, climbs to the ruins on the hill past a row of single-storied cottages which look southwest over the Bay. In the third cottage—near the middle of the row, snuggled between its massive masonry chimneys—John Philip Holland was born.

The most probable date of Holland's birth was 24 February 1841.[1] Parish records in Liscannor were not kept until 1842, and they do not mention John Holland. The register of the Christian Brothers in Limerick contains the notation: "J. P. Holland," then a resident of that city, "entered June 15, 1858, aged 17." This would fix 1841 as the year of his birth. Furthermore, a manuscript in Holland's own handwriting states: "The subject of the following sketch was born February 24, 1841."[2] In recent years, the problem of Holland's birth date was complicated by the recollection of his daughter Marguerite, who asserted that her father's birthday fell on 29 February—a leap year rarity—which would have meant he was born in 1840. But the facts do not warrant this recollection.

John Holland's father, also named John Holland, was for many years employed by the British Coastguard Service. This Service, organized originally under customs solely to prevent smuggling, had been converted into a defensive one at the time of Napoleon's threat to the British Isles. In a constant vigil against smugglers and foreign expeditionary forces, it used revenue cutters for patrolling the coastal waters and employed officers for riding circuit along the headlands. It is presumed that John Holland, Senior, was a riding officer. In 1831, he was transferred to Liscannor from the fashionable watering place of Kilkee on Malbay. His first wife, Anne Foley, probably a native of Kilkee, accompanied him.

This scenic but forbidding coast of County Clare was a bleak land in winter, and survival was difficult at best. In spring and summer, however, it was the Emerald Isle. Green fields, dotted with haycocks, alternated with darker plots of cultivated earth; and the stone-lined patches reached as far inland as the eye could see. But this was before the failure of the potato crop and the ensuing famine; before the depletion of the population by starvation, cholera, civil strife, and emigration.

In 1835, Anne Foley Holland died and was buried in Kilmacreehy Cemetery in Liscannor. John soon remarried; and his second wife, Mary Scanlon, of Killaloe, bore him four sons in the cottage on Castle Street. The first son was Alfred, but the date of his birth is unknown. Then came John Philip in 1841. Robert was born in 1845 and died two years later of cholera in the year of the Great Famine. The youngest son was Michael Joseph, born in 1848.

Before young John was ten years old, he had witnessed famine and disease. He had lost a brother and two uncles of cholera, had seen his youngest brother ill with smallpox, and had shared in the miseries that inflicted the neighborhood. But as long as his father remained in the Coastguard, the family had the right to live in the Coastguard cottage and so quite literally had a roof over its head. But the boy must have seen, heard, and remembered the unique eviction proceedings that befell those less fortunate. "Levelling," they called it. The local constabulary maintained the peace, while the landlord's agent proceeded with the eviction. The tenant's belongings were hustled out into the street, and then the thatched roof was so completely dismantled as to preclude any reoccupation. Such "levelled" cottages stood out bleakly against the landscape. They were a kind of ruin the people understood, more real and threatening than the ancient, towering rubble of O'Connor Castle.

There can be little doubt that the early events in the life of John Philip Holland filled him with a deep resentment toward an England that he and his countrymen felt was responsible for their misery and poverty, and that this resentment prodded him later to devise an instrument that would bend the will of the Mistress of the Seas. Three factors, however, tempered his feelings and checked them at that border of bitterness beyond which so many of his fellow countrymen chose to trod.

Primarily, the occupation of John Holland, Senior, did not tie them to the soil. The children were free, when the time came, to move to the larger towns and to seek employment in more urban pursuits. One can easily eulogize the tiller of the soil, the satisfaction and peace that he must know, but not in times like these.

Secondly, the father's livelihood demanded at least an outward allegiance to Her Majesty's government. It is certain that John Holland, Senior, took no part in the insurrection of 1848, but he must have cautiously followed the extraordinary journalism of John Mitchel, Smith O'Brien, John Martin, and the host of literary geniuses who wrote for the Irish national press.

The third factor which molded young John was the family devotion to the Roman Catholic Church and his own experiences in the teaching Order of the Christian Brothers. This Order was a rigidly disciplined body from which an exemplary outward behavior of its members could be expected, although its sympathies for the dissolution of the Union with England were well known. At the age of seventeen, John Philip Holland joined the Irish Christian Brothers, submitting to a discipline which was to temper any desire he might have to manifest open rebellion against British rule.

Little is known of John Holland's boyhood. He attended the new St. Macreehy's National School, a short walk down the hill from the Coastguard cottage on Castle Street. As a part of the system of the National Schools of Ireland, the two-storied Liscannor establishment was then under the management of the Bishop of Kilfenora. Here, John Holland began his study of English, for Gaelic was his mother's language and that spoken in his home.

If little remains to be told of young John's formal education in his native Liscannor, it is likely that his informal education consisted of his father's stories of the sea and an occasional trip with his father on his rounds to Hags Head beyond O'Connor Castle, perhaps even as far as the impressive Cliffs of Moher. John's older brother, Alfred, was a strong lad with a keen mind; together they could explore the ruins of the old castle. From its eminence on the hill, they could look out on the broad Atlantic or southward across the Bay to the cluster of white houses that composed Lahinch. When the tide was out, the Bay floor was a kind of Devil's Causeway, strewn with boulders which trapped marine life in tidal pools. Then there were stories to be gleaned from the fishermen returning to Lower Quay. But in those years of hardship, Liscannor must have been a town that time forgot. It was, as one Irishman put it, "a dreary place to be born."

Later, for perhaps a year, John attended the secondary school of the Christian Brothers at Ennistymon, five miles out on the road toward Lahinch. Then, in 1853, the family moved from Liscannor to Limerick on the River Shannon, and young John entered the Monastery School on Sexton Street.[3] The elder Holland died just before or soon after the family reached Limerick. According to rumor, he had been suffering from a minor ailment for which a friend advised a homemade remedy consisting mostly of potash. Within a few hours after taking the recommended "sure-cure," John Holland, Senior, was dead.

In the school at Limerick, young John applied himself earnestly to his studies, and the teaching Brothers marked his aptitude for the physical sciences. He would rise early each morning, climb a tree near his home, and in this elevated retreat prepare his lessons for the coming day.[4] John's thoughts were turning to a career at sea. In 1854 he passed a navigation examination, but his poor eyesight was a stumbling block. "No one would trust me even to row a two-oared boat, much less navigate a ship," he once said.[5] His father's death put an end to such dreams and interrupted his schooling, for the family needed his help.

Blessed with what the Irish would call "the power of learning" and already knowledgeable beyond his years, young John soon found a way by which to continue his education and to earn a living at the same time. He would become a member of the teaching Order of the Irish Christian Brothers. On 15 June 1858, Holland took the initial vows and was accepted into the Order. The Brothers rejoiced, as their need for teachers was great. The National School System, dominated by the Church of England, could not cope with the increase in pupils of school age; and the Christian Brothers struggled to fill the gap.

After a brief novitiate in Limerick, John Holland was sent to the famous North Monastery School in Cork for further training and apprentice teaching. The historical and beautiful city of Cork on the River Lee proved fascinating to the young man from rural County Clare. For the first time, he could revel at meaningful historic ground. Here was Drake's Pool where the great English navigator sought refuge from the Spanish; here Cromwell landed and melted the bells of Cork's many churches into cannon to be used against John Holland's own countrymen; here Patrick Redmond survived his own hanging. From this very harbor, twenty years earlier, the *Sirius* embarked for America to complete the first passage of the Atlantic under steam alone. Here, too, were many small craft skimming the harbor, sailing from the Cork Water Club, one of the first yacht clubs of the world. But the city groaned under harder times, and its citizens feared the approach of another winter. The jubilant church bells that greeted the American food ship in 1847 were now silent, though the humanitarian gesture had not been forgotten.

Meanwhile, among the cluster of sedate buildings at the North Monastery, Holland mingled with his new Brothers, coming under the influence of Brother James Dominick Burke, a noted science teacher and the founder of vocational education in Ireland. Brother Burke recognized the youth's mechanical aptitude, drafting skill and mathematical acumen, and encouraged his development of these talents. This influence came at a most propitious time in young Holland's life. He soon began to teach, and teaching afforded him the very tools he needed to satisfy his curiosity about the natural world and to develop his gifts. Shy, inquisitive, and witty, he surprised his students with impressive demonstrations of scientific principles.

But Holland lacked physical stamina; and, in 1860, ill health forced him to give up teaching. He was advised to seek a more favorable climate, such as the Madeira Islands, but this was financially impossible.[6] Instead, he took up lodgings in Ashburton on Clanmire Hill in the eastern section of Cork, where for nearly two years he read, sketched, studied, and rested.

There, one day in the spring of 1862, he read in the *Cork Examiner* the electrifying news of the engagement between the Union *Monitor* and the Confederate *Merrimack*. This strange encounter of ironclad vessels in the American Civil War caught the imagination of the recuperating school teacher. His keen mind saw the end of wooden warships. He foresaw the usual delays and parliamentary debates before the conservative Admiralty would adopt the iron vessel, but adoption was certain, and with it the continuation of British naval supremacy. That was a thought to make any Irishman shudder. But suppose John Ericsson's "cheese box on a raft" had failed to engage the *Merrimack*? "The successful result of that encounter," wrote Holland later, "alone saved her from being classed as the most conspicuous failure of modern naval construction."[7] Twenty years later Holland would be negotiating with the famous designer of the *Monitor* for projectiles to be used in the pneumatic gun on board his second submarine.

It was obvious that a wooden British fleet could be demoralized or annihilated by a vessel such as the "cheese box on a raft"; her defensive armor and low freeboard would make her an almost impossible target for the conventional surface ship. If she were a vessel completely submerged, she would "present the unique spectacle, when used in attack, of a weapon against which there is no defense."[8] These thoughts of Holland belonged to later years, but the basic insights may have presented themselves to his mind on the first reading of the extraordinary naval battle in Hampton Roads. Certainly there was time for reflection at Ashburton. For all true Irishmen, the American Civil War was a struggle to be watched. Indeed, Irish emigrants to the United States were involved in that great conflict, and the experience they were acquiring would one day be of use in the militant Fenian movement for Irish independence. If British favoritism toward the Confederacy sufficiently provoked the United States, perhaps Ireland's strike for independence would be at hand.

In early 1861, his health having improved, Holland was sent to the Irish Christian Brothers School in Maryborough (now Portlaiose), a small market town some fifty miles southwest of Dublin. From there he was sent to Enniscorthy, a mill community in County Wexford. Turning again to mechanical interests, he spent hours watching the great water wheel in a neighboring mill, and here he first thought about a flying machine.

"My first design was made in 1863, shortly before I began the study of submarines, but I had no suspicion of the chief, almost the only force employed by every flying animal. . . ."[9] This line is important, not only for its indication of Holland's serious study of flight, but also for its proof that the problems of submarine navigation had not yet concerned him. Despite his interest in the *Monitor-Merrimack* affair, there is no justification for the impression that the engagement set him immediately at work improving a supposedly earlier design of an underwater craft claimed by some to have been sketched as early as 1859.

Holland's interest in flying was more understandable. He lived on a coast that might be said to belong to the birds: the turnstones, with their sleek, chevroned wings; the mergansers that darted in over the ebb tide; and the other waterfowl that were the true masters of the headlands. Their flight was certain to intrigue the curious and thoughtful, for in proportion to their size and energy, the formidable tasks they performed were nothing short of miraculous. The young and keenly observant Holland felt that a reasonable explanation could be found only by careful and persistent study. Let people go their confused way. "Almost without exception they maintain absurd theories that cannot in the nature of things be true, that are refuted before their faces every day by every flying thing, and that are far from being reasonable and simple as are the natural functions regarding which they dogmatize."[10] Had he read Newton's statement of the principle of parsimony—in nature, "more is superfluous when less will do"?

Holland correctly held suspect the reaction-equal-to-weight theory. The force needed to propel birds through the air he calculated to be in the order of nine times their weight, and yet this force was not sufficient to account for sustained flight during the negative, or upward, stroke of the wings. What then kept these birds aloft? He was not satisfied to dismiss this question by invoking mysteries. His understanding of the principles of aerodynamics remained far ahead of his times, and his later efforts in this direction deserve more recognition than they have yet received. Though his major work on the problems of mechanical flight belongs to another chapter in his life, the beginnings had been made in Enniscorthy. It is totally erroneous for one of the chief sources on the life of this man to conclude that Holland's first attempts at a flying machine were assigned to oblivion.[11]

In 1865, Holland was assigned to Drogheda, a busy seaport on the River Boyne, in County Lough north of Dublin. Here, he quietly passed the tenth anniversary of his entrance into the teaching Order.

At this time, Irish-British friction again broke out in open rebellion at various places in Ireland. British retaliation was immediate and harsh, and Fenian leaders such as John Devoy and Jeremiah O'Donovan Rossa were sentenced to long prison terms. Holland's connection with the disturbing events of the years from 1865 to 1867 was remote. But it was the Fenian leaders who would one day provide him with the means to build his first two submarine boats. In the meantime, the unrest in Ireland was of genuine concern to him. His mother was still in Limerick, scene of one of the uprisings. His older brother, Alfred, could be trusted to take care of himself, although it appears that he edited one of the small "semi-revolutionary" weeklies then published in Dublin.[12] His younger brother, Michael, an open separationist, was his chief concern, but Michael soon "escaped" to the United States.

In the summer of 1869, John Holland was transferred to a post at Dundalk, where his principal pedagogical efforts were devoted to music. In the memory of a Christian Brother living in Galway, Holland "was an excellent and gifted music teacher."[13] He is credited with introducing the Tonic-Solfa system of musical instruction into his country's schools. Here, too, he exhibited his versatility. In the hedged yard of the school, he erected a sundial of his own design. Later, he possessed a telescope with which he revealed the wonders of the heavens to his students.

While at Dundalk, Holland first seriously occupied himself with thoughts of submarines. Sketching the principles he had in mind, he modestly began with a one-man craft of iron. According to local tradition, he experimented with a clock-driven submarine model in a large wooden tub filled with water. Accounts reached Ireland at this time of the experiments with the *Intelligent Whale* in New York Harbor. The United States government, mindful of the psychological effect of the Confederate *Hunley*'s attack on the *Housatonic* during the Civil War, was willing to invest in Halstead's *Whale*.[14] These accounts must have encouraged Holland to continue with his own experiments.

Again, the pace of his activities at Dundalk began to tell on the health of Brother Holland. He grew tired, his hair receded at the temples, and his weight dropped to one hundred and forty pounds. The twinkle in the eyes behind the thick, rimless spectacles became less frequent. After the abortive uprising in Limerick, he worried about his mother and his brother Alfred. Then, in the spring of 1872, they passed through

Dundalk en route to Liverpool, where they embarked for America to join Michael.

Now there were no longer any family ties in Ireland, no longer a home in Limerick. For Brother Holland the months dragged on into winter, and again his health failed. On 26 May 1873, not having taken final vows in the Order, John Philip Holland withdrew from the congregation of the Irish Christian Brothers. On the grounds of his health, a dispensation was granted by his Superior, Brother Yorke.[15]

Holland was now free to join other members of his family in Boston. His stipend at Dundalk had not exceeded thirty pounds per year, so he was forced to make the passage in steerage.

Thus, Holland's Irish years came to a close when he was at the age of thirty-two. He packed his valise for the long ocean voyage; among his few belongings was the sketch of his first submarine design. There were doubts to be quieted and hopes to be fanned. Holland's recollection of the thoughts that stirred within him at the time are revealing:

> I knew that in a country where coal and iron and mechanical skill were as plenty as they were in England, the development of large armor-plated ships must come first. Therefore I must get to a place where mechanics in shipbuilding were less advanced, and the available material for big iron-clad vessels scarcer. Then, too, I was an Irishman. I had never taken part in any political agitation, but my sympathies were with my own country, and I had no mind to do anything that would make John Bull any stronger and more domineering than we had already found him.[16]

The transition from school teacher to inventor would still take time. John Holland was not a trained mechanical engineer. It was evident from his early career in teaching that his mind was not disciplined in the academic sense: navigation, astronomy, aerodynamics, hydrostatics, music, and history had each, in turn, occupied his interest. In his later life, some of Holland's less scrupulous associates would be eager to pronounce him "untutored" and "an ignoramus" who "was content to impart elementary knowledge to elementary pupils," and who, as a pedagogue, "did not advance beyond that grade."[17] These unkind and indeed untruthful commentators failed to observe that this "untutored" man had within him some seed of genius: intellectual curiosity, a fruitful imagination, mechanical ability, and an unrelenting conviction in the rightness of his insights. The transition from school teacher to inventor would take time, but it was a more rapid transformation than Holland could have anticipated as he sailed westward across the Atlantic in 1873.

CHAPTER THREE

THE FIRST SUBMARINE
1873-1879

Holland had time to turn his thoughts to the submarine soon after his arrival in Boston in November, 1873, for he slipped on an icy city street, suffered a broken leg and a slight brain concussion in the mishap, and was confined to his rooms. "I had a search made through my effects for my former solution to the problem," he told the *Washington Star* in 1900, "and fortunately the friend that I had entrusted with the duty found them. When I was on the point of opening the envelope containing them, it occurred to me it would be better to begin at the beginning of the subject and study it over again from the start without looking at what I had done before."[1] Holland was surprised and delighted to find that his conception of the principles involved had not changed substantially from his earlier understanding. He concluded that he must therefore be correct in his approach to the solution of the basic problems in submarine navigation.

In the meantime, Holland was invited to turn again to teaching; and, in 1874, he joined the Christian Brothers as a lay teacher in the boys' division of St. John's Parochial School in Paterson, New Jersey. The submarine plans were put aside for another two years.[2]

According to tradition, the father of a boy whom Holland tutored was a friend of Navy Secretary George M. Robeson and this parent urged the inventor to submit his submarine plans to the government. In any event, the papers which were sent to the Navy Department in February, 1875, seem to be a refinement of a rough sketch which appears in Burgoyne's *Submarine Navigation, Past and Present* (Vol. II, p. 1) as Holland's first submarine design. The Burgoyne sketch may well be the drawing which Holland prepared in Boston.

Later in the same year, the papers which Holland had mailed to Washington were included in Lieutenant F. M. Barber's "Lecture on Submarine Boats and Their Application to Torpedo Operations," which Barber delivered at the Naval Torpedo Station in Newport, Rhode Island. Printed copies of this lecture were available at the

Torpedo Station. Barber gave a complete drawing and description of Holland's treadle-operated, fifteen-and-one-half-foot, one-man boat with its ingenious division of air reservoirs achieved by oiled silk partitions. "I can remember scarcely anything of what I described," Holland wrote later, "but I know I held a good deal back, and described something I didn't want to do, as I believed they would have no regard to my desire for secrecy."[3] In view of Barber's unauthorized publication, the suspicions of Holland were fully justified.

The Holland papers had been sent from Washington to Captain Edward Simpson at the Torpedo Station for his comment. The captain had returned them with the observation that the whole scheme was impractical. In his opinion, the operator had no means of visually determining his course; therefore, navigating the submersible would be an exaggerated case of a pilot steering in a fog. Holland was not satisfied with this meager commentary and drily observed, in a letter to Captain Simpson, that the captain probably had had no experience navigating by compass under water. The captain's answer was prophetic of the long battles which Holland was later to wage with officialdom—no one would go down in such a craft and the inventor should drop the whole matter, for "to put anything through in Washington was uphill work."[4]

A lesser man would have been discouraged by the captain's reply, but not John Holland. In his classroom at St. John's, long after his students had left for home, he drew sketches on the blackboard. Often William Dunkerley, an engineer, would join him at the school. Together they would draw on the board the details for a one-man submarine, erasing this line, adding that line, and correcting the calculations to match. Each improvement would then be transferred to paper.

A third drawing of the foot-treadled, one-man boat, the drawing most frequently reproduced, is almost identical to the original Barber plate, with three notable exceptions. First, the print and notes surrounding the longitudinal section are in Holland's own handwriting. The notes state that this was the submarine in which the inventor carried out certain experiments in the Passaic River in May and June of 1878. It is shown as twelve and one-half feet long, displacing one and one-third tons. Equally baffling is the fact that this version of the boat includes a simple periscope (or *camera lucida*), as though in direct answer to the criticism of Captain Simpson. But of the six boats which Holland was to construct, only two, the *Zalinski Boat* and the unsuccessful *Plunger*, carried such an instrument. Hence it is not possible to consider this third plan as derived from the blackboard sketches he worked out with Dunkerley. Rather, it appears to be a much later, idealized reminiscence indulged in by the inventor in his own effort to reconstruct the evolution of his ideas. And thirdly, the sectional view amidships, shown in Barber's plan, is not represented in this sketch by Holland. The final, constructed product of all these efforts, the so-called *Boat No. 1*, actually bore little resemblance to the three known drawings of the foot-powered submarine.

While Holland worked at his blackboard, certain stirring events far beyond the confines of the classroom in Paterson were releasing forces which would enable him to build his first underwater boat. These events centered around the struggle of his countrymen for the political independence of Ireland. It would be difficult to understand the rise and fall of the inventor's fortunes in the years between 1875 and 1883 without some appreciation for the magnitude of the Irish rebellion and familiarity with the daring, intelligent, and often conniving expatriate leaders who had sought political asylum in the United States.

The Irish Revolutionary Brotherhood (IRB) was established on St. Patrick's Day in 1858 by James Stephens and Thomas Luby. Its American counterpart was the Fenian Brotherhood organized by Michael Doheny and John O'Mahonley in the early 1860's. On this side of the Atlantic, many Irish patriots had received military experience in the American Civil War. These members of the Brotherhood were particularly militant, and their revolutionary schemes were not always sanctioned by their compatriots, so the organization soon split into three major factions. One group of dissenters, known as the United Irishmen, or the Canadian wing of the Brotherhood, made two unsuccessful raids on Canada, one in 1866 and the other in 1870. The United States government was forced to intervene in order to check such uprisings. The Fenians became *persona non grata* in their adopted country. John Mitchel, writing in the *Irish Citizen* in February, 1868, complained of the incompetence of the Irish-American patriots. "They are in sad confusion with respect to mode of action [whether it be on land or sea], the place [whether in Ireland or Canada] and the opportunity."[5]

The Fenians, although divided, were able to secure a sympathetic American press which hammered away at the atrocities perpetrated by the British on the Irish leaders in the prisons of Millbank and Portland. Then, Prime Minister William E. Gladstone issued a general amnesty changing the sentences of fourteen Irish revolutionaries from prison terms to exile.

The "Irish Exiles" were already heroes by the time they arrived in New York in 1871. There were two groups: one of five on board the Cunard steamship *Cuba*, and one of nine on board the *Russia*. The Exiles faced a confusing array of receptions, from that of the vote-hungry Tammany leaders who met them at Quarantine to an affair before President Grant on the steps of the White House. The Fenian factions also vied for their support. Disheartened by the dissension he found among the Irish-

Americans, John Devoy of the "Cuban Five" set out to bring some semblance of unity to the organization of Irishmen residing in the United States. He formed the short-lived Irish Confederation, headed by an Exile Directory with Jeremiah O'Donovan Rossa as chairman and himself as secretary. It was not long before Devoy realized that the real source of unity could emerge only from the Clan-na-Gael (United Brotherhood, or V.C.) which, under Jerome J. Collins, had attracted members from all three wings of Fenianism. The Exiles shifted their strength to the Clan-na-Gael, and a new fervor for the Irish cause spread throughout America. Irishmen everywhere now had reason to hope that punishing blows would be struck against British tyranny.

The question arises as to whether or not John Holland was ever a member of the Fenian Brotherhood. It would be easy to make this assumption, and some writers have done so. But the evidence does not exist. As a Christian Brother in Ireland, it is unlikely that he took an active role in the secret societies of Fenianism, even though he had not taken final vows in the teaching Order and in spite of the Christian Brothers' being openly in favor of independence. Furthermore, Holland had not been in the United States long before he was again associated in a lay capacity with the Christian Brothers in Paterson.

Holland's chief contact with Fenianism came through his younger brother, Michael, who registered as a member of the O'Donovan Rossa Circle No. 159 as early as April, 1869, more than four years before John came to the United States.[6] Many years later, Michael wrote to John Devoy: "I see by the papers that the boat [Holland's first submarine] was built in 1877. That's wrong. As I am the man who started the negotiations which finally resulted in the building of the boat, I think I ought to know."[7] Michael introduced John to Rossa sometime in the middle of 1876. Rossa, in turn, gave Holland a letter of introduction to Jerome Collins, founder of the Clan-na-Gael. At the time of the Rossa letter, which is quoted below, Collins was scientific and meteorological editor of the *New York Herald*.

July 6/76

Dear Mr. Collins:

I introduce to you a Mr. Holland of Patterson [Paterson]. He visited me in connection with a torpedo [boat] he has invented, and I wish you would have a few minutes conversation with him.

Yours truly,
Jer. O'Donovan Rossa[8]

As casual as Rossa's letter appears, the significance of this meeting with Collins should not be underestimated. Up until this time, Holland's acquaintance with men capable of appreciating his ability had been limited indeed. True, the circle into which

he was now introduced was composed of his fellow ⸱
thought were on the lunatic fringe of the Irish natio
they were numbered among the prominent men of thei
law, and industrial development. John Holland had need
sympathized with the whole Irish effort to achieve indepenc
willing to co-operate and to use his talents in promoting the
have done otherwise when one considers the early suffering ⸱
through famine and rebellion during his more than thirty years

There was a mildness and sensitivity about John Holland ⸱⸱ nim shy in
crowds, in sharp contrast to such physically and intellectually vigorous men as Devoy
and Rossa. They were men of action; he was a dreamer by comparison. In all of Holland's articles, notes, and voluminous correspondence that is still available, there is not
the slightest indication, no *Erin Go Bragh*, that could be interpreted as referring to active membership in any wing of the Irish revolutionary movement.

The impatience of American Fenians for action against the British was answered in
the summer of 1876, when the rescue of the Irish political prisoners from the British
penal colony at Freemantle, Australia, was announced with banner headlines in newspapers around the world. The New Bedford whaler *Catalpa*, under Yankee Captain
George S. Anthony, was sailing toward America bearing to freedom the escaped "convicts." It was an historic rescue.[9]

John Devoy, who was chairman of the Fenian Executive Committee, and John J.
Breslin, who had gone out to Australia under the alias of James Collins, were the real
heroes behind the expedition. The *Catalpa* arrived in New York Harbor on 19 August
1876, and the Fenian leaders received the prisoners and Breslin at the Battery. The
Brotherhood took the freed men under its wing and prepared a reception in their
honor.

John Holland was present at this reception, and it was here that he first met Devoy
and Breslin. He repeated for them his submarine proposal which he had made earlier
in the year to O'Donovan Rossa and Jerome Collins. Devoy's own recollection of this
meeting with the professor from Paterson is sharp and concise. "He [Holland] was
well informed of Irish affairs and was anti-English and with clear and definite ideas of
the proper method of fighting England. He was cool, good-tempered, and talked to us
as a schoolmaster would to his children."[10]

It is not difficult to imagine the persuasiveness of Holland before the leaders of the
United Brotherhood. A submarine was exactly the kind of weapon the Fenians
needed. The cost to the Brotherhood would be small compared to the cost to the Brit-

ch a vessel be successful. The place to strike John Bull was at sea, not on
e boat would be small; and smallness would be an advantage, for she could
transported to the scene of combat on board a larger vessel. Furthermore, Holland
insisted that a properly built and aptly handled submarine was invulnerable. A Skirmishing Fund to promote just such activities had been proposed late in 1875 by O'Donovan Rossa. The following April the *Irish World* had endorsed Rossa's fund and
launched a campaign for contributions. Irishmen throughout the country had responded generously. The hard-earned money of laborers, farmers, and domestics, as
well as the large contributions of lawyers, doctors, writers, priests, and politicians, had
poured into the fund. Holland observed, however, that the old fee of ten cents per
week per member would never free the Irish nation.[11] Flushed with the victory of the
Catalpa affair, the Fenian leaders knew that Holland was right.

The Trustees of the Skirmishing Fund appointed John Breslin to look into the submarine proposal. Breslin was an imposing man—slightly above average height and
with an excellent physique. His light brown hair and flowing beard accentuated his
strong blue-gray eyes. He was more than just another Irishman; he was the hero of
his people, a symbol of their resistance. He had delivered James Stephens from Richmond Prison, Dublin, in 1865; and now Breslin was known the world over as the
daring leader of the *Catalpa* rescue. To this adventurer, the quiet Paterson teacher
would have to demonstrate the practical application of his paper dreams.

Holland constructed a thirty-inch working model of his submarine, an improvement
on his Dundalk experiment. A metal hull was built around the clockwork mechanism;
rudder and diving planes were added to the hull. Breslin and a small group of Fenian
observers watched Holland demonstrate the model at Coney Island. Satisfied that this
inventor, though not technically trained, was something of a mechanical genius who
knew what he was about, Breslin assured Holland of financial support from Rossa's
Skirmishing Fund. Before 1877 had come to a close, arrangements had been made
with the iron works on Albany Street in New York City to begin the construction of
Boat No. 1. This diminutive craft was to measure fourteen feet six inches in length,
to have a three-foot beam, and to be two feet six inches in height, not including the
turret—making her probably the smallest submarine ever built. The original plans for
this boat are not known to exist. They are best represented by William Dunkerley's
freehand drawings made from memory and published in the *Paterson Sunday Chronicle* in 1916.[12]

On the first of February 1877, Dr. William Carroll, chairman of the Executive
Board of the Clan-na-Gael, wrote to John Devoy: "The salt water enterprise I

fully endorse. We *can* do it and we mean to try . . . it is a business must be handled, at least talked about, very gingerly. No loose pavement nor barroom palaver will do for that work."[13] There was no need to worry about Holland. In his dealings with the United States government he had already proved that he knew the value of secrecy in such matters. Not that one could hide an operational submarine in one's vest pocket, but as poet-editor O'Reilly of the *Boston Pilot* had suggested in the *Catalpa* affair, many might know, but few would know how. Details surrounding the submarine were well kept, and the local papers could report only that some wealthy friend of Mr. Holland's had provided the necessary financial backing. Where this "friend" was known publicly as Jacobs, Senior, of Jacobs and Company, the deception was effective, for these were the Clan's code names for Rossa and the Skirmishing Fund, respectively. To make the ruse complete, Breslin was known as Jacobs, Junior. Even the figures released as to the cost of the venture were erroneous, the most often quoted being $6,000. The Trustees of the Skirmishing Fund, according to more reliable sources, allocated $5,000 for the enterprise, $4,000 for the boat and $1,000 annually to John Breslin for overseeing the operation for the Clan-na-Gael.

Sometime in the spring of 1878, the *Holland No. 1* was moved from the Albany Iron Works to the shops of J. C. Todd and Company (later known as Todd & Rafferty) in Paterson. This was probably the engine shop on Van Houton Street and not the boiler works of the same company on Railroad Avenue. Several reasons support the former location. It was more conveniently situated for Holland on his way to and from his home and school. Also, a machine shop was needed to install the new engine patented by George Brayton in 1874. The discovery of a petroleum engine, which could possibly replace the foot pedals of the earlier designs, held promise for greater propulsion power. Such an engine would remove one of the most persistent obstacles to successful submarine navigation, an obstacle which had plagued inventors ever since Van Drebbel first submerged in the Thames River in the early 1620's. Now that the *Holland No. 1* was in Paterson, the inventor could forego the tedious trips to and from New York City; and the time saved could be devoted to the final installation and adjustment of the internal machinery.

By the afternoon of 22 May 1878, all was in readiness for the launching of John Holland's first submarine. Clusters of mill hands heading home that afternoon from silk factories and locomotive works gathered on the Spruce Street bridge above the Falls in Paterson to watch the proceedings below. On the right bank of the Passaic River, beside John Lister's boathouse, they could see a small group of men cautiously coaxing eight pairs of stallions to back a large wagon to the water's edge. The spectators could observe on the wagon a strange, lozenge-shaped mass of metal, about fourteen feet long and topped with a circular turret.

Occasionally someone on the bridge broke the silence with a comment, such as, "I see that the professor has built a coffin for himself." The intended reaction followed. Then the group was silent again; and only the constant rush of the Falls was heard, punctuated now and again by shouted commands from the men below.

When the two-and-one-quarter-ton craft slid from the wagon into the waters of the Upper Passaic and floated free of the shore at the end of her towline, a murmur of approval went up from the people on the bridge. The crowd began to disperse, but the more curious remained to see what would happen to John Holland's "wrecking boat." The word "submarine" was not a part of their vocabulary. Rumor had it that the professor from St. John's School over on Oliver Street was bent on building an underwater craft which could be used to "wreck" other vessels. No doubt the rumor started in Holland's own classroom, and was carried home by his students who told of the exciting prophecies of their teacher—man would one day navigate under the oceans and fly like a bird through the air. So the curious stayed on. They saw the slim, bespectacled professor standing to one side anxiously watching every detail of the launching. They saw Captain John Lister and Engineer William Dunkerley pull on the towline which led to the large ring in the bow of the boat. But something was wrong. The boat settled rapidly in the water. Then she disappeared. The two men hauled hurriedly on the line. Slowly the submarine emerged and was drawn with comparative ease to the river bank, much to the amazement of the onlookers who understood little about buoyancy.

For the following two days, the Paterson newspapers gave their own versions of the event. Under the headline, "Down Among the Fishes," one paper reported the "success" of the launching and observed that the wrecking boat "went immediately to the bottom; and this without even the assistance of the captain."[14]

John P. Holland must have had much on his mind as he went to his home on Willis Street that May evening. What had gone wrong? Had he calculated the buoyancy of his craft for salt water? The waters of the Upper Passaic were fresh. This was Dunkerley's theory many years later. Were the valves controlling the two five-eights-of-an-inch intake plugs in the bottom of the central compartment left open by mistake? Or had Dunkerley himself failed to dog securely the hatch cover on the turret and in the jostling had the hatch been pried loose? Whatever the cause, Holland had come too far to abandon the project. The opportunity had arrived to prove that his ideas would work. It might not present itself again. If he failed, if he betrayed a lack of confidence in his own ability, his fellow Irish patriots would close the purse strings to the Fenian

Skirmishing Fund; and he could not continue his experiments on a teacher's salary.

Holland must have rehearsed all of these possibilities in his mind as he attempted to rest from the excitement of the launching. Was this to be at once the alpha and omega of his efforts? Would Breslin report the failure; would O'Donovan Rossa call the Trustees of the Skirmishing Fund together; would they vote to shut off the flow of money before he had a chance to learn anything from the little boat? It seemed unlikely. Their investment was already too substantial to bring all to a sudden close.

After two more days of preparation, the *Holland No. 1* was ready for her first test. Air, under twenty-five pounds pressure, was pumped into the bow and stern tanks, but again there was discouragement. The stern sank slowly in the water, and it was evident that faulty riveting was responsible for the leak. On the twenty-ninth of May, the inventor succeeded in getting the boat to float on a fairly even keel; nevertheless, as a precaution against a fatal accident, two flat-bottomed rowboats were lashed to either side of the submarine with lines attached in slinglike fashion. Dunkerley drove his steam launch out from Lister's boathouse, maneuvered it into position, and picked up the line attached to the submarine's bow. Slowly the little flotilla moved upstream beyond the island and out of sight of the curious who might tarry on the Spruce Street bridge. All day the men worked, experimenting with ballast, until they had secured the proper trim.

The Brayton engine, mounted on angle irons in the central compartment forward of the operator, did not live up to Holland's expectations, nor to the specifications claimed for it by the designer. It was a two-cylinder affair with ordinary slide valves opening into a single pressure chamber. It might have been operated by steam or compressed air, but nothing would induce it to explode gasoline. Undefeated by such a discovery, Holland ingeniously attached a rubber hose to the top of the pressure chamber. Then he ran it through a watertight hole in the turret and over the side to Dunkerley's launch, where he fastened the far end to a valve on the launch's boiler. Awkward though this contraption was, it would nevertheless enable Holland to operate the submarine under borrowed power, and would permit him to check the then more vital problems of diving and rising to the surface.

By 6 June, Holland was ready to demonstrate his principles of submarine navigation before O'Donovan Rossa, who was accompanied by two brother Fenians from Paterson, Thomas Riley and Judge Thomas Casey. They joined Captain John Lister, Joseph Risk, and William Dunkerley on board the steam launch. John Holland slid through the turret of the submarine into his cramped quarters, an area three feet wide, three feet eight inches long, and slightly over two feet high. His head remained entirely within the turret from which he could see to navigate by looking through small deadlights in the coaming. Forward between his knees were the two cylinders of the Brayton engine mounted horizontally in a fashion that permitted Holland to connect the drive shafts eccentrically to flywheels on either side of the operator's seat. These flywheels were originally designed to be rotated by foot pedals, but the conversion to engine-driven action was readily accomplished. Shafts ran aft from the geared centers of the wheels to another geared arrangement, behind the operator, that drove a single shaft leading to the propeller. Only a man as small and slight as Holland could have managed in such cramped quarters. Holland reached between his knees and connected the steam hose to the central firing chamber. He signaled to Dunkerley from the open hatch. The pistons responded to the steam released from the launch's boiler, and the little submarine slid into the channel of the placid Passaic and headed upstream in tandem with the launch.

When the boats reached a clear stretch of water opposite the Pennington House which stood on the east bank, Holland flooded the two tanks, one just forward of his compartment and one just aft. The two additional tanks located in the extreme bow and stern were sealed and provided the small reserve of positive buoyancy which was a basic feature of the Holland design. (The submarine was not double-hulled, as later claimed by Cable and other authorities.) She settled in the water, only her turret remaining awash. Then the inventor pushed forward the lever that operated a single transverse axle connected to a pair of diving planes mounted outboard on either side of the craft just forward of the turret, pivoted at the center of buoyancy. The headway of three and one-half miles per hour was noticeably checked as the bow plunged deep into the water. The turret slowly disappeared, and the submarine was completely submerged. A tense silence fell over the men on the launch. Dunkerley payed out on the steam hose and estimated that Holland had reached a depth of twelve feet below the surface. Then the bow reappeared some distance off, and the craft leveled once again on the waters of the river. The hatch cover opened. The Paterson professor emerged from his "coffin" smiling.

On the steam launch a momentary excitement occurred when one of the men spotted a suspicious individual leaning against a rock on the River Road, field glasses trained on the scene in midstream. O'Donovan Rossa had reason to suspect a British spy, perhaps the one who had tipped off the Canadians to the second Fenian raid of 1870. This same man was later to haunt Holland at the Gap in Jersey City and to plant dissension in Irish ranks over the accounting of the Skirmishing Fund, especially as it concerned Holland's second boat. Yes, this could have been the notorious Major

Henri LeCaron, alias Thomas Beach, of Braidwood, Illinois, whom Devoy was to call "the prince of spies."[15] But nothing came of the incident in June, 1878.

Toward evening of this same day, John Holland demonstrated to his backers the ability of his craft to stay submerged for a considerable period of time. After lines had been attached to the bow and stern of the submarine, Holland again slipped through the turret and closed the hatch. The tanks were flooded, and then the sea cocks in the bottom of the center compartment were opened in order to produce a negative buoyancy. The air about the inventor was compressed, holding back the rising water. According to contemporary accounts the time was 5:45 P.M. Once again silence fell over the observers. The minutes passed slowly: 6:00 o'clock, 6:15, 6:30. At 6:45 bubbles stirred the water where Holland and his boat had vanished. Two minutes later the submarine rose to the surface and settled at her designed water line. The hatch was flung open, and again there emerged a smiling Holland. The inventor then offered Dunkerley, or anyone in the official party, an opportunity "to take her down," but no one volunteered. In subsequent years, writers have declared that Holland once stayed submerged in this submarine for a period of twenty-four hours, but these reports are unquestionably exaggerated. Not only do all contemporary accounts belie the claim, but there is also Holland's own modest assertion: "The longest time spent under water in this little boat was one hour."[16]

The success of these early experiments is summed up in understatement by the inventor himself: ". . . my financial supporters, the Trustees of the Fenian Skirmishing Fund, determined to build a larger boat."[17] Holland's first tests of an operational submarine were over. The little craft had served him well. He removed the engine and other machinery, and scuttled the boat in about fourteen feet of water just above the Spruce Street bridge. Some local citizens, thinking the metal could be used for scrap, attempted to raise the hull with tackle lowered from the bridge. Fearing that the bridge structure might be damaged, the city officials interrupted their operations, but not before the salvagers had torn the turret from its mounting. Nearly half a century later, the hull was again located and raised from the river bottom by a group of enterprising students who presented the submarine to the Paterson Museum where it may still be seen, minus its turret.[18]

What did Holland conclude from the 1878 experiments on the Upper Passaic River? He had tested pragmatically important principles of submarine navigation the solution to which had escaped many of his predecessors. He had demonstrated the merits of maintaining a constant reserve of positive buoyancy in conjunction with a low and fixed center of gravity in order to assure both lateral and longitudinal stability. He had taken a step forward toward the perfection of the porpoising principle of submergence first introduced in the *Nautilus* by Robert Fulton. This advance in Holland's thinking came about in the form of negative results obtained in his experiments with the lateral hydroplanes. These hydroplanes proved cumbersome, retarded forward motion, and required too much power to drive the craft under water. Now, there was no question in his mind about the proper location of the horizontal planes. They did not have to be located at the center of buoyancy. Less power would be needed to submerge the vessel if a single pair were located aft, perpendicular to the rudder. Though the Brayton power plant was in many respects a failure, it did convince Holland that a small petroleum engine could be perfected. He need no longer depend on manual or foot power to which the majority of his predecessors had been confined.

The inventor also planned to abandon his original scheme, which envisaged a submarine with its operator dressed in a diving suit of the type introduced by Rouquayrol and Denayrouze in 1865. "The first thing I found out was that it was folly to be bothered with either respirators or air purifying apparatus. They need lots of attention that can't be spared for them, and a fair supply of compressed air, that can be easily stored, render them superfluous."[19]

By foregoing the idea of dressing in a diving suit, Holland was forced to omit any demonstrations before the Fenian leaders of modes of attacking other vessels. Originally, the operator, protected by his helmet and respirator, was to build up pressure within the hull, open the hatch, remove torpedoes attached to the sides of the boat—the earlier drawings showed these torpedoes hung along the inside of the hull—affix a deadeye to the bottom of the enemy ship, and pull the torpedo against the ship by means of a lanyard. But the Paterson teacher observed that this would require great care, and he knew that any explosion in the water nearby might detonate the torpedoes prematurely to the decided detriment of both operator and underwater craft. Though it all looked feasible on paper, he observed, "One man could never manage it." Ezra Lee's frustrations in the *Turtle* were worth remembering. But before the experiments with his first submarine were completed and the little boat settled for her long rest on the bottom of the Passaic River, John Holland had determined to employ a gun in his next underwater boat.

O'Donovan Rossa must have made an enthusiastic report to the Trustees of the Skirmishing Fund. He saw a potentially potent weapon in the little submarine. And now the Fenian Brotherhood watched with interest the growing tensions between England and Russia. If war broke out, a Holland submarine might suddenly change the course of history. From Boston, James J. O'Kelly wrote to John Devoy on 11 October 1878: "I had a long talk with O'Reilly [editor of the *Pilot*] today about the 'National Fund' [a synonym for the Skirmishing Fund] during which I explained to him the *intelligent use* we hope to make of it. He was quite surprised—said it had never been so explained to him and that from Rossa's ravings he thought we simply meant to use it recklessly during times of peace. . . . If the fight between England and Russia begins *our time has struck*, or we are done forever."[20] This seems clearly to refer to the submarine venture, for in spite of "Rossa's ravings," it was always clear to Devoy that the submarine could only be used in times of war. Though the Fund did support many peacetime skirmishes, Devoy recollected in 1923: "As the submarine could only be used in case of war and its final use would require the expenditure of a very large amount of money, the boat had necessarily to lie idle until the opportunity should present itself."[21] This, of course, is commentary on Holland's second boat, but it unquestionably represented the official policy of the Clan from the inception of its negotiations with the Paterson inventor. Still hopeful that the time might strike when a submarine legitimately could be employed against the Mistress of the Seas to the greater glory and freedom of Ireland, the Trustees ordered Holland to build a larger underwater boat, one fully armed for combat and capable of breaking any enemy blockade. They also extended Breslin's appointment and salary. Work was to begin as soon as Holland was able to complete the drawings that he had already begun.

The future held new promise for thirty-seven-year-old John Holland, inventor. He put away his chalk and closed his school books; eighteen years of teaching was a career in itself.[22] Yet, he would not leave the classroom without regrets. Later, he was to confide in his daughter, Marguerite, "I loved the children because they were the only ones who didn't think I was crazy." Teaching, too, leaves its mark on a man in habits of directness, critical mindfulness, and quiet conviction. For years thereafter his friends and associates continued to address him as "Professor Holland."

CHAPTER FOUR

THE FENIAN RAM

1879-1883

There was every need for secrecy in what Dr. William Carroll called "'the salt water enterprise." As Chairman of the Executive Board of the Clan-na-Gael, Carroll had warned against "loose pavement" and "barroom palaver." Now rivalries within the Clan threatened the continuation of the submarine project. O'Donovan Rossa objected to the misuse of the Skirmishing Fund for non-revolutionary purposes, and he published his discontent in the columns of the *Irish World*, "conspiring aloud" against the Trustees of the Fund. Rossa's breach with his old friends of the Cuban Five widened as his militancy increased under the influence of liquor. Carroll and John Devoy tried to understand, but Rossa continued to fall back "into his old groove." One Dr. Dennis Mulcahy was sent to Ireland with the remains of one of the founders of the Brotherhood, John O'Mahonley, expenses to be paid out of the Fund. Mulcahy found himself in Dublin waiting for the promised money and threatened to bring an injunction against the Trustees unless his debts were paid. At this point John Devoy had had enough. He wrote to a leading Fenian Brother proffering his resignation as a Trustee. The letter was suppressed. On 6 February 1878 he restated his intent to resign:

> In my [former] letter I said we were in a nice position with a lunatic on one side threatening us with a lawsuit and on the other a drunken man bringing us into disgrace by raving in the papers. I waited somewhat impatiently to give both lunatic and drunkard time to think. . . . I do not propose to fritter away my life in endless squabbles nor do I think it safe to go into serious revolutionary work with men who cannot keep a secret.[1]

Amidst the internal bickering of the Clan-na-Gael, John Philip Holland quietly, persistently, and with the greatest discretion proceeded with his plans for his second submarine. This new craft, he believed, embodied all the principles and equipment for a three-man, fully operational engine of war. Secrecy would therefore be essential. After all, he had been careful to scuttle his first submarine above the Falls on the Passaic River. Now, he was fully on his guard as he approached C. H. Delamater and George H. Robinson of the Delamater Iron Works at the foot of West 13th Street,

New York City, and requested that their old and reputable firm build his second submarine.[2]

"But what is the boat intended for, and who is backing you?"

Holland replied that he could not divulge such information.

How then could the company be sure that it would be paid for the job?

Holland assured the two men that they would be paid in cash, in greenbacks, but he must first know something of the possible cost. The officials of the company carefully scrutinized the plans which Holland rolled out on the drafting board. They observed the water line of the peculiar, cigar-shaped vessel. It showed that in a floating position three-quarters of the boat would be submerged. Surely this was the conception of a "mad Irishman." The boat would sink on launching. But if Holland really wanted to go ahead with it, they were satisfied with his proposed arrangements, and the cost would not exceed $20,000.

Work began on the second submarine on 3 May 1879, but her construction was delayed by the continual argument and skepticism of every employee of the Delamater Iron Works. Holland recalled:

> Many objections were urged against her, especially by men who should have known better, but the trouble with them was almost the same as I encountered later among the staff officers of the navy, viz: they were, almost without exception, of English, Welsh, or Scotch descent, experienced in all kind of shipbuilding.[3]

Holland's Irish was showing through in the subtle and biting wit so characteristic of most of his writing.

As the months passed the submarine slowly took shape. An air of mystery surrounded her construction. Strange dignitaries came and went at the Delamater yard: Irish Fenians, Swedes, Russians, Italians, and Germans, as well as two Turkish envoys, Ali Ritza and Hassan Effendi. The latter gentlemen, Holland noted, were delightful observers, who behaved without the usual caution that stiffened other diplomats where matters of military secrecy were concerned. "But, very clearly to me, they had no idea of the importance of what was expected from the machine, or, much more likely, they had been persuaded by their acquaintances of English connections that the project would never amount to anything because it did not originate in England."[4] The representatives of the Sultan asked Holland to build a submarine for their government, perhaps half suspecting the psychological effect such a secret weapon would have upon their most recent foe, the Russian giant. But Holland begged off, declaring that his submarine boats were merely in the experimental stage.

The launching of the submarine took place about the first of May in 1881, two years after construction had begun. While the boat was on the stocks, John Breslin had resigned his post as Jacobs, Junior, to become editor of Devoy's *Irish Nation,* but he remained influential in Holland's work. Rossa had been ousted from the Clan-na-Gael. The *Irish World* had printed a front page article on the Rossa-Devoy fall out and the failure of Devoy to respect the "intent of the donors" to the Fund by departing from "the original 'skirmishing' policy" of open and rebellious acts against British tyranny. Rossa had stated his case succinctly in a letter to Thomas Bourke, a Trustee of the Fund. "You want 'honorable warfare.' Well wait till England will let you have it and you'll wait till you'll lie down and die."[5]

"Honorable warfare" won out, and the earlier wounds slowly healed, but not without leaving the Fenians rather severely splintered. The Convention of the Clan-na-Gael in May, 1881, revealed that $90,453 had been contributed to the Skirmishing Fund. During the years 1877 through 1880, the monthly receipts had averaged more than $2,000. Present at the Convention was a Fenian Brother serving as an agent for the notorious spy, LeCaron, to whom he gave the complete figures and all the financial circulars issued by the Convention. LeCaron's purpose was to provoke Irish patriots into demanding an accounting of the Skirmishing Fund. Devoy, recalling LeCaron's tactics, complained, "England always gets her dirty work done among Irishmen by ardent 'patriots' who want value for their money and ten cents worth of revolution every week, or an Englishman killed every once in a while, and the breed is with us yet."[6]

It was fortunate for the Clan that the statements which fell into the hands of LeCaron were not itemized, and he was unable to tell how much had been spent on "the salt water enterprise." John Holland later revealed that Robinson of Delamater's Iron Works closed the submarine account at $18,000. This figure, however, did not include all the machinery, some of which still remained to be installed. The best estimate of the total amount paid out of the Skirmishing Fund for all of Holland's submarine experiments ran to $60,000, no mean sum for those days.[7]

The second Holland submarine had already attracted considerable attention in the press. A reporter from the *New York Sun,* Blakely Hall, unwittingly enhanced the fame of the boat in the summer of 1881. He doggedly pursued Holland and begged the inventor to let him examine the inside of the submarine. Holland politely refused him admission. Hall argued that Holland was foolish not to publicize his work, for the press was full of reports that indicated the interest of various governments in submarine development. The French had continued to make strides since the days when Bourgois and Brun had completed *Le Plongeur.* In England, the Reverend George

W. Garrett had launched the *Resurgam*. The Russians had been more than mildly interested in the boats of Drzewiecki.[8] All these experiments had captured headlines in the world's press. But John Holland was not to be dissuaded.

Nevertheless, the *New York Sun* of the next day carried Hall's account of a mysterious "Fenian Ram," a name well chosen to indicate Holland's sponsors and what Hall believed to be the *modus operandi* of the strange vessel. Hall speculated further that her size deliberately matched that of a railroad boxcar and that she might even be hoisted on board a freighter and shipped to English waters to harass British shipping. Holland was amused by the article, but secretly grateful. The name *Fenian Ram* stuck. Henceforth, the little submarine never slid from her berth or returned without the presence of a crowd of curious spectators.

The *Fenian Ram* was towed from her launching site on the Hudson across the river to the little-used Morris Canal Basin above the New Jersey Central Railroad's ferry piers which jutted into the harbor. Holland wrote, "She laid at the Morris and Cummings Dredging Company's dock in Jersey City until July 3, 1883, during which time many experiments were made with her. . . . The first run on the surface was made in the Basin, or passage, east of the Lehigh Valley Railroad."[9] This passage was popularly called "the Gap."

The second submarine was thirty-one feet over-all, six feet in beam, and drew seven feet four inches. She had a gross displacement of nineteen tons. When Blakely Hall called her a "ram," there was some justification for his choice of the word. The *Ram* was ruggedly constructed of eleven-sixteenths-inch charcoal flange iron, and her "ramming power" was estimated by her inventor at a formidable forty-nine to fifty tons, sufficient to smash the plating of a ship's bottom in the days before double hulls were common. Holland declared with his usual frankness: "We had a demonstration once by running into the end of our pier at about six miles speed owing to my bad steering or forgetfulness of the tide. We split a twelve inch spile and lifted a horizontal tie having a load of four feet of stone ballast over it, and hurt nothing but the engineer's respect for good English."[10]

For power, the *Ram* used an improved Brayton petroleum engine meeting specifications laid down by Holland, whose experience with engines had been decidedly limited. The engine was a twin-cylinder affair with double action, thus firing twice for a single revolution of the flywheel. It was rated between fifteen and seventeen horsepower. On John Holland's own word, the engine drove the boat at nine miles per hour on the surface, but he admits that he never measured her speed submerged, though he had always intended to do so. "Observers said invariably that it [the submerged speed] appeared greater, the boat always rising farther away, in short dives, than where they expected. There is no telling for certain, but I think it was no slower than surface speed."[11]

This was probably no idle boast. The *Ram* was built to excellent proportions for her underwater function. An astute observer of nature, Holland strove to emulate the conformation of a porpoise; and he often compared his boats to this most expert swimmer of the underwater creatures. Designers of the first half of the twentieth century were to forget the need for observing basic hydrodynamic principles so clearly recognized by Holland in the *Fenian Ram* and in all the boats he was later to construct. Naval architects were too eager, in Holland's view, to clutter the upper surface of submarines with decks "for officers to strut on," or to mount on these decks guns and other paraphernalia that belonged to surface ships. Not until the advent of the diesel-powered *Albacore* and the nuclear-powered *Skipjack,* more than seventy years later, did naval architects revive the lines that characterized Holland's submarines, and thereby regain—and eventually exceed—the one-to-one ratio between speeds attained submerged and speeds attained on the surface.

The *Fenian Ram* was a three-man boat. The operator sat in a kind of bucket seat perched over the engine. On the port side, the large flywheel revolved, driving an eccentrically fastened rod that operated a compressor mounted forward over a high-pressure air tank. On the starboard side, a second eccentric drove a similar compressor. Two upright levers served as controls, joy-stick fashion: the left one controlled the rudder; the right, the diving planes.

The second member of the crew served as engineer. His task was to regulate flow through the numerous valves as required, check the gauges for pressure, or blow the fixed ballast tanks if an emergency required such action. Holland had masterfully designed the *Fenian Ram* to assure longitudinal stability, a problem that plagued such contemporaries as Goubet and such later rivals as Garrett and Nordenfeldt. This was achieved by meeting two fundamental requirements which he always set for himself: a fixed center of gravity and a constant reserve of positive buoyancy. The long, tapered bow and stern each held a sealed compressed air reservoir calculated to assure positive buoyancy. Between each reservoir and the crew's central control room, separate water ballast compartments were provided. The central location of these tanks proved a decided advantage. The after tank was always kept full when running submerged in order to prevent any disturbance from the motion of water within it. The forward tank was kept "nearly full, allowing a little to compensate for changing weights," including oil consumption and projectiles expended. This arrangement was far ahead of its time and enabled Holland to maintain a fixed center of gravity and the longitudinal stability he rightly felt to be so essential.[12]

A third member of the crew was the gunner who operated the sole piece of armament on board the *Ram*. This consisted of a pneumatic gun constructed of a nine-inch tube. Approximately eleven feet long, the gun tube ran through the center of the forward air reservoir. Its breech of heavy iron casting was centered in the forward water-ballast tank, opening by means of a hinged door into the control compartment. With the pointed bow cap screwed down into a watertight position, the gunner's task was to undog the inner door, load a six-foot projectile into the tube, shut the inner door, turn a crank which opened the bow cap, reach down and unscrew the balance valve sending a four-hundred-pound air charge into the breech, and thus fire the projectile. Water rushed in to fill the tube. The gunner cranked the bow cap closed. Then he blew the tube, forcing the water into the ballast tank that surrounded it and restoring the fixed center of gravity.[13]

Would such a complicated machine really work? It is a tribute to Holland's faith in his own boats, and to his courage, that he always tested his own submarines. After several surface runs in the Morris Canal Basin to check out the engines and the clutch, the big moment came. Here is Holland's own account of that important day in June of 1881:

Accordingly [George M.] Richards, the engineer, and myself entered the boat and closed the hatch. This shut us off from the air, and our breathing now depended entirely on the compressed air reserve. After waiting a few moments and finding no ill-effects from the compressed air, I decided to submerge. I drew back the little iron levers on either side of my head (these operated the Kingston valves in the bottom, through which water was admitted to the ballast tanks). Almost immediately the boat began to settle giving us the suggestion of slowly descending in an elevator. I now looked through the ports in the superstructure and observed that the bow had entirely disappeared and the water was within a few inches of the glass. A second or two later everything grew dark and we were entirely submerged and nothing could be seen through the ports except a dark green blur.

Our next suggestion was a slight jar when the vessel struck bottom. [The depth presumably was fourteen feet.] It might also be mentioned here that we had no light except the glow that came through the conning tower. This just about sufficed to read the gauges, but was too poor to be of interest to the engineer. The engine was not needed at the time, however, but we decided to carry a small lantern [in the future], to be used when any adjustment was necessary, but not otherwise, as it [would consume] too much of our precious oxygen.

Richards having made an examination and found everything tight, I decided to blow out the ballast and come up. Accordingly I opened the valve admitting air to the ballast tank, and at once heard a hiss that told me that the air was driving out the water. The green blur on the ports in the conning tower grew lighter as I gazed through them until suddenly the light of full day burst through, almost dazzling me. After blinking my eyes a few times, I looked out again and saw the familiar surroundings of the Gap. I now opened the hatch and stood on the seat, thus causing my head and shoulders to protrude from the tower. As soon as I was observed doing this, a cheer burst from the crowd of observers on the dock, among whom opinion was equally divided as to whether we would emerge alive from our dive or not. We had now demonstrated that our boat was tight, that our air was sufficient for breathing, and that our ballasting system was perfect.[14]

The next day, on a bet, the two men took the little submarine down and remained submerged for two and one-half hours, so alarming the men who remained on the dock that they began to grapple for the hull in an effort to raise her. "The man that wanted to bet was satisfied and badly frightened," wrote Holland of the incident.[15]

But several questions remained unanswered. Running under her own power, would the *Ram* dive and remain under water? Would the engine exhaust itself at a depth of ten or more feet? Many were the prophets who answered these questions in the negative—the professor had built himself another coffin; and, they predicted, this one would bury not one but three men.

But Holland understood what he was doing. The engine would exhaust itself outboard through the check valve and "breathe" the air from the surrounding compartment—all with little fuss, provided the interior pressure always equaled the pressure outside the hull. He was confident that the engine would work well at depths of forty feet or more, though the pressure endured by the crew might be "unreasonably high." He had planned to install a special pump to take care of the ventilation for the crew, while air for the engine was to be supplied directly from the tanks, leaving the regulating valves free to maintain a constant atmospheric pressure within the submarine. What he did not know was that events beyond his control were to prevent him from experimenting with such devices.

The tests began. Again it was Holland who made the first trial run, accompanied by Richards, the engineer.

With the clutch engaged, the *Fenian Ram* slid away from the Morris and Cummings pier and slowly proceeded into the Basin. When she had reached the far side, observers saw her turn and almost simultaneously settle until only the nine inches of her streamlined turret lay awash. A hand appeared and drew the hatch closed. Then, almost imperceptibly, she disappeared. Three hundred feet from where she had submerged, the *Fenian Ram* arose, first the turret, then a quarter of the hull that slanted off toward the bow and stern. When the hatch opened, a great shout from the spectators on the pier reached the men in the submarine.

Holland was jubilant over the results. The leading edges of the diving planes forward of their fulcrum points would have to be sawed off to achieve greater maneuverability, but this was a small matter. She behaved like a porpoise, and that was exactly what he wanted. The soundness of the "diving boat" principle seemed assured. "There is scarcely anything required of a good submarine boat that this one did not do well enough, or fairly well," wrote Holland of the *Ram*. "It could remain quite a long time submerged, probably three days; it could shoot a torpedo [projectile] containing a 100 pound charge to 50 or 60 yards in a straight line underwater and to some uncertain range, probably 300 yards over water."[16]

The automobile torpedo of the Luppis-Whitehead type[17] had been perfected several years before the construction of Holland's second boat, but means of launching it had been confined to tubes mounted on surface vessels. The pneumatic gun on the *Fenian Ram* was used to fire a projectile, or in more modern parlance, a missile containing a warhead charged with gunpowder. Holland's missiles were not, however, self-propelling. The Paterson inventor faced many difficulties in procuring the correct projectiles for use in the gun. His machinist was compelled to test the effectiveness of the firing mechanism by resorting to such ammunition as a nail keg, until someone at Delamater's described the submarine to Captain John Ericsson of *Monitor* fame. Ericsson's *Destroyer* was under construction at the yard that had just completed Holland's submarine. The captain sent a note to Professor Holland offering to supply him with several dummy projectiles of his own design.

Holland recalled that day in Ashburton, Cork, twenty years earlier, when he had first read about the designer of the revolutionary Union ironclad. Now, here was a note from the famous Ericsson offering his assistance. It was that measure of recognition which genius needs to feed upon. Holland, in his firm and clearly legible handwriting, accepted Captain Ericsson's offer.

The first Ericsson projectile was fired under a pressure of only three hundred pounds per square inch to avoid hitting a floating dry dock moored in the Basin. The *Ram* was submerged to a depth which put the bow cap of the pneumatic gun about three feet below the surface. The firing valve was released. The projectile cleared the muzzle by eight or ten feet. Then, it leaped out of the water and rose sixty to seventy feet in the air to plunge downward and bury itself irretrievably in the mud at the bottom of the Basin.[18]

The career of the second Ericsson dummy projectile was even more eventful than the first. The bow of the *Fenian Ram* was deliberately dipped about five degrees below the horizontal and swung to port to keep the projectile clear of the moored dock. On this second shot the projectile doubled its course under water, again leaped into the air, passed over the breakwater on the far side of the Basin, and struck hard against a piling. From behind the breakwater came a frightened shout, "What's that!" The head of an unsuspecting fisherman popped up from behind a rock. Holland felt that he would have to improve on the design of Ericsson's dummy projectiles.

The inventor's more immediate concern, however, was effective submarine navigation. The master spy, LeCaron, was at work again in the summer of 1881. Supposedly he, or one of his cohorts, informed the British Consul General at New York of the experiments of the Holland torpedo boat. Reports on the *Ram*'s success prompted the Consul General to put pressure on Washington to intervene. Orders were sent to the Collector for the Port of New York, a Mr. Robertson, to keep an eye on the *Fenian Ram* and her inventor. It appears that the British were more alarmed by the proceedings in the Basin than were the officials in Washington. The American attitude was that an inventor merely wished to experiment with his creation, and there was no need to make an international incident of the affair. So the concern of officialdom subsided and Holland was free to continue his investigations.[19]

To determine the *Fenian Ram*'s potential as an effective submarine, John Holland needed deeper water than was available around the Basin. On 3 July 1883, the craft got under way with the inventor at the helm and George Richards standing by below in the engine room. The boat had been sealed at the dock for diving. She headed down New York Harbor to seek the depths of the Narrows. She had just passed Robbins Reef Lighthouse when Holland noticed that his view of Staten Island ahead and of Bay Ridge to port was obscured by what he described as "a pair of brown rags hanging on either side of the turret." This was both disconcerting and inexplicable. The water roughened. The deadlights in the turret were washed with spray. Then a strange scuffling could be heard overhead, clearly indicating to Holland that some unwelcomed visitor was astride his submarine. The inventor swung the *Fenian Ram* upstream to run with the waves. The hatch was opened, and there sat a Negro boy grimly clinging by his knees to the turret like a bareback rider in a circus. Convinced that it would be dangerous to proceed with anyone so precariously perched atop the slippery skin of the submarine, Holland invited the frightened stowaway below. The boy would have none of it. He assured Holland that he was perfectly safe where he was and he promised to hang on. There was no recourse but to proceed cautiously for the unfamiliar Brooklyn shore.

As the *Ram* approached within a thousand feet of the Bay Ridge ferry slip, two curious boys rowed their little boat into shouting range. "What's that thing?" they cried. Holland disengaged the clutch, and the *Ram* slowed down, enabling the boys to pull alongside. Holland, the school teacher, kindly invited the boys to satisfy their curiosity.

They went below, inspected the small central compartment with great interest, and expressed their incredulity at the strangest boat they had ever seen. By now the sun was setting, and the crew of the *Ram* was anxious to find a berth for the night. Where could they dock? The boys, Tunis Bergen and his cousin, Henry Midgley, were both sure that Tunis' brother, Vanderbilt Bergen, would be happy to provide a slip for the *Fenian Ram*. Eagerly they jumped into their rowboat, attached a painter to a ring on the fishlike heap of metal, and headed for shore. Convinced that they led some important though vague mission, they guided the submarine to Mr. Bergen's dock near the Crescent Yacht Club station. Thus were Holland and the *Ram* introduced to the Bergen yard which was ideally situated for experimental runs in the Narrows and which was later to be a base of operations for the boat that was the final and climatic achievement of Holland's life.

Experiments and trial runs out of Bay Ridge continued through the months of July and August. On one occasion, the captain of the ferryboat *St. Johns*, which was running off Stapleton across the Narrows, observed a strange metal monster spouting a mass of water as it reared up in a steep, porpoise-like dive. He brought the ferryboat to a sudden stop; whereupon, the monster disappeared below the surface of the harbor. Shaken by the apparition, the captain as suddenly turned his vessel in a hasty retreat for shore. Returning from a trial run in the *Fenian Ram* that day, Holland noticed that the men on Bergen's dock were "jumping around and acting as if demented."

"Oh, you frightened the devil out of the *St. Johns*," commented Bergen.

The mild professor admitted that he, too, was somewhat baffled, for he had heard the unmistakeable chugging of paddle wheels and had dived to a depth of twenty feet to avoid a possible collision. When the sound had suddenly stopped for no apparent reason, he decided it was safe to surface; upon surfacing, no large vessel was in sight.

In September, 1883, the *Fenian Ram* returned to her berth at the Morris and Cummings docks in Jersey City. John Holland had every reason to be proud of her achievements. He could now take her out from her slip as casually as a yachtsman might take his pleasure craft out for a day's sail. In fact, several trips made from the Basin took on the air of pleasure cruises. On a cold November day, Holland and Richards, with two guests on board and with a sloop containing a party of six in tow, headed up the Hudson River for an outing. The little submarine labored as she made her way through the ice floes in the river. When Holland was forced to reduce speed in order to let a steamer cross his bows, the towline to the sloop slackened. It caught in the submarine's propeller and was instantly severed, casting the little sloop and its party adrift in the ice-clogged waters. Snugly ensconced within the submarine, Holland and his crew were totally unaware of what had happened; and the closed hatch prevented them from hearing the frantic cries of the people in the drifting sloop. The *Ram* proceeded for a mile upriver before Holland realized that the submarine was no longer laboring with her tow.

On another occasion, off the grounds of the Stevens Institute of Technology at Castle Heights, Hoboken, Holland took the *Fenian Ram* down within a few feet of the bottom of the river. The professor estimated the depth to be between thirty-seven and forty-seven feet, and charts of the area indicate a probable forty-five-foot descent. Some writers have claimed that the *Ram* once reached sixty feet in the waters of the Narrows below Stapleton, and Holland himself declared that in November of 1883 he not only reached the sixty-foot mark, but that he remained at that depth for an hour. Certainly the *Fenian Ram* was capable of such a feat.

The amusement park atmosphere wherever the submarine was berthed helped to conceal the determination and singleness of purpose which motivated John Holland. Between trial runs in the *Ram*, he was fully occupied at the Gannon and Cooper shop in Jersey City where he spent his spare time supervising the construction of his third submarine, an all-metal, sixteen-foot, one-ton replica of the successful *Fenian Ram*. Only in size was his third craft reminiscent of his first little boat, which lay in the mud of the Upper Passaic River. The new boat's purpose was vastly different. It was a working model designed to incorporate improvements suggested by the trials of the *Ram*. With this diminutive craft, Holland hoped to test hitherto unexplored principles of submarine navigation which he had been unable to exhaust in previous experiments.

During one of Holland's absences from dockside, Engineer Richards decided to try out the *Ram* on his own. Dropping downstream from the Gap, he passed dangerously close to a tug and the barge which she was towing. The wash from the boats lapped over the open turret into the engine compartment. The *Fenian Ram* began to settle rapidly. In another moment, Richards was literally blown out of the turret through the hatch. As Holland wrote: "He happened to be just below the hatch . . . and was blown out by the escaping air from within the boat." The crew of the tug hastened to his rescue. Sadly Holland noted, "It cost my backers $3,000 to raise the boat and put her in shape again."

In the meantime, all was not well in the ranks of John Holland's backers. The Fenian Brotherhood had financed the three submarines, but not without dissension from impatient members who wanted their "ten cents worth of revolution every week." Pilfering of the Skirmishing Fund for purposes other than those for which it was intended put the Holland venture in a precarious position. The Mulcahy case was being heard in the Supreme Court of New York in 1883. Mulcahy's suit sought an injunction to restrain the Trustees of the Fund from using any money in the treasury without the jurisdiction of the court. The suit named Rossa, Devoy, Luby, Breslin, Carroll, and Reynolds as defendants. Simultaneously, reports were being circulated that clearly showed dissatisfaction with Breslin's handling of the submarine project, though after 1881 his association with the work had been somewhat modified by his assumption of the duties of editor on the staff of Devoy's *Irish Nation*. That Breslin continued to play an important role in the enterprise is evident from his letter to Devoy of 14 April 1883: "The *Ram* has been the excitement of the week in the papers here. We simply moved her to a place more convenient to paint her and make a few experiments. The impression has got afloat that she is gone to sea."[20]

Holland, too, may have muddied the waters. He claimed that George Brayton had asked more for the engine used in the *Ram* than the engine was worth and, if Devoy is correct, was prepared to make his point at law.[21] Breslin, already threatened by the Mulcahy suit and the growing unrest in the Clan, criticized Holland for his inopportune complaint. Holland, in turn, sought the advice of James Reynolds of New Haven, the former owner of the *Catalpa*. Reynolds wrote to Breslin on 8 October 1883: "Mr. Holland spent the whole of yesterday with me and after a very long explanation I think I find the difference between you is in the main imaginary."[22] Reynolds then urged Breslin to call a special meeting of the Trustees of the Fund in order that they might vote on Reynolds' proposal to offer an additional sum of $1,500 to Holland for his services.

How this matter was finally adjudicated is not clear, but Breslin was certain that the time had come to act. He felt it was necessary to protect the Brotherhood from possible legal attachment of its properties. His action brought the affairs of the *Fenian Ram* and her sixteen-foot companion submarine to a dramatic conclusion.

On a dark night in late November of 1883, Breslin and a few fellow Fenians, armed with a pass bearing the forged signature of John P. Holland, gained access to the docks at the Morris and Cummings pier in the Canal Basin at the Gap.[23] The night watchman apparently did not think it unusual for a tug to pull up at the slip. At any rate, the pass assured him that the unpredictable Irishman could well have ordered the transfer of his submarine under cover of darkness, for the strange craft had been surrounded with an aura of mystery ever since her inception. The Fenians deftly placed the *Ram* in tow and then slid the blocks from under the sixteen-foot model which rested on ways near the water's edge. The smaller craft was tied astern of the *Ram*, and the strange convoy made its way into New York Harbor. The tug rounded

Manhattan during the night and proceeded up the East River. By the time she reached Whitestone Point, the wind was blowing in strongly from Long Island Sound. The model boat's turret had not been completely closed, and no gasket sealed the hatch. In the choppy waters she foundered, snapped her towline, and settled to the bottom in one hundred and ten feet of water.[24] The tug forged ahead into the Sound with only the *Ram* astern. The next day she reached New Haven and cautiously worked her way toward the Brass Foundry of James Reynolds on the Mill River.

Breslin and Reynolds attempted to operate the *Ram* in New Haven Harbor, but the little submarine was poorly managed. Considering her to be a menace to navigation, the harbor master prohibited any further experiments. Holland complained to Devoy about Breslin's clandestine action, but to no avail.[25] He later wrote of the "theft" of the *Fenian Ram* with surprising finality: "I received no notice of the contemplated move then, nor was I notified after. . . . I have no intention of advancing any excuses for the incident, as no official explanation was ever made to me concerning it. As a result, I never bothered again with my backers nor they with me."[26] Fully aware that his erstwhile partners could not operate the submarine, he let the matter stand by declaring prophetically, "I'll let her rot on their hands."[27]

The final fate of so notable a boat in the annals of submarine navigation deserves some mention. In 1888, Mulcahy was still attempting to lay claims on the underwater craft in order to assure the payment of the debt he felt due him. Devoy wrote to Reynolds: "I am so sick of the boat and Mulcahy's insane war on us that I should be inclined to let him take the thing and have it for a white elephant if I did not believe there is a prospect of selling it, if it was only put in decent condition."[28] The rumor that she was offered to Russia may have been correct, but in any case no one attempted to revive her. She was placed in a lumber shed on the Mill River, and her Brayton engine was removed to operate a forge in Reynolds' foundry. In 1916, the hull was taken from the shed and carted to New York City where she was exhibited at a Madison Square Garden bazaar which was held to raise money for the victims of the Irish Uprising of that year. Here, the *Fenian Ram* performed her last service in the cause of Irish independence.

For some time, the *Ram* was on the grounds of the New York State Marine School at Clason Point. Then, in 1927, she was purchased by Edward A. Browne of Paterson, New Jersey, and set up in West Side Park, within a few hundred yards of the spot where Holland first descended in the *Holland No. 1* beneath the waters of the Upper Passaic. There she stands today, a most appropriate monument to the genius of her creator.

Michael Holland rightly deserves the credit for securing the initial backing from the Fenians for his brother John's submarine proposals. Writing to John Devoy in the year of the Irish Benefit at Madison Square Garden, Michael spoke with feeling about the famous *Ram:* "I hate to think of that boat becoming a curiosity in a museum. She is the only boat that John P. ever built that he didn't have somebody to tell him what to do and how to do it also. . . . I suppose you will lose interest in the boat now that she has become merely a curiosity? But to me she will always be 'the boat'."[29]

In many respects the *Ram* was, indeed, "the boat." Frank T. Cable has correctly asserted that "it belongs to the record to say that the Irish question produced the modern submarine."[30] And one of the first American naval men to recognize the potential of the submarine, Admiral Philip Hichborn, said of Holland and the *Fenian Ram:* "After the completion of this boat Holland led the world far and away in the solution of submarine problems and for a couple of years demonstrated that he could perfectly control his craft in the vertical plane."[31]

CHAPTER FIVE

THE LEAN YEARS
1883-1893

John Philip Holland had lost the financial backing which he needed to continue his practical investigations into the problems of submarine navigation. When American-Irish patriots saw their hopes for war between the United States and Great Britain shattered by the amicable settlement at Geneva of the *Alabama* affair, when Fenianism failed to make a *cause célèbre* of the Phoenix Park murders, and when the expenditures of the Skirmishing Fund, composed of the hard-earned nickels and dimes of Irish laborers and domestics, came under legal scrutiny creating new factionalisms within the Clan-na-Gael, John Holland knew that the stolen *Ram* marked the end of a chapter in his life. Furthermore, he was an American citizen now, and his loyalties lay beyond Ireland. Yet he did owe a debt to the United Brotherhood for giving him the opportunity to explore his peculiar mechanical bent in the direction of underwater craft. He was not one to forget the Brotherhood's contribution.

But what did the future hold for Holland? He could return to teaching; however, there was much to be said against such a course of action. He was now forty-two years old. The former youthful, clean-shaven, slender school teacher of St. John's School in Paterson betrayed the marks of his more recent efforts. His hairline had continued to recede at the temples. The full but firm lips were now shaded by a mustache which was to become, like the ever-present bowler hat and rimless spectacles, a kind of trademark of the man. Though he kept in touch with his friends in Paterson, including one Margaret Foley, he had shifted his lodgings to Newark. The three Fenian submarines had brought him recognition, if not notoriety, and had opened for him a whole new circle of American acquaintances. With their assistance, he foresaw the possibility of further exploiting his mechanical interests. So he decided not to return to teaching.

Holland's faith in his American friends was to prove wholly warranted. Vanderbilt Bergen at Bay Ridge would be a connection of considerable value to him in the development of the epoch-making *Holland VI*. Charles A. Morris, a young engineer of the Morris and Cummings Dredging Company, had been among the few who did not

49

scoff at the *Ram* when she had been tied up at the company's docks. Holland had used this man's experience when fitting out the sixteen-foot companion to the *Ram*. Then, before the dissension over the theft of the boats had fully subsided, Holland met Lieutenant William W. Kimball, United States Navy. Without Kimball's devotion, Holland's ultimate success might have been irreparably delayed. To him Holland also owed his introduction to Lieutenant Edmund L. Zalinski of the Fifth U. S. Artillery.

The circumstances of the first meeting with Lieutenant Kimball revealed the extent to which Holland's reputation had spread. While Breslin and Reynolds pondered over the question of what to do with the *Fenian Ram*, the inventor found employment as a draftsman in Roland's Iron Works in New York City. Holland's assignment was to work with the aging George Brayton in an effort to improve the Brayton petroleum engine. While so employed, late in 1883, Holland received a note inviting him to dine on board the flagship of the Naval Artillery Station at the Brooklyn Navy Yard. The note was signed by Kimball.[1]

The young naval officer warmly received John Holland. At dinner in his quarters, the two men plunged into a discussion of the future of underwater boats. Kimball spoke of Lieutenant Barber's lecture on submarine boats, which had been published in pamphlet form by the U. S. Torpedo Station at Newport and which included an account of an early design submitted to the government by Holland. Kimball was cognizant of the press reports of Holland's experiments in the Passaic River and of his adventures with the *Fenian Ram*. Now, what did this Irishman really know about the principles of controlling and maneuvering a vessel beneath the surface of the sea?

Holland recognized at once a sympathetic and intelligent audience in this naval officer. Without hesitation, he began to explain what he had learned from his three boats. A submarine must first meet two fundamental requirements: a reserve of positive buoyancy and a fixed center of gravity. Furthermore, a submarine must be highly maneuverable if she is to be an efficient engine of war. "It is worse than useless to provide that the boat shall always descend and rise on an even keel," whether by creating a negative buoyancy or forcing it up and down with awkward and dangerously protruding vertical-thrust propellers.[2] Such an agonizing descent involved precious moments and made the submarine more vulnerable to attack from surface vessels. Rather, Holland insisted, a submarine should be steered down by horizontal planes affixed to the stern, using the engine to force the buoyant hull beneath the surface of the water. If the engine failed, the boat would always rise to the surface automatically, a safety measure not to be overlooked. She should dive like a porpoise and rise like one.

"Of course we discussed many details," wrote Kimball, "as to how to get the requisite low but safe metacenter fore-and-aft height, so as to make the craft handy on her vertical helm and at the same time stable enough to be safe, and many others."[3]

The naval officer was impressed by the three principles discussed. If he could arrange it, would Holland come to work for the Navy Department as a draftsman? Kimball would see that a "cast-iron contract" was drawn up that would compensate Holland for his own creative designs and would pay additional sums to the inventor if the Department decided, in the interest of military secrecy, that it should hold title to his designs and inventions. "Holland was delighted with such a prospect."

On this note the two men parted company. Kimball was off on an extended cruise to foreign waters, but he gave "the submarine question a little fillip in the Navy Department" before he sailed. Holland waited for word from him. There was no doubt now in Holland's mind that he could assist in adding a new arm to the naval services of his adopted country, provided the country could be convinced of its need for a submarine service.

In Kimball's words, "Holland waited. I was bound away to southward. Just before sailing, Zalinski came to me and asked who knew anything about submarines. I told him that Holland was far and away the best submarine man in the United States, if not in the world, but that he, Zalinski, was to keep hands off, as the Navy Department might make Holland an offer."[4] As Holland watched the mail for a letter from Kimball, he must have recalled Captain Edward Simpson's comment of 1875, "to put anything through in Washington was uphill work." The captain was indeed right.

In the meantime, Lieutenant Zalinski offered Holland a position in his Pneumatic Gun Company. Reluctantly Holland wrote to Kimball, who was then cruising in the Caribbean, and explained that his financial circumstances were such that he could no longer wait for the Navy contract. Had this contract materialized, as Kimball desired, the history of the submarine in the United States would have been vastly different. The control of Holland patents would have remained in the Navy Department; and, in addition to a probable saving to the American taxpayer, the United States might well have been able to maintain its lead in submarine development over the other naval powers later involved in World War I. In the hands of private interests, Holland's patent rights were more readily secured by foreign companies. Such reflection is, however, speculation and cannot alter the record. Holland accepted the position in the Pneumatic Gun Company.

Zalinski, an ordnance expert, was a well-known inventor of military devices. He had developed a telescopic sight for large artillery, and had devised a range and position finding system for coastal guns. Prior to his promotion to second lieutenant in the

Fifth U. S. Artillery, Zalinski had been a professor of military science at the Massachusetts Institute of Technology. In 1883, he was on active duty at Fort Hamilton in Brooklyn.

Encouraged by Holland's acceptance of his offer, Zalinski began at once a promotion scheme among his employees and friends to finance the construction of a submarine that would employ his dynamite gun. His negotiations and Holland's quiet confidence attracted sufficient private capital for the two men to establish the Nautilus Submarine Boat Company. There was a kind of mockery in the fact that Holland was about to build his fourth submarine without the support of naval authorities; indeed, that craft was made possible largely through the efforts of an officer in the United States Army.

During the year 1884, John Holland divided his time between New York City and the parade grounds at old Fort Lafayette, on an island off the Brooklyn shore below Bay Ridge. This building site was chosen because of Zalinski's post at nearby Fort Hamilton. Behind a screen designed to discourage the curious, Holland supervised the construction of the submarine which became known simply as the *Zalinski Boat*.

Once again the professor from Paterson seized the opportunity not merely to repeat what he already knew, but to test new features of design and new equipment. In the *Zalinski Boat*, he wished to experiment with a system of tubular air reservoirs originally intended for the *Fenian Ram* but abandoned on the earlier boat to cut expenses. There was an improved *camera lucida* to be tried in an effort to extend underwater visibility. It is important to note Holland's desire to check the usefulness of the Wallaston prism that replaced the simple mirrors of earlier tubes. Reporters, accustomed to the more primitive instrument used to sketch scenes in the days before photography became common, insisted on referring to the tube in the *Zalinski Boat* as a "simple *camera lucida*." The *camera obscura*, however, included a darkened chamber which was in effect provided in the turret of a submerged submarine. Thus the tube in the *Zalinski Boat* was a hybrid instrument which foreshadowed the periscope. Holland, writing of his trials in the *Fenian Ram*, observed: "It was proved that guiding the boat by direct vision while submerged was impracticable, that steering a straight course under water, although not regarded as a difficulty by anyone up to that date, was a problem that must be solved before submarine warfare could be made practicable under modern conditions."[5] The fourth submarine also enabled Holland to test an automatic steering vane mounted above the vertical planes of the conventional rudder. This mechanism had been placed on the sixteen-foot model which his former partners had stolen and lost. The inventor therefore welcomed the chance to try his patented pilot on a new boat.[6]

Lieutenant Zalinski had his own interests in the submarine. He wished to prove the merits of his pneumatic dynamite gun, and Holland's boat was precisely what he wanted to demonstrate the versatility of this piece of armament. In 1886, Zalinski declared in an article in *The Forum:* "The boat may be considered as a floating gun carriage." He claimed that his pneumatic gun could hurl a two-hundred to five-hundred-pound charge of high explosives to a distance of twenty-four hundred feet— nearly half a mile. The dynamite gun tube was mounted in the bow just above the pointed stem of the submarine. When running submerged, the helmsman would spot his target through the viewing tube, bring the bow to the surface at an appropriate angle from the horizontal, and fire the projectile containing the dynamite charge. With the diving lever forward, the boat would quickly plunge downward again under the combined action of the gun's recoil and the thrust of her propellers. For a brief moment the submarine would expose a small, difficult-to-observe portion of her hull, and then quickly disappear from the scene of action. Zalinski knew that only a Holland-type submarine could execute such a maneuver successfully.

Hopes were high when the two men first discussed their plans. Construction was another matter. The amount of capital at the command of the Nautilus Submarine Boat Company was limited. Some economies would have to be effected, so it was decided to construct the hull of wood on frames of iron. Cyrus Plant, of Brooklyn, contracted to build the boat. She was to be fifty feet long, and the diameter of her largest frame amidships was to measure eight feet—by far the largest craft Holland had attempted. Certain contemporary sketches gave her a stubby appearance, but she was in fact so elongated that the popular description of "cigar-shaped" aptly applied. She was even more spindly than the *Ram*. A platform below the conning tower enabled the operator to stand at the controls with his head and shoulders in the turret. This arrangement had certain advantages over the control areas of Holland's earlier submarines. The operator's position was more independent of the machinery below. Also, such a relatively commodious control room enabled a single individual to manage all the principal functions of the vessel. The diving planes answered to the helmsman's movement of a bar lever which was pushed forward for submerging and aft for surfacing. Another lever was used for steering. The depth gauges, the control that shifted the manual steering mechanism over to the automatic pilot vane, the levers for operating the Kingston flood valves and the throttle, all were within the pilot's reach. Both the

Ram and the *Zalinski Boat* thus heralded the mid-twentieth century efforts of naval architects to design a one-man control system for submarines. Increased submerged speeds and greater maneuverability, made possible by the combined use of nuclear power for propulsion and a hull shape designed for greater efficiency submerged than surfaced—a Holland principle—have dictated a revival of the control system employed by Holland.[7]

While the *Zalinski Boat* was still on her blocks on the old parade ground, the lieutenant was surprised one day to see a uniformed visitor peer around the canvas screen which enclosed the construction area. Lieutenant Kimball had come to pay them a visit. The screen, Zalinski explained, was merely a device to reduce the newspaper reporter nuisance which had plagued their work from the beginning. Holland was at work inside the boat, and Zalinski called to him. "Holland appeared from the bowels of the spindle-of-revolution-shaped craft on ways in the Fort. His face," Kimball recalled, "was smudged and his brow careworn."[8]

Holland was plainly discouraged, and he spoke of his dissatisfaction in a private conversation with Kimball. The boat had proved nothing, except to satisfy the stockholders of the Nautilus Company that a man could live in its interior at atmospheric pressure and in normally pure air for a considerable length of time. He thought that the petroleum engine was far from adequate to propel the craft; he was equally dubious about the armament proposed by Zalinski. The *camera lucida*, he felt, was useless. The apparent hopes of the stockholders that the submarine could be sold for use in the Sino-French War had dimmed, for hostilities in that struggle were over.

On Friday, 4 September 1885, the submarine was prepared for launching. Ways led from the parade ground of the Fort out over the high sea wall to the water below. It was an almost impossible launching site. The greatest skill would be required for a successful launching, and Cyrus Plant insisted that it should be supervised by a naval officer who knew about such matters. Holland remembered that "This part of the program was in the hands of a young engineer who had either insufficient knowledge of the subject or lacked the ability to put his knowledge to practical use."[9]

At the command of "down daggers" from the naval engineer, the yardmen knocked the dog shores from under the submarine. She began to move down the tallowed ways. Suddenly it became evident that she was picking up too much speed. At this moment the span of ways over the edge of the wall collapsed, hurling the craft into some pilings at the edge of the water and staving a hole in her bottom. In the traditions of the sea, this was an ill-omened launching, to say the least.

The *Zalinski Boat* was raised and repaired. In the summer of 1886 she made sever-

al trial runs in the Narrows of lower New York Harbor, presumably more at the insistence of the Army lieutenant than from any enthusiasm on the part of her
inventor.[10] By the winter of 1886, the Nautilus Submarine Boat Company was a matter of history. How Zalinski squared accounts with the stockholders is not fully known.
Holland said that the boat was dismantled, and the engine and other machinery were
removed and sold to reimburse partially the investors in the Company.

It is doubtful whether Holland's fourth submarine contributed much to the still un-
solved problems of submarine navigation. From Holland's point of view, the *Zalinski
Boat* was really a gamble by which the inventor hoped to keep his paper dreams alive in
the real world of practical construction.

For most of his adult life, Holland had devoted himself almost completely to his vo-
cation, first teaching and then submarine navigation. Absorbed in the task at hand, he
had little leisure. Yet early in 1887 there came a significant change. In Brooklyn, on
17 January, he married Margaret Foley, of his old neighborhood in Paterson. He was
forty-six years old, and his late marriage may have come as a surprise to those who
were not familiar with his frequent weekend visits to Paterson. John was Margaret's
senior by at least a dozen years. His bride's father, John Foley, an immigrant from
Ireland, had been employed in the silk mills of Paterson, and Margaret had been born
in that city. By the time of her marriage to John, both her parents were dead.[11]

It was not a propitious year for the couple to marry. The former school teacher was
now famous, but his latest venture had ended in failure. He was without the source of
income one usually associates with a man contemplating marriage. On the other hand,
it is certain that Margaret considered it no risk to join fortunes with a man who in
forty-six years had accomplished more than most men were able to do in a lifetime.
Sustained by friends in Paterson and by an unwavering faith in their church, John and
Margaret settled in the Newark parish of St. Patrick's Cathedral to which Monsignor
P. Whalen, Holland's first benefactor in America, was later assigned.

In the following year, Holland found time to bring himself abreast of the latest developments in submarine design as reported in the technical journals and daily press.
In the United States, there were the experiments of another professor, J. H. L. Tuck,
creator of the *Peacemaker*. The name of this boat, Tuck's second submarine attempt,
was most suggestive. His first boat had a central propeller placed in a recess under the
hull, designed to drive the craft up or down; but the *Peacemaker* used horizontal
planes both fore and aft, anticipating the level-keel principle of submersion later perfected by Simon Lake. In Tuck's day, this principle was accepted almost universally as
the only safe mode of operation for a submarine "by those," as Holland observed,

"who should have known better." The unique feature of the *Peacemaker* was her patented Honigman's natron boiler, a fireless method of generating steam by the use of caustic soda. Tuck claimed that a fifteen-hundred-pound charge of caustic soda at ninety-five per cent saturation could furnish sufficient steam power to drive the fourteen-horsepower Westinghouse engine for five hours. While Holland was busy completing the *Zalinski Boat*, the *Peacemaker* underwent a series of trials in New York Harbor, and not without semiofficial notice of naval observers. Holland knew that he had a rival in Professor Tuck.[12]

The Swedish inventor of machine guns and torpedoes, Thorsten Nordenfeldt, represented to Holland an even more formidable competitor than Tuck. Nordenfeldt published a description of his first submarine in 1886. She had the startling length of sixty-four feet and was nine feet in diameter. The plating of her hull varied in thickness, but averaged one-half inch. Propelled by steam, the Nordenfeldt boat had three engines. One, of course, was for forward propulsion. The two smaller engines performed the dual function of driving air blowers when running awash and of activating two vertical propellers encased in sponsons on either side of the vessel amidships when submerged. The vertical propellers, working in conjunction with horizontal bow planes, made possible descent and ascent on an even keel.

It was never difficult to find a crew for the Nordenfeldt boat, because men felt secure in the presence of the familiar steam engine. Besides, the vessel was "sanely designed" to keep her decks horizontal.

Perhaps the most ingenious device incorporated in the Nordenfeldt design was the internal counterweight. This device automatically corrected the bow planes when the vessel plunged too steeply and brought the submarine back to the horizontal without the aid of the pilot. It might be presumed that this mechanism assured longitudinal stability, but, as Holland accurately observed, Nordenfeldt's boat did not have a fixed center of gravity. Rather, the center moved as a result of "empty spaces in her large submerging tanks, and steam space in her hot water tanks, and to the want of an automatic system of compensating for weights expended."[13] The counterbalance attached to the bow planes would not overcome these defects. Kimball, too, sensed that the Nordenfeldt boats "would have been successful had they been designed for diving instead of for rising and sinking."[14]

The Greek government purchased the first Nordenfeldt submarine after the inventor had been prevailed upon to add to the outside hull a launching tube for a White-head torpedo that would supplement the inventor's own torpedo device. The boat had been successfully demonstrated in the Sound of Landskrona, off the Swedish coast, before an impressive array of representatives from the principal naval powers of Europe. These trials had taken place a few days after the unsuccessful launching of Holland's *Zalinski Boat*. In the following April, Greek officials witnessed an experimental run of their newly purchased submarine in the Bay of Salamis. Their country now possessed a new "Greek fire" with which to frighten its enemies.

Neighboring Turkey, excited by the submarine's reported success and fearful lest a traditional enemy might threaten her with this unconventional weapon, ordered Nordenfeldt to build two large submarine torpedo boats for her developing navy.

While an interest in underwater craft was slowly penetrating the more liberal elements of the naval staffs of the great powers, the official position was still that submarines were meant for the weaker nations. Indeed, submarines were considered an anathema by the great powers, threatening the very existence of a jealously guarded hierarchy of surface-ship admirals. Upon reading of the Greek and Turkish orders for Nordenfeldt boats, Holland remembered how that old seadog, Earl St. Vincent, had chastised Pitt for encouraging Robert Fulton: "Pitt was the greatest fool that ever existed to encourage a mode of war which they who commanded the seas did not want, and which, if successful, would deprive them of it."[15]

John Holland realized that the Swedish munitions manufacturer would bear additional watching, since the chief designer behind his boats was the Reverend George W. Garrett, an English clergyman and the creator of the submersibles *Resurgam* I and II. Nordenfeldt had combined forces with Garrett to produce the Turkish boats.

In the early 1880's, France was the only major power seriously intent upon solving the problems of submarine navigation. Although that country's interest dated back to *Le Plongeur* of Siméon Bourgois and Charles Brun, her practical concern began with the sixteen-foot, two-ton boat of Claude Goubet, presumably intended for the Russian government. She used accumulators (storage batteries) which operated an Edison-type dynamo, possibly the third submarine in history to employ successfully electric power as the sole means for propulsion.[16] But this boat was abandoned when it was found that she would not stay at the depth set for her, nor could she maintain the proper longitudinal stability.

The *Goubet II*, launched in 1889, was a two-man craft with an attractive interior, a true rival of the earlier *Fenian Ram*. Much of the apparatus on board the *Goubet II* was operated electrically. She even had installed on the bow an electric "headlight," though Zalinski made clear in his treatise on "Submarine Navigation" that such a device was really useless below the surface unless it were carried ahead of the boat on a kind of automobile fish which he appropriately designated "a pilot fish." Somehow

Goubet had solved the problem of longitudinal stability in his second boat, but, like her predecessor, she stubbornly refused to remain at the depth set for her by her helmsman.[17]

Gustave Zédé's *Gymnote* holds the distinction of being the first submarine accepted by a major naval power. She became the basic unit in the subsequent submarine fleet of France. Designed by Dupuy de Lôme, and incorporating improvements by the famous naval engineer and shipbuilder, Zédé, the *Gymnote* was launched in September, 1888. The fifty-six-foot, thirty-ton, cylindro-conical hull was re-enforced by thirty-one spherical frames braced longitudinally. She was operated by an electric motor capable of fifty-five horsepower, the current being supplied by a battery of five hundred and sixty-four accumulators. The result was a speed of eight knots on the surface when the propeller was turning at two hundred and eighty revolutions per minute, a quite satisfactory performance. [Max Laubeuf's *Narval* came more than a decade later.]

Although certain pieces of equipment used on the first French submarine were not completely successful, they did suggest the direction future developments were to take. She carried a compass attached to a gyroscope which, on all reports, was none too satisfactory. For improved visibility she used a *camera lucida* and a primitive prismatic periscope, though the former consistently proved more reliable. And as Holland pointed out, the *Gymnote* could not proceed far from her base of operations, since she had no internal means for rejuvenating her accumulators. He felt, nevertheless, that in spite of all her defects, her acceptance by the French Ministry of Marine might possibly stimulate a squelching of resistance to submarine boat construction in United States naval circles. Where naval men were themselves the innovators, as in the case of France, the cause of the submarine almost always appeared to advance without delay. Wherever this was not the case, as with most of the underwater craft developed to that date, the obstacles to official approval seemed insurmountable.

Lesser experiments with underwater boats, such as the *Porpoise* of J. F. Waddington, the *Nautilus* of A. Campbell and J. Ash, and the Italian *L'Audace*, may also have come to John Holland's attention. It is possible that Holland had heard, too, of Lieutenant Isaac Peral of the Spanish Navy who began the construction of a submarine in 1888. He launched the electrically driven *Peral* in 1889. This boat passed all tests and successfully fired three Whitehead torpedoes, but politics within the Spanish Navy caused her rejection by naval authorities. The impact of Peral's experiments was not to be felt in America until the growing tensions with Spain made the United States realize the military potential of underwater vessels.

By 1887, Holland probably knew that Montgomery Sicard, Chief of the Ordnance

Bureau, later Admiral Sicard, was bent on persuading William C. Whitney, President S. Grover Cleveland's Secretary of the Navy, to open a competition for an experimental submarine design. Holland could rely on Kimball to keep him informed of the mysterious ways in which the Navy Department functioned. In remarks not typical of Holland's usual modesty and quiet confidence, but rather more characteristic of those periods in his life when circumstances prevented him from occupying himself with the practical application of his ideas, and when bitterness was more likely to replace his customary composure, he wrote:

> About this time the United States Navy Department was mildly interested in the performance of submarines in France, where they had attained some slight degree of success. The designs of these boats, I am sure, were based on certain fundamental points of my *Fenian Ram* design. As I have said previously, there were a number of foreign officers present at Delameter's [Delamater's] Yard from 1879 to 1881, while the boat was in the course of construction, and it is hardly to be expected that they failed to take notes. However, the knowledge they secured did them very little good, because, while they secured a lot of valuable data, their inexperience caused them to disregard the most vital points, with the result that their boats never attained any degree of success. However, I do not wish to convey the impression that the United States Navy Department was at this time considering building submarines as a result of the French experiments; far from it. Had it not been informed of the success of my *Fenian Ram*, which was far more interesting and wonderful than anything the French had done, and still remained unconvinced? I was totally sick and disgusted with its action, and was seriously tempted to abandon all further attempts to convince and awake it from its lethargy.[18]

Of course Holland did not "abandon all further attempts to convince," for such inaction would have been completely contrary to his nature. Instead, he wrote an article entitled "Can New York be Bombarded?"[19] The purpose of the author was not merely to show the "pitiable condition" of coastal defenses, but to demonstrate "the superiority of the submarine over torpedo boats and gunboats, the two arms of defense on which the Navy placed all its confidence at the time."

Then, in 1888, the United States Navy Department announced an open competition for the design of a submarine torpedo boat that would meet the following specifications:

1. Speed: 15 knots on the surface, 8 knots submerged.
2. Power endurance: 2 hours submerged at 8 knots, provisions for 90 hours.
3. Ease of maneuvering: circle in no greater space than 4 times her length.
4. Stability: assured normal or positive buoyancy at all times.
5. Structural strength: sufficient to withstand pressure at depth of 150 feet.
6. Power of offense: torpedoes with 100-pound charge of gun cotton.

Designs could range from 40 to 200 tons displacement submerged, and it was suggested that the main engine be capable of developing 1,000 horsepower.[20]

Secretary Whitney had been assured of an appropriation of two million dollars to build the craft from the design which was chosen.

John Holland was requested to submit his plan through the Cramps Shipbuilding Company of Philadelphia.[21] It must have been somewhat disconcerting to Holland to learn that the opportunity to submit designs was open to all comers: professionals and amateurs, domestic and foreign inventors. Nevertheless, he was warmed by the old confidence which again surged within him. His competitors, as he suspected, were no amateurs. Cramps not only represented his interests in the competition, but also those of Nordenfeldt. Twelve years later, Holland testified before the House Committee on Naval Affairs that four designs were presented in answer to the Circular of 1888. In addition to his own plans and those of Nordenfeldt, there were the proposals of George Baker "and one other." The fourth design unquestionably was Professor Tuck's *Peacemaker*. One journalistic account maintained that the Danish engineer, G. W. Hovgaard, filed his design of a submarine which appeared in his book, *Submarine Boats* (1887), but there is no evidence to confirm this assertion.[22]

It is possible that the noted Swedish inventor submitted the plans for the boat called the *Nordenfeldt*, intended for Russia, but which was wrecked on the Horne Reef off Jutland, 18 September 1888. The specifications for this craft are given in Alan Burgoyne's work, *Submarine Navigation, Past and Present*. Burgoyne states, "It may not be generally known that although Mr. Nordenfeldt as a rule receives all the praise for the invention and construction of these four [Nordenfeldt] boats, it was really Mr. Garret[t], the designer of the *Resurgam*, who proposed and planned them."

Of the other designs submitted, Professor Tuck's *Peacemaker* has already been described. George C. Baker of Chicago submitted two designs, both essentially identical except for the shape of the hulls. Baker had not built his boat by the time he sent his papers to Washington, and this boat was not launched until 1892. He had none of the practical experience of his rivals, nonetheless his planning was sound and his innovations by no means minor. He combined two independent sources of power, steam for surface propulsion and an electric motor for running submerged. A clutch connection with the steam engine enabled it to drive the electric motor as a dynamo to charge the accumulators while cruising awash. This presented a notable advance over previous all-electric boats, since the latter were forced to return to their stations to recharge their batteries. But the novel feature of Baker's boat consisted of two lateral propellers on either beam. These were fitted with beveled gears on shafts in such a way as to provide for their rotation through one hundred and eighty degrees. They were used to drive the vessel down, forward, or back to the surface.

These then were the men and designs against which Holland had to compete. His own plan is not known, though it may have been an improvement on the steam-driven submarine drawn in 1886, the plans for which may still be seen in the Paterson Museum. All steam-driven submarines had to be designed with retractable smokestacks, and Holland was perfectly aware of the fact that such a system was both cumbersome and unsatisfactory. To achieve the horsepower rating set forth in the government's specifications, there could be no alternative to steam. Yet Holland persisted in his efforts to improve the Brayton engine, as though an uncanny instinct told him that the internal combustion engine could remove the inconveniences of size, weight per horsepower, heat, and other awkward problems associated with a steam plant.

Anxious days were spent with his wife in their home at 185 Court Street, Newark, while he awaited word from the Navy Department on the results of the competition for a submarine torpedo boat. One can well imagine that Holland rehearsed over and over in his mind the government specifications. He must have wondered if his boat would meet each of the requirements. As time passed he probably became less certain, for some of the requirements were clearly unreasonable in view of the state of mechanical development in 1888. He guessed that the decision of the Naval Board might be narrowed to a choice between Nordenfeldt and himself. In fact, when Lieutenant Kimball visited the Cramps work to inquire about the competition, he intimated to Charles Cramp that since the latter held the plans of the two leading submarine authorities he, Charley Cramp, could not lose. "You seem to wish to grab all the submarines," Kimball chided. "You want the earth."

"Not at all," replied Cramp. "We want the sea only, and all that goes into it."[23]

Eventually the announcement came—John P. Holland had won the government competition of 1888. His elation, unfortunately, was short-lived. When the Cramps Shipbuilding Company failed to guarantee the fulfillment of the six specific requirements of the Navy, the Board in Washington withdrew its agreement and recommended to Secretary Whitney that new designs be sought.

The contest reopened the following year, the previous submarine designs were reviewed, and Holland again was declared the winner. But before a contract could be issued, President Cleveland's first administration came to an end. Under President Benjamin Harrison's new Secretary of the Navy, General Benjamin F. Tracy, the appropriation originally allocated for submarines was reassigned to complete surface craft already under construction.

Discouraged and financially embarrassed, Holland hoped to find someone who would build his improved petroleum engine. He visited Charles A. Morris, who had supported him in the days of the *Fenian Ram*, at the Pine Street offices of the Morris and Cummings Dredging Company in New York. Morris could sympathize with the professor's predicament. He, too, knew that the lot of an inventor was insecurity, for he came from a family who had worked creatively with mechanical devices since Colonial times. His grandfather, Ephriam, had designed the inclined planes on the Morris Canal, and had become director of the Canal; his father, Augustus, held original patents on the clam bucket and other harbor dredging equipment and was president of the Morris and Cummings Dredging Company at whose docks the *Fenian Ram* had been berthed.

Throughout 1889, Holland saw much of Morris. Their visits revealed a kind of desperation on the part of Morris to put his friend in touch with people who might give the inventor another chance to establish himself in a creative enterprise. Their conversations rekindled Holland's old interest in flying machines.

At this low point in Holland's career, it might be considered that the problems of mechanical flight were pursued solely for the purpose of assuaging his disappointment over his failure to exhaust solutions to the problems of submarine navigation. But the diaries of Charles Morris record that both men spent months on the flying machine project. This concern culminated in a twenty-eight-page document, completed by Holland on 21 April 1891 and entitled "The Practicality of Mechanical Flight."[24] Appended to the document were twenty-one drawings. The result was far different from the inventor's first scribblings on the subject in Dundalk in 1863, and from the goose feathers on a broomstick which he had used in his classroom in Paterson to demonstrate the principles of mechanical flight. It was the work of a self-trained engineer. The details, understanding, and calculations have been appraised by those competent to judge as an extraordinary achievement for a time when the Wright brothers were contemplating the opening of a bicycle shop. The paper demonstrated a thorough knowledge of all the experiments with model flying machines prior to 1891, including Hiram Maxim's "War Kite."

"It must be noted," wrote Holland, "that none of the experimenters named employed screws that were properly designed for lifting the greatest possible weight. All had rigid propellers incapable of accommodating the pitch to the work and therefore very wasteful of power." Only Messrs. Dahlstrom and Lohman of Copenhagen had attempted to vary by hand the pitch of their propellers, but their experiments proved unsatisfactory. Now, Holland proposed a flying machine with two four-bladed propellers, the pitch of each to be automatically regulated by springs in response to the amount of power exerted. The propellers were mounted on the opposite ends of a longitudinal beam which could be rotated from the horizontal to a vertical position with the fulcrum in the center of the spindle-shaped fuselage. In the horizontal position the thrust of the propellers was directed downward for lift-off; the beam was then slowly brought to the vertical position to push the aeroplane ahead. Here was a machine that at once anticipated and combined the concept of the helicopter and the aeroplane.

The proposed flying machine was to be operated by four steam-driven pistons mounted near the hub of the beam which carried the propellers. Holland, writing in considerable detail, describes an improved tubular boiler efficiently fired by petroleum injected into the burner with air. Accepting as the basis for his argument the British Aeronautical Society's estimate of a lifting power of thirty-six and two-thirds pounds per horsepower, a figure which the inventor proved was much too low, he calculated the performance of his two-man flying machine. He claimed it would fly for four and one-half hours at an average speed of sixty-three miles per hour and at a top speed of eighty, with a cruising radius of two hundred eighty-eight miles—all with a four-hundred-pound payload. With petroleum priced at four cents a gallon, he estimated the total cost of such a flight at $34.12.

To his paper on mechanical flight, Holland added two designs (one machine carried two pairs of propellers) by which he proposed to double and treble the flight and nearly double the speed. At a quick glance it appears that his computations gave little consideration to the airfoil qualities of his "aeroplanes," or wings, but the drawings indicate that these were fully considered. In fact, to determine the surface area of his biplane, he worked out the proportions of wing surface to total weight by using the comparable figures for the Australian crane.

Charles Morris attempted to find a backer who was willing to finance the building of the aircraft. He took Holland's paper on mechanical flight to several prominent business acquaintances; and, on one occasion, went over the proposal at a luncheon meeting with Colonel Edwin A. Stevens, son of the founder of the Stevens Institute of Technology where Morris had been trained. There was deep interest in the project, but no takers. The manner in which these conversations always reverted to submarines left no doubt as to where confidence in Holland lay. Therefore, it must have been with considerable reluctance and humility that Morris finally offered Holland a position as a draftsman in his company.

Holland went to work for the Morris and Cummings Dredging Company on the first of May 1890, gratefully accepting the pittance of $4.00 per day. In the meantime, Holland had submitted to the Navy a new design for a "submergible torpedo boat," for which a patent was pending, but he had received no reply from the Bureau of Ordnance.[25] Therefore, on 17 July, when Morris called in a young lawyer, Elihu B. Frost, known to his friends as "E. B.," to inquire about a legal suit pending within the dredging company, he also discussed Holland's problem. Frost expressed a keen interest in the inventor's determination. He promised that he would urge his father, Calvin Frost of Washington, to write to Secretary Tracy to see why a reply to Holland had not been forthcoming.

The months passed slowly for John Holland. Laying out the drawings for buckets and other dredging apparatus must have seemed a hapless and unwelcomed diversion. He found encouragement, however, in Morris' enthusiasm for submarines, petroleum engines, and flying machines. Indeed, Morris spent so much time trying to find capital for Holland's schemes he scarcely realized that his own interests in the dredging company were on the verge of collapse. Early in 1891, Morris was legally without a business of his own, having lost out to Cummings in a court decision. Yet, he continued to employ Holland to draw the buckets ordered under patents which he retained after the legal separation from his father's business. In 1882 he had designed the pump which Holland had used to operate the compressor on the third submarine, the sixteen-foot companion model of the *Fenian Ram*. Now both men worked to improve, combine, and patent their devices. Once again they sought investors who would finance the production of their inventions.

In the meantime, Morris had secured a contract to manage the New York Dredging Company's operations in the channels of Dorchester and Chelsea in Boston Harbor, and had moved his office to the World Building, New York's first skyscraper. When Morris departed for Boston, Holland remained in New York to perfect the drawings of the barge and dredge to be used in the Bay State project. He continued as a business associate of Morris into the spring of 1893.

The 1892 elections put Grover Cleveland back in the White House. E. B. Frost, encouraged by the political shift in Washington, told Charles Morris on 28 February 1893 that he was ready to consider forming a company to provide Holland with the necessary capital to continue his experiments with submarine torpedo boats. Frost planned to get affidavits from those people who knew intimately of Holland's work— specifically from Dunkerley, Lister, Morris, the Bergen brothers, Zalinski, and Plant.

On 3 March 1893, Congress passed an appropriation of $200,000 to cover the reopening of the competition for an experimental submarine. The Naval Committees of both houses of Congress gave the bill their blessing. The United States Navy was dangerously weak; strained relations existed with Great Britain over the Venezuela boundary line; the French reportedly were making new strides in submarine construction—all facts which could no longer be ignored. On the first of April, the Navy Department formally issued a new call for designs, repeating the requirements contained in the Circular of 1888.

About this time, a revealing conversation is supposed to have taken place between E. B. Frost and Holland during a luncheon in a New York restaurant to which Frost had invited the inventor.

"I know I can win the competition and build the boat for the government," Holland told the young lawyer. "But I need to raise some money to pay for fees and other expenses in preparing the drawings. I need exactly $347.19."

"What do you want the nineteen cents for?" Frost asked.

Holland did not hesitate. "To buy a certain kind of ruler I need for drawing my plans."

Frost was delighted. "If you have figured it out as closely as all that, I'll take a chance and lend you the money."[26]

John Holland ferreted out his old papers and returned to his own drawing board. He had the plans for the *Fenian Ram* and for the *Zalinski Boat*, the design for the steam submarine that had won two previous competitions, and the drawings of the submergible torpedo boat which eventually had elicited a favorable report from the Bureau of Ordnance during the regime of General Tracy. He also had in his papers a gun patent, a steering apparatus for submarine vessels patented early in 1893, and another submarine design for which a patent was still pending.[27]

On Holland's board there slowly emerged the plans for a new underwater vessel. On 4 June 1893, he signed the drawing which was to serve as the principal guide for the construction of his fifth submarine.

Then, a few weeks later, he went to Washington to witness the examination of the designs. His lean years were over.

CHAPTER SIX

THE GOVERNMENT CONTRACT
1893-1896

The John P. Holland Torpedo Boat Company was incorporated under the laws of the State of New York in the spring of 1893. E. B. Frost assumed the difficult role of secretary-treasurer of the new company; but he had influential backing in Washington through his father, Calvin Frost, and through attorney Charles E. Creecy. John Holland became manager of the company bearing his name at a salary of $50.00 per month. Young Frost collected the affidavits testifying to the successful submarine experiences of the inventor, and he used these testimonials deftly to secure the support of investors. The Navy Department required that a deposit of $7,500 accompany each design. This deposit was raised, as were the sureties for a bond of $90,000 to be held in the event that the accepted boat failed to meet the specifications laid down by the government's circular.

Armed with the financial assurance of his company, John Holland arrived in Washington on 30 June 1893 for the opening of the designs.[1] He found that the lounge adjoining the Secretary of the Navy's office was crowded with an impressive gathering of people. In the Yankee tradition of "inquire around, but don't ask any questions," Holland quickly ascertained that only three designs had been submitted: his own, one by George Baker (a former contestant), and one by an unknown young man from Baltimore whose name was Simon Lake. Across the room from where Holland stood, he noticed a round-faced, fair-complexioned, young man who was rather nervously engaged in conversation with George Baker's son. Holland correctly surmised that this boyish individual was the third competitor.

Simon Lake asked innocently of Baker's son whether all the gentlemen in the room were there to file submarine plans with the Secretary. The Chicago youth laughed and then obligingly replied by identifying Holland as the only inventor present. The others were congressmen, and Baker's son startled his companion by at once proceeding to name them. Lake wrote later of this meeting: "I said to myself, 'Well, Lakey, it looks as though you were not going to have much of a show here.' I submitted my plans and specifications, however, and returned to Baltimore and to my other business."[2]

Holland himself might well have returned to New York, for he was given no information on the kind of competition he faced. While rumors were in his favor, a company cannot be built on rumors. There was something ominous about the ensuing silence from officialdom. A month passed before Holland heard from the Board on Submarine Torpedo Boats in the Bureau of Ordnance, and then it was a request from Lieutenant Commander C. S. Sperry for further descriptions and calculations to support Holland's drawings. Such an inquiry could only mean that pressure was being placed on the Board to postpone a final decision. Baker's influence in Washington was impressive. He was, in fact, considered by most observers to be the original instigator of the congressional appropriation of 3 March 1893, and thus his stake in the competition loomed large. E. B. Frost set out to counteract the Baker lobby. He requested Holland to find a shipbuilder for the submarine should he, Frost, be able to negotiate a contract with the Navy.

What happened in Washington during the summer of 1893 is a complicated story. Baker had completed the actual construction of his boat one year prior to these events, and he was fully prepared to demonstrate her on Lake Michigan for the benefit of the Navy. Senator William B. Allison of Iowa and General C. M. Shelley, Baker's lawyer, persuaded the Secretary of the Navy that the Board on Submarine Torpedo Boats should put Baker's little vessel through her paces. The Board, in fairness to Holland, Baker's major competitor, offered him the opportunity to present a boat of his own. Holland objected to these tactics, for he knew through former Secretary Whitney and others that his design had received the approval of the Board. His reply to the Board's invitation was both masterful and clear.

The *Fenian Ram*, he wrote, still existed, but vandals had stripped her of gauges and other machinery; and she lay in a state of neglect in the yard of James Reynolds in New Haven. The cost of refitting her would be considerable; and his company, already financially embarrassed as a result of the design competition, should not have to bear this expense. Furthermore, the circular advertised for designs only; it said nothing about pitting completed boats against each other. If *The New York Times* report of 28 July was correct, the Holland design had been accepted by the Board. Did the Board now intend to change the tenor of its report? The final paragraph of the appeal was another demonstration of Holland's rare ability to convert the matter-of-fact into subtle and often biting Irish wit: "If the newspaper description of Mr. Baker's boat is anywhere near accurate, I entreat you to examine the structure carefully before you submerge its center below 20 to 25 feet. My motive for this request is—I admit a very selfish one—of objecting to the risk of having to wait for a decision until a new Board can be appointed."[3]

The Board was stung by the sharpness of Holland's objections to its procedures and replied that *The New York Times,* or any newspaper in the country for that matter, was not the official organ of the Navy Department. The Board also asserted that, when a boat such as Baker's existed, it was quite proper to desire to test her. The case rested there as far as the Navy was concerned.

At the time of the trials of the Baker boat, Frost's father was in Chicago. Holland urged him to report carefully on the effect of Baker's unique lateral propellers when the submarine descended. Holland prophesied that the disturbance on the surface would be so great as to reveal the vessel's presence over a considerable distance. The time of descent should also be noted, Holland insisted, for if rapid submergence were to be achieved Baker would have to redesign his craft to include a system of automatic compensation devices to assure fore and aft stability.

The summer was nearly over when John Holland received a telegram from Lieutenant Commander Sperry announcing that the long-awaited report of the Board was about to be released. Holland replied cheerfully, "Said report contains good news for somebody, and as this is one of my lucky days I just guess who it is."[4] E. B. Frost, equally excited over the news, wrote the following letter on 13 September to the Honorable Hilary A. Herbert, Secretary of the Navy:

Dear Sir:

From the newspapers I learn that the board on submarine boats has again reported in favor of the Holland boat. If this is true, may I call your attention to the fact that already considerable delay has been incurred by reason of the Board's going to Chicago, at Mr. Baker's request, to inspect his boat? The company which I represent endeavored to put no obstacle in the way of the fullest investigation on this subject by your board. This having been done and a decision having been arrived at, I think I should be pardoned in respectfully asking that the company which I represent be awarded the contract as soon as it may suit your convenience, in order that the building of the boat may be commenced at the earliest moment possible.

Yours respectfully,
Elihu B. Frost[5]

In spite of the optimism among the officials of the John P. Holland Torpedo Boat Company over the decision of the Board, other circles in Washington set out to delay the Secretary's approval. In fact, when the report reached the Secretary's desk, he decided not to issue the contract for the construction of the Holland boat. He claimed the appropriation should be diverted to other naval construction. Was this the result of the political influence Baker was able to command? If so, Frost would attempt to undermine Baker's power, as Creecy urged him to do. The officials of the Company were prepared to gamble. They would suggest that Baker join them in exchange for $200,000 in Holland Company stock, provided that Baker assign his patents, "free of all encumbrances," to the Holland interests.[6] As a feeler, Frost sent to Baker's lawyer, General Shelley, a substantial block of shares for "services or services to be rendered." Frost was later forced to apologize for this action; he declared he had not been fully aware that Baker was still the general's client.[7] In any event, the Holland-Baker combine never materialized.

Newspapers indicated that the Secretary of the Navy was determined to credit the submarine boat appropriation to other construction, and Frost used every means in his power to stop this diversion of the funds. He sought a resolution in Congress to prevent the move, while urging prominent senators and high ranking naval officials to dissuade the Secretary. In November, 1893, the whole question was about to explode into a major exposé of the consequences of political influence in high places.

As Frost saw the issue, the facts were clear. Not only had the Secretary refused to acknowledge the judgment of his appointed Board on Submarine Torpedo Boats, but also he had succumbed to the proposal of Senator Allison and General Shelley that the Board be sent to Chicago to review the performance of the Baker boat. Upon the Board's return from Chicago, it had reiterated its stand in favor of the Holland design. Then, the Secretary, still adamant, had proposed to turn the appropriation over to yards in which surface vessels were nearing completion. If this record were published in the press, Frost knew it could embarrass the Secretary. With considerable deftness, the lawyer saw to it that this possibility reached Mr. Herbert. The cards were down. Again the officers of the Holland Company openly expressed their confidence to shipbuilders, declaring that the contract would soon be in their hands.

The Secretary, however, was not so easily perturbed. He still held a trump card. Once again Frost and Holland learned of the Secretary's latest scheme through news releases. The Navy Department was directed to test the safety of submarines by exploding a torpedo near a submerged vessel to measure the effects of concussion from underwater explosions on living creatures confined within the vessel.

After some secrecy, it was revealed that the experiment actually took place late in December at the Naval Torpedo Station in Newport, Rhode Island. The tests consisted of submerging a crude, watertight tank in which were held captive a cat, a rabbit, a rooster, and a dove. Several charges of gun cotton were detonated, each succeeding charge being closer to the tank than the one before it, until the last charge exploded within one hundred feet of the mock submarine. The cat and the rooster survived, but their companions were dead. The tank was unharmed.

A few weeks before the Newport event, John Holland wrote to Secretary Herbert: "Your experiments will prove, I think, that when the torpedo passes under the net and explodes against the ship nothing more than noise and vibration and possibly some movement will be felt by those in the boat."[8] Holland must have thought that the experiment as actually performed was both senseless and bizarre. "I am making no experiments with animals in order to determine the effect of concussion," he assured Creecy's secretary when rumors of the nature of the tests held at Newport were reported in the newspapers.[9] Rather, he had hoped that the Navy's investigations might yield data on the effectiveness of the submarine as compared to the surface torpedo boat; and there was little doubt in his mind as to which boat would have received the higher rating.

Secretary Herbert had accomplished two objectives: first, he had prevented the mounting antagonisms in Washington and elsewhere from blowing up in his face; second, he had gained time before yielding to those who felt the country should build submarine torpedo boats. When the report on the Newport experiment reached his desk, he could mull it over-and perhaps still save the appropriation for a "great white fleet" of surface vessels in the more reliable tradition of the leading naval powers. With the private sector of the economy in no mood to risk its capital on speculative enterprises, certainly the taxpayers' money should be spent only on the tried and true.

The year 1893 closed with the John P. Holland Torpedo Boat Company as far from holding a government contract as it had been back in April. Its manager had seen his salary increased from $50 to $150 per month; but, by December, Holland was willing to settle for $100, if Frost could raise the money. Holland now had two sons; there were doctor's bills to pay and the rent to meet. His brother, Alfred, had joined the growing ranks of the unemployed, and this too disturbed John, for he had always considered Alfred the capable, dependable member of the family. He turned to Frost, asking the young lawyer to use his wide circle of acquaintances to help Alfred to find work. Frost was eager to be of assistance. He wrote a letter to his friend, Richard Deming, who managed Pier 36 in New York City:

Dear Dick—

This will introduce you to Alfred Holland who is seeking some employment. He is the brother of the inventor of the Holland submarine boat, so that I chance to have a pretty intimate acquaintance with that branch of the family. Mr. Holland is honest, sober and a man of remarkable cultivations of mind. It may occur to you that it is funny that he should be willing to take a position of fireman or laborer about the dock, when there are so many higher positions for a man of his ability to fill. The reason is that he has for many years been professor in classics in various institutions. Through reasons of overwork in youth, he has become over sensitive and diffident and prefers some position where there is little or no responsibility. I speak thus highly of Mr. Holland on the authority of his brother in whose word I have implicit confidence. I have sent Mr. Holland to you knowing you would help him if you can, thinking you might find in Mr. Holland an invaluable man in some position.

Remember me kindly to your wife.

Yours truly,
E. B. Frost[10]

Alfred's short but vigorous career as a youthful journalist in Ireland had ended shortly after his arrival in the United States. Unlike such Irish-born journalists as John B. O'Reilly of the *Boston Pilot*, Jerome Collins of the *New York Herald*, and John Devoy, all of whom rose to prominence, Alfred's pen either could not or would not compete. He followed his younger brother's example and turned to teaching. But the classroom seemed remote from the tasks of living in an industrial society dominated by more mundane interests than Latin or Greek. His earlier revolutionary leanings arose to confuse him. If he was to leave the classroom, then he would join the labor force where he could serve without pretension and without responsibility. He accepted the job at Pier 36.

For John Holland, one of the brighter moments at the close of the year came with a letter from his friend, Lieutenant Kimball, who was then in Panama. Kimball shared Holland's depression over the course of events: "I find myself very much astonished and exceedingly disgusted at the prospect that there is to be not only no submarine boat, but also no submerger, and no anything."[11] At least Kimball understood the importance of continuing submarine development. If the Navy Department would keep him at home, Holland's prospects might improve.

In an attempt to force a contract from the United States government for the construction of the Holland submarine torpedo boat and to satisfy the investors in the Company that every effort was being made to sell a submarine, E. B. Frost built up a system of foreign patents on Holland designs and established agencies abroad which were empowered to negotiate contracts with interested governments. The Company made it clear, however, that no contract could be honored until one year after the completion of the submarine proposed for the United States. Old and trusted friends were chosen as Company representatives and were sent abroad to establish foreign agencies. Captain Edmund Zalinski went to South America, where he appointed William Eyre, Grace and Company of Valparaiso, as agent for Chile, Peru, and Ecuador. A month later Zalinski was in Rome. With Frost's approval, he then returned to South America with permission to make the necessary arrangements to establish an agency in Argentina. Commander F. M. Barber, who had delivered the lecture on

72

submarine boats at Newport in 1875, represented the Company's interests in Japan twenty years later. When Zalinski joined Barber in Tokyo in June, 1895, Frost wrote to him: "If you and Barber cannot sell a boat in Japan, I'll be surprised."[12]

The question of foreign patents was a touchy one. Five years later, when Holland appeared before the House Committee on Naval Affairs, the matter of foreign interests in his designs was thoroughly reviewed. It was obvious that the Navy Department, because of its interminable procrastination, had lost control over Holland patents, other than the one submitted on 30 June 1893. The consequences of the delay may be seen in the following exchange between Holland and the chairman of the committee:

Question: You can build them [submarines] for whom you please?

Mr. Holland: For whom we please, because some of our patents are published in foreign countries.

Question: You are a citizen of the United States, Mr. Holland?

Mr. Holland: Oh, yes, sir: I am a citizen. . . .

Question: And you would be in a position to make a contract with this Government whereby this Government will control this process or your plant?

Mr. Holland: Yes, sir. By the way, what the Government asked to control was only the American patents. They have not made us any proposition at all to buy the sole right out. . . .

Question: What would be the advantage to the Government of controlling your process if you had foreign patents by which the [other] Governments are advised of the construction and mechanism of the ship?

Mr. Holland: The advantage to the Government would be only the saving in the expense of building. [Holland's reply showed the sharpness of his understanding of the potential investments involved.]

Question: Does your transfer to the Government transfer all rights under foreign patents?

Mr. Holland: They have never asked us to do that.

Question: Would you be willing to transfer to this Government all rights under all patents?

Mr. Holland: I will be only too glad if the Government will do it.[13]

Holland's reply this time unquestionably reflected his own personal opinion and not that of the Board of Directors of the Holland Torpedo Boat Company, for the Board was soon to make certain that not even John Holland himself was to have legal claim on his own patents.

In the meantime, the effect of the Company's foreign activities must have been felt in Washington. On 3 March 1895, Frost received the $200,000 government contract for a submarine torpedo boat of Holland patent. He signed the contract on the same day and returned it to the Navy Department for the signature of the reluctant Secretary of the Navy. Mr. Herbert finally signed it on 26 March. It had taken the Company two years to achieve this victory, but for John Philip Holland the struggle had begun with the first Navy Department circular in August of 1888, nearly seven years earlier.

Holland was again in high spirits. Work agreed with him. From his office at 120 Broadway, he wrote letters to shipbuilders from Maine to Florida. Holland's friends shared his happiness at the sudden change of his fortunes. Kimball was elated by the Navy Department's decision. Charles Morris, a friend since the days of the *Ram* and a charter investor in the new company, busied himself trying to find a yard that would undertake the construction of Holland's next submarine.[14] Zalinski was abroad promoting Holland designs on three continents. E. B. Frost, who had managed to keep the stockholders together through months of financial panic and seemingly endless weeks of political banter, still confidently held the reins of their growing enterprise.

Holland had other reasons for rejoicing. At home in Newark, there was a daughter in the family, little Julia, to check, somewhat, the growing exuberance of young John and Robert.

In April, John Holland learned of the death of George B. Brayton and wrote to his widow paying full tribute to her husband's ceaseless efforts to develop a small and efficient petroleum engine. More touching for its thoughtful restraint and dignity than for promises which could not be fulfilled, the letter expressed his regrets that he had been unable to keep the name of the Brayton engine in the forefront of submarine navigation. He knew that had the Brayton engine continued to be used for submarine propulsion, the widow would have been assured an income from the patents. But now John Holland found himself apologizing, in effect, for turning to steam. He did not want to offend the memory of the man whose engine he had used in all his previous submarine boats.[15]

The choice of a shipbuilder finally focused on William T. Malster's yard at the Columbian Iron Works and Dry Dock Company on Locust Point in the harbor of Baltimore. E. B. Frost felt that the selection might be unwise. What would their friend, Lewis Nixon, the chief of construction at Cramps, say of the choice? "How will Nixon like the matter of giving Malster all the boats?" he asked Creecy.[16] By "all the boats," Frost was referring not only to the proposed Holland submarine, but also to Simon Lake's *Argonaut*, which Malster was already building. Furthermore, Malster was shareholder and treasurer of the newly formed Lake Submarine Boat Company. Holland's solution to Frost's dilemma was to appoint Lewis Nixon, shortly thereafter, as his consulting engineer at the Iron Works. Nixon was further persuaded to find a position at Cramps for J. Alvah Scott, a draftsman at the Mosher Boiler Works, until operations for the submarine's construction could be started at Baltimore. The Company would need Scott's services in connection with the installation of the huge steam plant proposed for the boat.

In August, John Holland set up temporary residence at 2423 Barclay Street, near 25th and Greenmount, in Baltimore. Daily visits to the Columbian Iron Works began, and his fifth submarine, which the government called the *Plunger,* took shape alongside the experimental boat of Simon Lake.

The *Plunger* was a huge craft: eighty-five feet long, eleven and one-half feet in diameter, with a total displacement of one hundred and sixty-eight tons submerged and one hundred and fifty-four tons light. The thirty-six-foot *Argonaut* was diminutive by comparison. The hull of the *Plunger* was constructed of one-half-inch, oil-tempered steel. Her heavy internal machinery occupied nearly every cubic inch of available space. In order to meet the guarantees given the Navy Department in the specifications, she carried two independently mounted triple-expansion engines capable of generating sixteen hundred and twenty-five horsepower at four hundred revolutions per minute to assure a fifteen-knot surface speed when running awash. For operating submerged, an electric motor, rated at seventy horsepower, was designed to propel the craft at eight knots. The storage batteries used to supply the current would be charged by a small compound steam engine. The three surface engines took their steam from a vast Mosher boiler occupying much of the central compartment directly below the conning tower. It contained twenty-five hundred square feet of heating surface and was rated to bring steam pressure to two thousand pounds per square inch.

J. Alvah Scott joined Holland in Baltimore to oversee the installation of the boiler. He caused something of a panic among Company officials when, at a crucial point in the early stages of construction, he requested a leave of absence in order to marry. Frost was firm. Scott could take time out for his wedding day, but he was not to enjoy a honeymoon. There "must be no prejudice to the Company's aim to complete the boat," Frost warned.[17]

The secretary-treasurer of the John P. Holland Torpedo Boat Company was busy with details that were more important than Scott's wedding plans. He now had the going concern he had struggled so hard to build. The man indispensable to the continued success of the enterprise was the inventor. If they lost Holland, the Company would collapse. To guard against such an eventuality, Frost took out a large insurance policy on the life of the inventor, designating the Company as beneficiary, though he was unable to persuade the Equitable Life Assurance Society to remove the clause which prevented recovery in the event that Holland lost his life as the result of a mishap in an underwater experiment.

Frost felt certain controls must now be consolidated. In 1893, he had realized that John Holland was a talented man who deserved support. Now, Frost was convinced that this Irish-born school teacher was a mechanical genius, who, properly handled, was worth millions of dollars to the Company. Holland was assigned a sizable share of stock, but not enough for a controlling interest; and the contract which named him manager carefully stipulated that all submarine patents, inventions, and devices, along with any improvements thereon, were to be the property of the Company. In May, 1895, Frost went so far as to urge Holland to secure affidavits from George M. Richards, former engineer of Holland's second submarine, authenticating the *Ram* plans and her pneumatic gun as Holland inventions. He then turned these documents over to the Company's patent lawyer to have them properly registered. There is also correspondence indicating that Frost was not averse to the thought of reassigning to the Company Holland patents not related to submarines.

An inventor is a kind of beggar who seeks financial support for patentable ideas, and a beggar cannot be a chooser. He is motivated by the desire to put his ideas to the pragmatic test. Since he is by nature a dreamer, he often comes to the practical test with no financial resources of his own. This was true of Holland, Morris, Lake, and a host of other men in nineteenth-century America who contributed to the country's affluence and material well-being. Some were more fortunate than Holland. Lake, for example, by a freak twist in management, became president of his own concern. But the more general pattern persisted until World War II when, as James B. Conant has so aptly observed, the inventor who was considered by the public as a scientist disappeared and the scientist became the inventor.[18]

At the end of 1895, Holland's fame was widespread. When he was asked to deliver a lecture on submarine navigation at Cornell University, Frost and Creecy, the latter now president of the Company, urged him to do so.[19] Holland's name appeared almost daily in the great metropolitan newspapers, and magazines sent feature writers to Baltimore to report on the progress of the *Plunger*. The press captured the public's imagination with headlines reading: "*Plunger:* Still Hunter of the Sea," "Fiction Has Been Outdone," and other similar phrases.[20]

By 1896, Holland sensed that all was not proceeding smoothly with the *Plunger*.

He felt cramped by the naval "brass" that constantly surrounded him, by the senseless modifications insisted upon by those who were not qualified to make recommendations, and by the fact that his own proposed changes had first to be submitted to the Navy Department for approval. The requirements laid down by the Navy were not only unrealistic, but they simply could not be met. The triple-screw arrangement had been a concession to demands for exaggerated surface speeds, when the single propeller mounted aft of the rudders on the central axis of the submarine would have been sufficient. Two additional propellers set in wells fore and aft for vertical propulsion were a further concession for the sake of even-keel submersion and in direct opposition to Holland's long-held principle of the diving boat.

The boiler in the *Plunger* was an unshielded monstrosity. It would retain enough heat when the vessel was submerged to roast the crew. Its position almost isolated the men in the forward torpedo area from those in the engine room, permitting only a crawl space on either side or over the top of the boiler. The awkward smokestack had a workable retraction mechanism, but it still necessitated a clumsy fairing around the conning tower hatchway.

Lewis Nixon had not deigned to visit the *Plunger* at Baltimore. Frost pleaded with him to take an interest in the project, anticipating the Company's need for Nixon should this boat result in additional contracts. Without Nixon, Holland was pressed for technical assistance to cover the many details of construction. He persuaded Frost to get in touch with his old friend, Charles Morris, whose office in New York was in the same building to which the Holland Company had moved a few months before. Morris, busy with dredging operations at Atlantic City, agreed to devote part of his time to the *Plunger*. He arrived in Baltimore on 25 August 1895 and made his way to the shipyard on Locust Point.

Later that day, Holland and Morris rode leisurely back to the city. They discussed the technical problems which threatened to delay the completion of the *Plunger*. Morris would go to work on the old compressor-pump design which neither man had had time to perfect. Once again Morris found himself volunteering to do more for Holland than was good for his own business. One winter night, when work on the compressor had kept him late at the Brooklyn Navy Yard, he confided to his diary: "This is too much."[21]

Toward the close of 1896 a fresh and determined spirit took hold of John Holland. The depression which surrounded the delays in the construction of the *Plunger* gave way to a new enthusiasm. The inventor was about to embark on an adventure which was to constitute the high-water mark of his creative genius. He was now nearly fifty-five years of age; yet, he looked like a man in his forties. Behind the thick, rimless spectacles, his eyes sparkled at the thought of a witticism or softened perceptibly to reflect his compassionate nature. The mustache was now bushy, and at times neglected and shaggy. Going about the shipyard in Baltimore, he wore an off-white, thigh-length smock and a soft felt hat. On more formal occasions, as a concession to his role as a public figure, he appeared in more distinguished attire—winged collar over a full and colorful cravat, stick pin, cut-away tweed jacket, and waistcoat crossed with a heavy gold watch chain. This was the man who stood on the threshold of a success that was to change the course of modern history.

On a Friday night in early December, Holland was returning home on the late train from Baltimore to New York, accompanied by Morris, who was describing the apartment he had leased for Holland and his family at the then fashionable address of 116th Street in New York City. Morris assured the submarine inventor that all arrangements for the transfer of his family from Newark to the city had been completed. But Holland seemed not to listen to his friend.

His Company had just decided to grant his request to begin the construction of his sixth submarine boat, and this exciting prospect occupied his thoughts. Work on the *Plunger* would continue. In the meantime, he had been authorized to build a new submarine under private contract, free from the red tape that hampered the completion of the *Plunger*, and above all, free from the interminable delays brought about by the carelessness of those whom Holland dubbed as "amateurs." The Company had agreed that the new proposal held better prospects of assuring future contracts than blind reliance on the outcome of the *Plunger*. When a private yard could be found to construct the new design, Holland informed his traveling companion, the Company would want the full-time services of Morris, who alone remained intimately familiar with the mechanical problems which Holland had faced ever since the days of the *Fenian Ram* in 1881. Morris would not commit himself. Perhaps he could arrange his commitments in the dredging business in such a way that they would not interfere. In any case, there could be no doubt of Morris' respect for his friend's determination to master the problems of submarine navigation. In all the history of the submarine, no one, not even the persistent Wilhelm Bauer, could now match the duration of the singleness of purpose that motivated John Philip Holland.[22]

The Company's decision to undertake an entirely new approach at its own expense was unquestionably a calculated risk, and yet the prospects for success were considerably fortified by the tone of the 1896 hearings before the Congressional Committee on Naval Affairs.[23]

CHAPTER SEVEN

THE HOLLAND VI
1896-1898

"Give me six Holland submarine boats, the officers and crew to be selected by me, and I will pledge my life to stand off the entire British squadron ten miles off Sandy Hook without any aid from our fleet." So testified Lieutenant Commander Kimball before the Senate Committee on Naval Affairs early in 1896. He was referring to the still untried *Plunger;* and he was backed by a similar pronouncement from then retired Rear Admiral James E. Jouett, a hero of Mobile Bay and a former president of the Board of Inspection and Survey.

Another influential witness to speak out in favor of the submarine boat was Captain Alfred Thayer Mahan, an acknowledged authority on naval policy and strategy and the author of *Influence of Sea Power Upon History* (1892).

"In our present unprotected position," the captain told the Senate Committee, "the risk of losing the money by the government by reason of the boat's [*Plunger's*] being a failure is more than counterbalanced by the protection the boat would be if a substantial success."

This hearing culminated in the Act of Congress of 10 June 1896 authorizing the Secretary of the Navy to contract for two submarines of the *Plunger* type, provided the vessel passed all the tests required of her. An appropriation of $350,000 was set aside for this purpose. In the nation's capital, the foggy atmosphere which had long enveloped submarine talk was slowly lifting. The indomitable inventor of the *Plunger* must therefore have faced his financial backers with confidence when he proposed that they should underwrite the private construction of a sixth and improved boat.

The *Holland VI* took shape at Nixon's Crescent Shipyard, Elizabethport, New Jersey, during the winter of 1896-97. E. B. Frost had persuaded Charles Morris to serve as superintending engineer, for Alvah Scott would have to remain in Baltimore to oversee the completion of the *Plunger*. There were numerous matters to check as the building progressed—a compressor of improved capacity, pressure regulators, valves, and sea cocks; the dismantling and redesigning of the turret; and a thousand lesser details—for the failure of any one of these items might spell disaster for the submarine and her crew.

While the *Plunger* had been very much in the news throughout the winter months, only vague rumors about the *Holland VI* had leaked to the press. Then, in March, 1897, the *New York Herald* carried a fair sketch of the strange vessel over the headline: "Fiction Has Been Outdone." The garbled story accompanying the drawing must have been among the first to touch off the chain reaction of publicity that led Alan Burgoyne to observe a few years later: "Of this vessel perhaps more has been heard than of any other ship or boat in the world."[1]

It was reported that John Holland had said his submarine was "being built to be placed on the market, and whoever has the price can buy the boat."[2] Endless speculation began: the Cuban refugees offered a fixed sum if the boat proved successful; the Holland Company was prepared to sell the submarine to the Spanish to quell the insurrection in Cuba; France was negotiating for the American boat.

The significant day of the launching came and went.[3] The visits of Holland and Morris to Elizabethport became more regular, though there were many side trips to the Brooklyn Navy Yard, Philadelphia, Perth Amboy, and other centers in search of rubber packing, a steam yacht tender, electric equipment, and countless devices needed for the complex machinery on board the submarine. In late June, Holland moved from 209 West 116th Street, New York City, to a house on Mt. Pleasant Avenue in Newark, in order to be nearer to the base of operations at Elizabethport.

The weeks dragged on into months. John Holland was determined to bring his latest underwater craft to a state of mechanical perfection hitherto unachieved, in keeping with his assertion to Lieutenant Commander Kimball that the design represented "a powerful and effective boat." He would not permit himself to be pressured into meeting arbitrary deadlines.

Engineer Morris understood his old friend's stubborn resolve. He labored on, checking out each piece of apparatus to be installed. By the summer's end, he may have been somewhat impatient with Holland's demands, for he turned again to his dredging business and became involved in lengthy, but futile, negotiations to secure a contract for digging the proposed Cape Cod Canal. It was indeed hard to serve two masters. The informal arrangement with the Holland Torpedo Boat Company did not demand his full time on the submarine, and his visits to Elizabethport became less frequent.

Then, on the night of Wednesday, 13 October 1897, a careless workman accidentally left open a small valve in the boat. All night the sea water seeped into her hull until the cigar-shaped vessel settled to the bottom of the slip at Nixon's yard. Salt water corroded the delicate machinery and electric wiring. No coating protected the armatures of either the main dynamotor or the smaller auxiliary used to drive the air compressor.

It is not difficult to imagine the depressed spirits of John Holland on Thursday morning as he arrived at the yard to inspect the damage. The boat could of course be raised, but could the machinery be overhauled within the hull? To remove the main dynamotor would mean first removing the Otto engine. Neither of these operations could be accomplished without dismantling most of the steel plates on the upper half of the hull.

Eighteen hours after the *Holland VI* sank, she floated again on the surface. A careful check of her machinery revealed that the motors and accumulators were badly grounded. The whole electric system was dead. The Company decided that, short of dismantling the boat, it would go to any expense to recondition her. Holland and E. B. Frost again turned to Morris, asking him to accept a full-time contract as superintending engineer in charge of the submarine.

Efforts were made to dry out the dynamo by applying external heat. Oil stoves were placed in the hull and kept burning day and night. Superheaters were applied directly to the motors. But after a month of such activities, the electrical system was as faulty as ever. Captain W. H. Jaques, then president of the Company, called a special meeting of the principals charged with renovating the *Holland VI*. It was decided to request The Electro-Dynamic Company of Philadelphia, makers of the dynamos, to send their best technician to Elizabethport.

On Friday, 26 November 1897, electrician Frank T. Cable reported to Morris at Nixon's yard. "After an examination I decided that there was only one way of remedying the trouble, and if this course was adopted there was a chance of restoring the boat."[4] The young electrician reversed the current in the armatures, ingeniously generating an internal heat. In less than a week he pronounced the dynamos ready for service and the order was given to recharge the accumulators. Workmen struggled to remove acid from the bilges and replace the dead cells in numerous batteries. Winter closed in. The *Holland VI* had not yet been tested, but hope for success returned with the new year.

The advent of Cable on the scene in the fall of 1897 marked his first acquaintance with the submarine and the men responsible for its development. Asked if he would like to go down in the vessel, he replied, "Not for anything would I attempt to do so."[5] Nevertheless, he had made an important contribution at a crucial moment in the boat's history. As a token of appreciation for his work, Morris prophetically presented Cable with a captain's hat. The young electrician's curiosity about the boat had been aroused. After his return to Philadelphia, he eagerly watched the papers for news of the submarine.

81

It came in exciting headlines on the morning of 25 February 1898: "The Holland a Success." The submarine had been towed by the tug *Erie* out of Nixon's yard into the Arthur Kill. The strange pair headed south for a presumed destination in Princess Bay. Opposite Kreischerville on Staten Island, the towline was dropped; and the submarine proceeded under her own power with the inventor at the controls. The *Erie* returned to Elizabethport for supplies.

"I plan to take a dip in her," Holland had told reporters at Nixon's. This was his casual way of indicating that he might submerge the boat. Holland was elated at the success of the first surface run and was totally oblivious to the concern he and his crew were causing others. A New York police boat lay off Nixon's yard under strict orders to keep an eye on the *Holland VI*; but, when the submarine appeared in the channel, the police boat was unable to get under way because of a mechanical failure. A telephone message was relayed to the Brooklyn Navy Yard, and Admiral Francis M. Bunce dispatched the Navy tender *Narkeeta* to Princess Bay to intercept the *Holland VI*. The happy skipper of the submarine quite unintentionally eluded his pursuers and slipped in behind an old canal barge alongside the docks at Perth Amboy.

"The submarine disappeared before our very eyes," declared observers along the shore. The illusion was understandable, since the vessel had an exceptionally low freeboard. Contrary to some press accounts, the little craft at all times remained on the surface, but nothing prevented the press from indulging in rumors: Holland was going to deliver his boat to the Cubans; no, she was going to blow up Admiral Cervera's cruiser *Viscaya* which lay at anchor in New York Harbor as a show of Spanish strength following the controversial explosion on board the USS *Maine* ten days earlier.

It was this news that greeted Frank Cable in a Philadelphia newspaper on the morning of the 25th. He immediately wrote:

Dear Mr. Morris:

I have been "waiting and watching" the papers for several weeks thinking I would see something about the "sub-marine" boat. Today my eager gaze was rewarded. If all I have read in today's paper is true, you deserve congratulating. I can imagine the load that is off your mind. I hope the dynamo did not "fail in time of need," for in that case I would not want to keep that hat.

I presume there will be a premium on sub-marine boats if the "Maine" disaster proves to have be [*sic*] caused by Spanish treachery.

Extend my congratulations to Mr. Holland. With best wishes for the success of the Company, I remain

Yours truly,
Frank T. Cable[6]

It was a fortnight later before John Holland attempted to test the submerging capabilities of his submarine. At seven o'clock in the evening of 11 March, the members of the crew slipped through the turret and took their places: Nathaniel Addison, the engineer; Henry L. Meyers, the electrician; William F. C. Nindemann and Walter W. Scott, the gunners. Holland was the last to enter. The lines were cast off, and the inventor calmly and firmly closed the hatch over his head. The boat moved out into the entrance to the slip, came to a stop, and then slowly began to settle in the water. President Jaques, Charles Morris, and Walter Thompson, superintendent of the Raritan Dry Dock where the boat was berthed, watched anxiously from the pier. The turret disappeared in the murky water. Moments later, the two ten-foot staffs mounted fore and aft on the superstructure also vanished. Only a confusion of bubbles marked the position of the submarine; and then they too subsided, leaving no trace of the boat. The depth was twenty feet at the point of descent. The *Holland VI* was resting quietly on the bottom.

There was a tense moment some thirty minutes later when the water began to churn into numerous whirlpools. Morris assured Captain Jaques that Holland had the vessel under control and that the submarine was surfacing. Shortly thereafter the inventor, smiling broadly, emerged from the turret to be greeted with congratulations from the small gathering on the pier. Holland mumbled something to Morris about ballast; and then, turning to the others, he announced he would "take her for a little dip" on Monday.

On that day a sizable crowd gathered at the docks at Perth Amboy in anticipation of the first full-dress demonstration of the *Holland VI*. After testing her agility on the surface, she was brought dockside in order to stow on board a considerable amount of pig iron ballast. Again in the broad entrance to the Arthur Kill, known locally as Staten Island Sound, running a course parallel to the shore, her skipper attempted to submerge her, but water only frothed around the turret. She would not go under. A second and third run proved equally unsuccessful. The spectators slowly dispersed, grumbling with dissatisfaction and open pronouncements of skepticism. The newspapers joined the critical chorus. In Philadelphia, Frank Cable clipped an account of the event from a local paper, pinned it to a sheet of stationery, and wrote: "Now will you be good!" He mailed the message to Charles Morris.

Holland, however, was not dismayed. He blamed himself for the fiasco and told the audience remaining on the dock that he could solve the problem by loading the submarine with the right amount of lead molded to fit the empty spaces along the bilge. "Lead will take up less room than pig iron of equal weight and the molding will remove any danger of shifting ballast." Furthermore, it is possible that the dry ballast was needed to reduce the buoyancy in the new waters of operation where the salinity of the water was higher than Holland had calculated.

By Thursday, 17 March 1898, the *Holland VI* was fitted with her new ballast and ready again for a trial run. It was two-thirty in the afternoon. A heavy drizzle dampened the enthusiasm of the Holland Company's party which prepared to board the tug *Sally B. Lindeman*. The members of the crew of the *Holland VI*, each in his turn, slipped through the hatch of the turret. Then came Holland, sprightly and cheerful, "acting more like twenty than a man in his fifty's." Before he closed the hatch over his head, the rain suddenly stopped. The sun broke through the clouds to the west, and a huge rainbow arched the dark sky over Staten Island. It was the luck of the Irish— and on St. Patrick's Day, too. Holland waved to the crowd in response to the omen, and the crowd responded with a great cheer.

It is not merely a legend that the first successful dive of the *Holland VI* took place on St. Patrick's Day. The little submarine performed exactly as her creator had intended. Even the press, prone to make Verne-like fiction out of the accounts of the boat and frank in its skepticism, now offered glowing praise of Holland's accomplishments. "If tomorrow's tests," wrote a *New York Herald* reporter, "realize today's promises, then Mr. Holland has made the most marvelous revolution in marine warfare since Ericsson invented the monitor."[7]

The trial, however, was not without its frustrations. Three times additional ballast had to be lowered from the decks of the *Sally B. Lindeman* to the narrow superstructure of the submarine and then carefully stowed below. Finally, when the submarine did submerge, only her jack and ensign remained above the water as she glided along for three hundred yards on an even keel at a speed that caused anxiety on board the escorting tug. Staten Island Sound was noted for its unpredictable mud banks. What if Holland ran her aground?

Four days later the boat descended until even her flagstaffs were completely under water. On that occasion, the imperturbable professor confessed he had not really intended to dive so deeply, but that the muddy water caused the light to fail within the conning tower so that he could not read the depth gauge. Some awareness of the risk involved in this maneuver was impressed on Holland and the crew when, shortly after surfacing, the submarine drifted onto one of the mud banks in the Sound and had to be pulled off by the tug *Erie*.

John Holland and E. B. Frost were now confident that it was time to invite the United States government to send an official observer from the Navy Department to witness the next experiment with the submarine. They scheduled the trial run for Sunday, 27 March. Preliminary exercises with the boat were held on the preceding day for the benefit of a number of the stockholders and friends of the Company. The plan was to take the boat into the deep water of Princess Bay, but Frost objected because of the roughness of the seas and the strong easterly wind. Holland was forced to concede, though he declared that he did so merely because he did not wish the guests of the Company to suffer from *mal de mer*. It was during this dress rehearsal for the main performance on Sunday that the *Holland VI* first carried her new electrician, Frank T. Cable.

Cable's arrival at Perth Amboy proved to be an event of no small importance for the subsequent history of submarines. Though a late comer to the confidential circle of acquaintances who surrounded John Philip Holland, and though a novice in the field of underwater craft, the tall, slender, thirty-five-year-old electrician, sporting sideburns and a small mustache, was about to embark upon a career to which he was to devote the remainder of his life.

Another newcomer to the group of Holland's associates was William F. C. Ninde-mann, who had joined the Company a year earlier. Forty-eight years old, Nindemann was small and heavy set, with a straggly brush of hair on his upper lip that rivaled Holland's own mustache. His serious demeanor could in part be explained by the hor-rors he had experienced in the Lena Delta during the tragic De Long arctic expedition of the *Jeannette*.[8] Later he had joined one of the rescue vessels sent to find Lieutenant Adolphus Greely's party on Ellesmere Land in 1884. Nindemann had already sur-vived more than most men would dare to contemplate, and now he turned to the still unknown and dangerous occupation of submarining. John Holland spoke of him as "a grand fellow," a jack-of-all-trades, and one to be relied upon in an emergency. Like Frank Cable, he too was to spend his remaining years in and out of submarines.

Aside from the necessary financial backers of the project, those who might endanger their capital but not their lives, and excepting such staunch friends as Kimball, the team most responsible for the success or failure of the *Holland VI* was now complete. Led by John Holland, the team included Elihu B. Frost, Charles A. Morris, William F. C. Nindemann, and Frank T. Cable.

It was raining on Sunday morning when Frost arrived at Perth Amboy with Lieu-tenant Nathan Sargent, who had been sent by the Board of Auxiliary Vessels to in-spect the submarine. Again the tug *Erie* served as a tender and, at the insistence of the lieutenant, only Company officials were allowed on board. The choppy water on the Sound forced Holland to close the turret hatch to keep heavy spray from being driven below as the submarine first ran through her paces awash. There was no rainbow this day to augur well for the trial. Dressed in heavy-weather gear and standing alone in the prow of the escort vessel, Sargent watched the submarine disappear, staffs and all, beneath the Sound. When the vessel surfaced again and Holland opened the hatch, Lieutenant Sargent waved congratulations to the submarine's skipper; and the little flotilla headed back for the Raritan docks.

Preparations were then made to test one of the dynamite guns. The bow of the boat was directed toward Tottenville on Staten Island, and small craft were cleared from the area. From the bowels of the submarine a hissing noise emerged, indicating that Nindemann had blown an air charge into the forward gun's breech; but Holland was disappointed to learn that only six hundred pounds of the one thousand he planned to use could be obtained from the air flask. The order to fire was shouted to Nindemann from the deck. A boom broke the silence, and spectators craned to follow the three-foot, fifty-pound, wooden dummy-projectile through its graceful trajectory three hundred yards out into the channel.

Lieutenant Sargent reported to his superiors that the submarine "fully proved her ability to propel herself, to dive, to come up, admit water to her ballast tanks, and to eject it again without difficulty."[9] In an informal discussion with the inventor, he remarked that the stern seemed to clear the water when she dived; and he thought this attitude a dangerous one. John Holland answered by observing that certain sea birds, noted for their ability to dive from a floating position, were also compelled to show their bottom sides before plunging into the depths. It was clear, however, that Sargent had been influenced by those who believed that level-keel submergence was the only safe means of descent.

Not satisfied that the Navy would be favorably moved by Sargent's report, E. B. Frost saw that the little *Holland VI* received her fair share of publicity. Reporters were invited to inspect the boat docked at Perth Amboy. *Harper's Weekly*, *Leslie's Weekly*, and the leading metropolitan newspapers published their versions of the strange craft, often in nothing short of the most sensational journalism.

In the meantime, John Holland concentrated on bringing his vessel to such a state of mechanical efficiency that the world could no longer ignore his accomplishments. He ordered the boat to be hauled at the Raritan Dry Dock. During two busy days, workmen gave her a new coat of slate grey paint, replaced the wide guard around the propeller with a narrow band of steel in the belief that she would thus better answer her helm, and constructed wooden fairings fore and aft of the circular turret to reduce the turbulence along her superstructure. The boat was floated again on 4 April, but for two additional weeks she remained at dockside as the workmen checked out all the apparatus on board.

While these improvements were being undertaken, the John P. Holland Torpedo Boat Company waited hopefully for official reaction from Washington. Tensions between the United States and Spain increased daily. President William McKinley asked Congress for authority to use military and naval forces should the situation warrant, and Congress granted the President's request. The day before the President sent his message to Congress, the Assistant Secretary of the Navy had dispatched a personal letter to Secretary John D. Long:

10 April 1898

My dear Mr. Secretary:

I think that the Holland submarine boat should be purchased. Evidently she has great possibilities in her for harbor defense. Sometimes she doesn't work perfectly, but often she does, and I don't think in the present emergency we can afford to let her slip. I recommend that you authorize me to enter into negotiations for her, or that you authorize the Bureau of Construction to do so, which would be just as well.

Very sincerely yours,
T. Roosevelt[10]

On the day President McKinley was voted his extraordinary powers, and the Congress passed its resolution declaring Cuba independent, Holland and his crew were on board the *Holland VI* in the open waters of Raritan Bay. They were waiting for signals from a Board of Inspection composed of Captain C. S. Sperry, the expert on surface torpedo boats; Commander Swift; and Assistant Naval Constructor George H. Rock, who still represented the government on the construction of the *Plunger* at Baltimore. The appointment of this Board may have been Secretary Long's answer to Theodore Roosevelt's inquiry. In any event, the proceedings at this trial of the *Holland VI* were only halfheartedly planned. All the Board hoped to ascertain was whether or not the submarine could dive, though such information was already available to it in the memorandum of Lieutenant Sargent.

The determined Mr. Holland decided that the opportunity was worthy of more than a simple demonstration. If the government was going to be indifferent about its inspection, he did not intend to be indifferent about his performance. He watched through the small one- by three-inch deadlights which ringed the turret, waiting for his signal from the heavy tug, *George P. Roe*, then wallowing in the choppy waters a mile or so south of Old Orchard Shoal Light. Cable, Meyers (now assistant electrician), Addison, and Nindemann were at their posts below, little suspecting what their skipper had in store for them. The signal came. Holland answered with the air whistle and set the submarine in motion. In a matter of seconds, the little boat was completely under water, her apparent speed of descent being accentuated by the lack of her familiar ten-foot staffs which she did not carry on this run.

Minutes passed—ten, fifteen—and someone on the tug remarked that she had now exceeded any previous time below the surface—then twenty, and thirty, and forty-five. If the officials on board the tug had been coolly unconcerned at the start of the exhibition, they were now alert and anxious. Someone on the opposite rail shouted that he saw the submarine, but by the time the spectators reached his side, the apparition had disappeared and there was a considerable expression of annoyance at the crewman's false report. But was it false? Holland could have brought the turret briefly to the surface, checked his bearings, and as suddenly vanished.

On the second escort tug, the *Lindeman,* Trial Captain Charles Morris ordered his vessel to get under way, setting out in the general direction in which the *Holland VI* had last been seen. Then, just short of an hour from the moment of descent, the submarine bobbed to the surface a few feet away. Her pilot must have taken particular delight in revealing that he and his crew had traveled several miles in a sweeping circle while submerged in the Bay. He had disobeyed the prearranged orders, but he had given the Board a show it had not expected.

The Board, in its report, quibbled over details. Small defects, which never would have been noticed had they not been pointed out by the inventor himself, were exaggerated. The Board complained that it had no assurance of the depth at which the submarine operated because the flagstaffs had been removed. Yet for all these observations, the distance of the run submerged was twice that demanded officially of the *Plunger* on completion, and the duration for a single dive far exceeded anything the government had required. But elsewhere in the world the results of the trial of 20 April were noted. President Jaques cabled from Birmingham, England, that he had a bona fide bid of $100,000 for the boat from the French government. Charles Creecy, the Company's representative in Washington, advised Frost not to act hastily on Jaques's information, implying that the Company was not without its supporters in the capital. Furthermore, there was a clamor for a congressional investigation of the unfavorable report submitted by the Board.

It is always a popular game to criticize those in power for being blind to significant innovations or for failing to recognize the work of genius. Such criticisms, however, are generally leveled by those who look backward from their vantage point in time and say: "How stupid the Navy was, not to see the importance of the submarine." Hindsight is so much more secure than foresight. Yet an invention is not really an invention until it is accepted.

Four days after the trial run in Raritan Bay, Spain declared war on the United States. The United States hardly needed to reciprocate, except for the record, since the newspapers across the nation had already declared war on Spain weeks earlier. Clearly the major encounters in the conflict would be resolved at sea. Not since the Clan-na-Gael secretly wished for open conflict with Britain to test John Holland's remarkable

Fenian Ram had the inventor seen any real hope of testing in combat the worth of his devices. Things might be different now. He had a vastly improved boat at his command, one he believed could meet all the claims he had made for her.

Holland was not a man to harbor grandiose schemes. If he made an offer, however absurd it might appear to others, he was willing to back it up with his own personal performance. By all accounts he was a modest man, though once convinced that he was right, he stubbornly adhered to his convictions. He rarely exhibited impatience, but when he did, it was often tinged with bitterness made the more poignant by his unfailing wit. "What will the Navy require next, that my boat should climb a tree?" And once when approached as an expert on underwater vessels, he replied, "So you sought me out as an authority on submarines? Go down to Washington, and you will find plenty of people there who will tell you that I know nothing about the subject, nothing at all."[11] He was fond, too, of defining an official committee, called a "board," as something that is "long, narrow and wooden." Yet the success of any course he now charted obviously depended on a favorable wind from Washington.

The public was of a different mind. It had come to accept the *Holland VI* as "warfare's newest and most awful weapon," the boat which alone could stand off an invading fleet in Ambrose Channel, a boat which the government must certainly use in prosecuting the war with Spain. Whenever a trial was announced, or wherever she was known to be docked, enthusiastic crowds gathered.

On the last day of April, 1898, with the launching ensign flying from her after staff, the submarine prepared to depart from Perth Amboy for her new station in the Erie Basin, Brooklyn. People assembled at the Raritan yard to pay tribute to Holland, Morris, and the crew of the boat. There were handshakes and congratulations. Then the *Erie* towed the little craft into the Sound. A cheer of farewell burst from the faithful on the docks.

The trip to Brooklyn was a leisurely one up the Arthur Kill, past Nixon's establishment, and into Mariners Harbor for the night. The next day, the tug with her strange tow made her way through the Kill Van Kull, crossed New York Harbor, and arrived at the Erie Basin in the evening of the first day of May. Simultaneously, in another part of the world, Admiral George Dewey's Asiatic Squadron steamed into Manila Bay. The admiral's young flag secretary, Ensign Harry H. Caldwell, who volunteered to man the five-inch battery on board the *Olympia*, was the same Harry Caldwell who would later command the *Holland* as the first submarine skipper in the United States Navy.

When it was confirmed that Spanish Admiral Cervera's Cape Verde Squadron was bottled up in the harbor of Santiago de Cuba, John Philip Holland persuaded his Company to hold a conference in its Broadway offices to hear his plan to test his submarine in combat. "If the government will transport the boat from the Erie Basin, where it now is, to some point near the entrance to the harbor of Santiago, and a crew can be secured to man the boat, Mr. Holland will undertake the job of sinking the Spanish fleet, if it be still in Santiago harbor, commanding the boat in person. If his offer be accepted, and he is successful in his undertaking, he will expect the government to buy his boat."[12]

Evidently the Company officials thought well of the offer to blow up Cervera's fleet, for Creecy and Holland left for Washington to put the proposal before the President and the Secretary of the Navy. In an interview before leaving New York, Holland declared that he had no desire to depart this life, but that there would be less risk for himself and his crew than for the Spanish sailors on board the warships. He would, of course, have to work his way through the minefields; but he was confident that he could explode a mine or two, while remaining unobserved, and return undetected to enter the harbor through the passage he had thus cleared.

Washington would have no part of Holland's daring plan, and it is futile to suppose the course of naval history had it been attempted. However, the scheme did capture the public's imagination. The journalism of the day played it up in bold headlines, presented imaginative drawings of how the attack would take place, and depicted the submarine shelling fortifications with its pneumatic guns. It was about this time that McAllister drew his well-known cartoon of the bespectacled, derby-headed inventor emerging from the conning tower of his submarine. The caption read simply: "What? Me Worry?"[13]

While Holland and Creecy were in Washington, the submarine was put in dry dock at the Erie Basin yard of John N. Robbins and Company at the foot of 50th Street, South Brooklyn. Morris supervised the installation of a larger, experimental propeller; made further modifications in the steering mechanism; and had the boat back in the water within twenty-four hours. On 2 June 1898, the boat steamed under her own power to a new site of operations, the Atlantic Yacht Basin at the foot of 55th Street. To John Holland this must have seemed like coming home, for from this base he had ventured forth in the *Fenian Ram* sixteen years earlier.[14]

The *Holland VI* underwent eight trial runs in June and July, the majority below Owl's Head Light off Bay Ridge in the crowded waters of New York Harbor. On at least two occasions the submarine and her crew barely escaped destruction. The first incident occurred on Saturday afternoon, 11 June. The submarine left the basin, skippered as usual by her inventor; she carried, in addition to the regular crew, Holland's old friend, Captain Edmund Zalinski. Somewhere off Bay Ridge, not far above Fort

Lafayette where the two men had witnessed the abortive launching of Holland's fourth boat more than a decade before, the skipper brought the submarine to a stop. The boat lay low in the water, her superstructure barely awash. Holland had turned from the conning tower to point out some piece of internal machinery to his friend. From the deck of the escort vessel, Morris noticed that the craft was drifting down on the towline of a harbor tug; he ordered the tender to close the submarine. With the deftness of one who had spent years around the waterfront, Morris lassoed the steel ring in the bow plate of the *Holland*. The submarine answered to the line, and was pulled out of danger. "Only for the promptness of the cool-headed Captain," wrote a reporter from the *Herald*, "two distinguished inventors of dynamite guns and dynamite boats would undoubtedly have been lost to the world."[15]

On a second occasion, 19 July, the Navy's Chief Engineer, John T. Lowe, made his first trip in the submarine. The *Holland VI* was running submerged in the Narrows; only the small pennants on her staff remained above water. Bowling up the harbor before a fresh southerly breeze came the lumber schooner *Lois V. Chapele* on a collision course. Captain Morris spotted the threat to the submarine and blew the tug's whistle in an attempt to attract the attention of the schooner's skipper. Just at the moment when the huge bowsprit of the sailing ship appeared to pass over the flags of the submerged boat, the two vessels veered apart. When the tug moved alongside the schooner, her master shouted, "Say, is that the *Holland?*" "It is," returned Morris from the bridge of the tug. Moments later the submarine bobbed to the surface, her little air whistle blasting away in disapproval.[16]

A few days after this near collision, a sea captain appeared in the Holland Company's offices in New York. He accosted the inventor: "Your boat dived under my craft as I came up the Narrows and struck her bottom, seriously damaging the copper sheathing, and I've come to collect the damages."

John Holland admitted he had seen the shadow of the hull of the schooner loom in the deadlights of his turret and that he had immediately altered course, but he was not going to be hoodwinked into paying damages on such an absurd allegation. "If such a thing were so," he quipped, "your copper bottom would have ripped off the top of my conning tower and I would not have been here to talk to you now."[17]

Throughout the summer and into the early fall, numerous dignitaries visited the Atlantic Yacht Basin to view the latest weapon of naval warfare. After the close of hostilities with Spain in August, an increasing number of prominent individuals observed the trial runs of the submarine either from the decks of the escort tug *Erie* or from Charles R. Flint's steam yacht *Nada*. Among the nearly two dozen men privileged to accompany the inventor-skipper in runs submerged were Commander W. W.

Kimball, back from his war assignment as commander of a torpedo boat flotilla; Naval Cadet F. Taylor Evans, son of Captain Robley ("Fighting Bob") Evans of the *Iowa* and a hero of Santiago; a Mr. Ferguson, a reporter from the *New York World;* Count Lieutenant Takashi Sasaki of the Japanese Navy; and. Captain Georg Strang of the Royal Norwegian Navy.[18]

Perhaps the most important guest to dive in the *Holland* during the summer of 1898, at least from the standpoint of the submarine's future, was Isaac L. Rice, versatile German-born entrepreneur, law professor, founder of *The Forum* magazine, and an authority on chess. Some sources claim that he first descended in the boat on 4 July, but the better evidence indicates that while he may have visited the boat at dockside on that date, he did not go down in the submarine until 3 September.[19] Mr. Rice held a monopoly in the storage battery business, building his first company in 1888 around the patent of Clement Payen's "chloride accumulator." He acquired control of the Electric Launch Company (later Elco); and upon the death of the president of The Electro-Dynamic Company, the former employers of Frank T. Cable, that enterprise also came under Rice's management. The use of his storage batteries to operate the dynamos of John Holland's underwater boat introduced him to the invention. There can be little doubt of Isaac Rice's enthusiasm for his adventure on board the submarine, for when capital was needed to make extensive alterations in the stern structure of the *Holland VI* during the winter of 1898-99, he did not hesitate to put up the money for the reconstruction. Later, Rice was to combine the John P. Holland Torpedo Boat Company with his own newly incorporated Electric Boat Company of 100 Broadway, New York City.[20]

In the meantime, all the events of the summer were aimed at securing another official exhibition of the *Holland VI* before a Naval Board of Inspection. In preparation for this event, which the Company hoped would lead to government acceptance of the boat, a new battery system was installed. Difficulties were at once encountered, for the new cells could not be brought up to their normal voltage. Writing from Baltimore, where presumably he had been sent to check out electric equipment on board the *Plunger,* Frank Cable complained to Morris: ". . . with all due respect to the people who installed the plant, it is the D—— mess I ever ran up against."[21]

In September, the *Holland VI* had been hauled on the marine railway at the yacht yard for a new coat of paint, a new and smaller propeller, and the reboring of the torpedo tube. Therefore, when Secretary Long finally appointed a Board of Inspection and Survey, the submarine torpedo boat was as ready for her test as her competent overseers could make her. On 4 November 1898, the Secretary directed the members of the Board to meet with Mr. Frost at the Battery in New York and to proceed to South Brooklyn on board the tug *John A. Bouker*.

The official trial of Saturday, 12 November, was exceptionally thorough. It had one serious defect, however, which may have influenced the final tone of the report of the chairman, Captain Frederick Rodgers. For the first time in twenty years of underwater experimentation, John Philip Holland temporarily relinquished the navigation of one of his vessels to other persons—Chief Engineer Lowe and Commander W. H. Emory, both former passengers on board the submarine. One can imagine the reluctance with which the inventor accepted this decision, as well as his consternation when he saw his crew, under the command of a naval officer, take a full twenty minutes to ballast the craft for diving.

Lieutenant W. J. Sears, an ordnance inspector from the Bliss Torpedo Factory in Brooklyn, had loaded a 17.7-inch Whitehead torpedo into the tube, using the cage designed by Morris. The cold November weather had caused the grease to congeal, delaying the loading process. Nevertheless, the torpedo, which did not carry a warhead, was successfully fired and struck its target three hundred yards out in the harbor. After the "fish" was retrieved, the little submarine motored out of her slip and headed south for the deep waters in the Lower Bay around Old Orchard Shoal Light. Lieutenant Nathan Sargent, the official recorder on board, clocked the surface speed of the *Holland VI* at six knots at three hundred rpm. Then the boat performed nineteen brief dives in the Princess Bay area, the eighth being of ten minutes duration and to a maximum depth of fifteen feet.

In its deliberations the following day, the Board considered the testimony of the naval personnel who had been on board the *Holland VI* during the exhibition. This part of the report was highly complimentary on many points, but in one key item it was critical. "The boat turns quickly, but the steering and diving gear did not work satisfactorily owing, we believe, to the inexperience of the crew." The Board focused on this negative evidence and recommended yet another inspection, expressing the wish that, when such a trial did take place, the crew would be "exercised by actual practice so as to be able to make required submerged runs and steer a straight course."[22]

The battle with the Navy Department was not yet won. Moreover, the November trial created a battle within the Holland Company. The inventor pointed out that the temporary commanders of the craft had not used his automatic steering vane designed to be put in operation when submerged. Cable insisted the compass was at fault, declaring that it was impossible to compensate a magnetic compass in a boat heavily shielded by a steel hull. Later, in his own account of submarine development, Cable claimed it was he who suggested that the yawing action was the result of the rudders and diving planes being placed forward of the propeller, but the records indicate that recognition of this mechanical disadvantage belonged to Morris.[23] To some degree, each man was correct in his estimate of the problem. Holland had great faith in his steering vane, an improved version of the original device used on his sixteen-foot boat which the Fenians stole with the *Ram* in 1883. Cable's contention about the deviation of the compass is further supported by the fact that the directional properties of the compass would be dampened by the magnetic properties of the vessel herself. As for the position of the propeller, this was a fundamental characteristic of Holland's design. Therefore, it was only after lengthy discussions that the inventor finally agreed to relocate the propeller in the conventional position forward of the steering and diving planes. With the propeller in this position, the pressures on the surfaces of the planes from the direct thrust of water from the blades would hopefully make her helm more sensitive. That these arguments produced their own friction is revealed in a laconic entry made by Morris in his diary of the period: "Cable is getting too smart for his own breeches."

The modifications of the stern were laid out on the drafting board, and Isaac Rice assured the Company he would underwrite the alterations. So the little boat was towed from the yacht basin in Brooklyn to the Gas Engine and Power Company yards at Morris Heights on the Harlem River. Frost placed Morris in charge of the extensive overhaul, and this work proceeded throughout the bitter winter that followed.

By the close of 1898, John Philip Holland was a tired and discouraged man. The buoyant enthusiasm of earlier months had waned with each new setback. The *Plunger*, launched 7 August 1897, proved in dockside trials to be the impossible monster which he had predicted she would be. The *Holland VI*, the submarine he was sure he could not improve upon, the one which he confidently trusted would replace the Baltimore boat in the eyes of the Navy, now seemed further from official acceptance than at any time in her brief career. Other matters disturbed him. Lake's *Argonaut I*, completed and launched alongside the *Plunger*, achieved considerable notoriety for her open-water passage from Norfolk to Sandy Hook in September, 1898. Holland was too astute not to recognize a serious competitor in Simon Lake, though, for the present, Lake appeared to be confining his efforts to salvage techniques. Furthermore, the new financial interests in the Holland Company threatened to complicate, if not subordinate, the inventor's role in controlling the destiny of his own creations. E. B. Frost, concerned about the health of his friend, urged Holland to plan a voyage to England and to visit his native Ireland. If his energies permitted, the Company would then send him on to the Continent to assess the foreign market for his submarine boats.

CHAPTER EIGHT

THE TWO YEARS OF DECISION
1898-1900

The extensive remodeling of the *Holland VI* progressed slowly through the winter of 1898-99. Bitter cold weather, faulty workmanship, hasty installation of inadequately tested equipment—these were some of the factors responsible for prolonging the work schedule set by the Holland Torpedo Boat Company. When the calendar showed that spring had arrived, the Harlem River remained jammed with ice, further delaying an early launching of the submarine.

In spite of these frustrations, the overhaul resulted in an improved arrangement of machinery on board the boat. The after dynamite gun was removed to provide space for an improved exhaust system for the gasoline engine. Two new after trimming tanks were fitted in the hull on either side of the propeller shaft. A series of small compensating tanks were added to take care of weight lost in the operation of the vessel. The use of these small tanks in conjunction with the trimming tanks did not present the dangers inherent in the practice of partially filling the large ballast tanks and then admitting water to bring about the required trim. Frank Cable had suggested this practice, but Holland always insisted that water allowed to surge about in the larger tanks could suddenly alter the center of gravity and produce disastrous results.

The major reconstruction entailed shortening of the porpoise-shaped hull at the stern, moving the propeller forward, and constructing a heavy skeg to which was tied, by a circular loop, three struts of angle iron to support the rudders and diving planes abaft the propeller. The automatic steering vane, in its v-shaped channel, was re-mounted on the upper rudder brace. This return to the conventional position of the propeller and rudders was the answer to the complaint of naval inspectors that the *Holland VI* yawed uncontrollably when running submerged.

Prior to the launching, the submarine was given two coats of a newly developed antifouling paint. Ten barrels of gasoline, of specific gravity 73, were delivered to the Gas and Engine Company yard at Morris Heights. The fuel was pumped on board the boat as she stood in her cradle on the railway. Engineer Morris, who had been in charge of the *Holland VI* throughout the winter, waited impatiently for a warm spell to melt the ice in the river. Finally, on 24 March, the submarine slid down the ways and was towed back to the Atlantic Yacht Basin in South Brooklyn.

In the meantime, a significant reorganization had taken place within the Holland Torpedo Boat Company. On 7 February, the Electric Boat Company was incorporated and the Holland Company became its major subsidiary. Certain privileged holders of Holland stock converted their assets into preferred shares of Electric Boat. The management of Holland's company did not change, but the power structure did. Isaac Rice became president of both companies; John Holland was retained as manager; Charles Morris continued as superintending engineer; Charles Creecy still represented the Holland interests in Washington as legal counsel. E. B. Frost, secretary-treasurer, emerged as the real overlord of the submarine enterprise. In a letter to an official of the newly formed Electric Boat Company, Frost protested with shrewd modesty:

> While I think it entirely natural and proper that the dominant stockholders should wish control of the treasuryship of both companies, I am convinced that if there is any field of usefulness for me in connection with the Company, it will be greatly impaired by divesting me of every official title. Personally I do not care for office or title; but as a matter of fact title and office in Washington are regarded as of some importance. . . . I would suggest that I be left with the simple title of Secretary, the duties of which involve very little detail, from which I am happy to be relieved. I should prefer so far as my work is concerned to remain upon a salary.[1]

The Electric Boat Company soon absorbed, into one vast combine, The Electro-Dynamic Company of Philadelphia and the Electric Launch Company, among other Rice enterprises. The full impact of this power shift on the fortunes of John Philip Holland and his associates became increasingly evident as the months advanced.

On 25 March 1899, John Holland sailed for Europe on the "pleasure trip" which Frost had encouraged him to take. However, business was to be mixed with pleasure. Before Holland's departure, Frost wrote numerous letters to individuals in Europe, informing them of Holland's proposed ports of call and prompting them to discuss submarine developments with the American inventor. Some of these men represented the Company's interests abroad, others were officials in the governments of their respective countries. Frost's plans were rather pretentious for a trip arranged ostensibly to benefit Holland's health. The itinerary, as Frost saw it, was to include London, Paris, Berlin, and St. Petersburg, with a possible sojourn in Ireland.

One such letter was sent to Captain F. M. Barber, former U.S. naval attaché at Rome and Berlin, then residing in the latter city—the same Barber who, as a young lieutenant, delivered the lecture on submarine boats at Newport in 1875.

Frost had written:

> Mr. Holland is anxious to discuss several matters with you regarding design. He is anxious to get a view of *Zédé* or some of the new French boats, and if possible, one of the German boats at Kiel. . . . I suggest that you make your arrangements most explicit as Mr. Holland has not the best memory in the world for business engagements, as you very well know. As I am writing this letter in his presence, I have taken the liberty of speaking thus frankly about him.[2]

This was not the last time that Frost was to chide Holland about his memory, publicly or privately.

A similar letter was dispatched to Captain A. Tromp of the Royal Dutch Navy, who was acting as an agent for the Company in Rotterdam. Frost explained to Captain Tromp that under the Company's reorganization the matter of policy regarding the sale of foreign patents, or the building of Holland submarines abroad, had not been established, but that Tromp was to regard their agreement prior to the amalgamation as binding until such time as he was informed to the contrary.[3]

For all the elaborate planning, it is apparent that John Holland confined his travels primarily to the British Isles. He left for Europe alone. Upon his arrival in England, he spent several days in London. He crossed the Channel to Rotterdam, but was forced to return to London to recover from an illness that befell him. He then proceeded to Ireland to join Mrs. Holland and the children, who had sailed from New York three days after his own departure, presumably landing in Queenstown.[4]

Little is known on either side of the Atlantic about John Holland's return to his native soil. There is not even a record to show that he went back to the little village of Liscannor. It is known that he was the guest of his old friend Brother Yorke, Superior of the Christian Brothers' community in Dundalk. One of the younger members at the school where Holland had taught recalled the excitement in the town on the famous inventor's arrival, observing: "Mr. Holland, as he then was, struck me as being a very gentle type of man, kindly and soft spoken. He was then in middle life and the subject of stories in the newspapers. He was frail in build, and I should say he would have found the discipline of the Brothers' life beyond his strength."[5]

Presumably Holland went alone to Dundalk, from which town he proceeded to Cork to meet his family. Together they returned to London for a brief visit before embarking on the Cunard liner *Etruria*, 26 April 1899. Cable comments:

> About this time he was in England in consultation with naval and shipbuilding officials. The humor of such a contact could not have been unrecognized by either party. The man who had set his heart on devising an instrument to cripple Great Britain's sea power had seen the way open to introducing his device into her navy, not as a destroying foe, but as a protecting auxiliary.[6]

97

The return passage on board the *Etruria* proved to be exceptionally rough. Three days out of the Port of New York, the 8,000-ton, 500-foot ship lurched unexpectedly in the heavy seas. John Holland was hurled against the casing of a cabin door. His glasses were smashed, injuring one eye; his head was cut and bleeding; and a wrist was badly sprained. His only complaint was that he could not read for the remainder of the voyage. "My wife thought I was killed," he confided later to Captain Tromp, "and the shock to her nerves was so great that she was taken sick soon after landing, and after inching between life and death for nearly one week, she began to recover slowly."[7] No doubt Frost was correct when he told Kimball he suspected that the trip had provided Holland with very little relaxation.[8]

During the first week following his return, Holland devoted his attention to his ailing wife. He asked that Morris be sent to see him, but beyond this he did not wish to be disturbed. One Sunday in May, Morris came to visit with his friend in Newark and to report on the developments which had occurred during Holland's absence.

When the submarine had reached the Atlantic Basin the day before Holland sailed, they turned her around in the slip under her own power and "the steering behaved beautifully." She was first "sunk" on 18 April and settled heavily in the stern. Inspection revealed a faulty rivet in the top of one of the after trimming tanks. The rivet was replaced the next day; all tanks were carefully checked and caulked, wherever they appeared to need such treatment.

Morris then told Holland of the plans to move the submarine's base of operations from the Bay Ridge area and the Narrows out to Wickford, Rhode Island, or to Greenport on Long Island, for it was the unanimous decision of all concerned that the crowded waters of Lower New York Harbor were dangerous grounds in which to navigate a submarine. Morris was expecting Frost to send him to Greenport to see if a suitable base might not be found for the establishment of a submarine station.

The *Holland VI* had been ready for a trial run several days before her inventor's return. On 13 May, it was decided not to delay the trial any longer; on that day, Morris, Cable, and the crew took the submarine through five dives off Bay Ridge. "We had to dip the bow very badly to get down," Morris reported. The depth gauge failed to function properly. "Told Frost about my gauge—Frost said 'put it in'—Said I had not done so on account of the fact that it was patented—He [Frost] said I was among friends now and for me to go ahead."[9] The twelve-inch diameter needle gauge, built from the engineer's patent and marked on its face "The Holland Torpedo Boat Company," was promptly installed just aft of the diving wheel.

By 17 May, John Holland resumed his duties. Everyone solicited his advice. Would he confer with Walter W. Scott about the status of the *Plunger?* Yes, the Company would negotiate for a diesel engine to replace the steam plant in the Baltimore boat, but would a diesel fit in the space now occupied by the steam engine and boiler without blocking access to other vital machinery? Yes, replied Holland, if Scott will use cardboard mock-ups to test the layout within the engine room. Would he and Morris take Lieutenant Carlo da Luca-Kennedy, naval attaché at the Italian Embassy in Washington, to lunch and later for a "spin" on board the *Holland VI?* Then there were papers to sign—would he get them back to Frost immediately? Would he do this? Would he do that?

In the letter to Captain Tromp in which Holland described his accident on board the *Etruria,* he revealed:

> I have not transferred my European patents to my present Co. Until last Friday I was under the impression that I had done so. On that day Mr. Frost handed me a bundle of papers requesting me to sign them. Instead of doing so there and then, as requested, I took them home to find what they were. You may guess how surprised I was to find that they were assignments of my rights in Europe.
>
> I shall take the whole bundle with your proposal which, by the way, appears to be very reasonable—to my lawyer this morning for his advice, and I strongly suspect that within a day or two Mr. Frost will find that I am not such a ———— fool as he thought.[10]

But it was Mr. Frost, the lawyer, who won the legal game; it was Mr. Holland, the inventor, who lost, probably by default in that he had allowed Frost to take care of his business affairs. It is more than a coincidence that the Company's secretary paid five years of back taxes on all of Holland's foreign patents—British, German, Swedish, and Belgian—on the very day he thought the designer was safely on board the *Etruria,* bound for Europe. Holland actually sailed on an American Line steamer a week later, an event which caught Frost off guard. Yet it is unlikely that Holland chanced to see this vital entry in the Company's books until some time after his return from abroad. If Frost did not have the patents tied up in the contract which the inventor had signed with the Company, at least he now had a lien on those patents. If Holland sought counsel on the matter, he was surely advised that the foreign rights were for all intents and purposes already assigned to the firm. In June, 1900, when he was demoted from manager to chief engineer, his five-year contract was made retroactive to 1 April 1899 to cover the period of the patent dispute.[11]

Nine years later, in testimony before a Special Committee of the House of Representatives appointed to investigate the charge that the Electric Boat Company had indulged in monopolistic practices against the Lake Submarine Boat Company and others, Isaac Rice observed that Holland was like all inventors in that he was "never satisfied with what he invented" and was constantly seeking something new. Rice advised him to be content with the public acclaim given him for his work.[12]

True to the image portrayed by Rice, Holland concluded his letter to Tromp by saying: "Europe is a free field for me so far as patents are concerned for the plain reason that the most important and vital devices are still in my head and nowhere else."

Meanwhile, Morris was sent to Greenport to investigate a possible site for future submarine experiments. His inquiries led him to the Goldsmith and Tuthill Yard in New Suffolk, a little summer resort on Cutchogue Harbor. The basin was excellently protected by extensive bulkheads and breakwaters; and only a mile away, beyond Little Hog Neck (now Nassau Point), lay the open waters of Little Peconic Bay. He reported his findings to the Company. The location was accepted on 27 May 1899, the basin and docks to be held to the exclusion of all other vessels for a monthly rental of ten dollars. The superintending engineer acquired several adjoining rooms for himself and family in the home of Harrison H. Tuthill.[13]

The *Holland VI* took her last run out of the Atlantic Yacht Basin on the first of June, her performance again witnessed by the Italian naval attaché, Carlo da Luca-Kennedy.

On Monday morning, 5 June, the lighter *Columbia* towed the *Holland VI* through the East River into Long Island Sound. Cable and several of the crew remained on board the submarine; Morris and the others stayed on the lighter. They passed Execution Light at four-thirty in the afternoon, and were scheduled to put in to Port Jefferson for the night. Morris had noted in his diary that the crew of the lighter had placed on board a large store of beer. By seven o'clock, the crew was too drunk to go on; and Morris ordered the little flotilla to anchor in Huntington Bay.

Later the towing company endeavored to secure charges for an additional day's service, and Frost was obliged to remind the agent of the fiasco on board the *Columbia*. "We went to the trouble of having our representative aboard your tug to see that our boat was properly towed and the results have shown that we were very wise in having so done, as certain members of the crew of your tug were for a portion of the time out of commission on this trip."[14]

By dawn of the next day, the lighter was under way. In the early afternoon the two boats passed safely through Plum Gut into Gardiners Bay. The little submarine, plowing along at the end of her towline, now sported an awning stretched between her flagstaffs to shade the skeleton crew from the June sun. A pilot boarded the *Columbia* at Greenport to guide them through the winding channel around Shelter Island, across Little Peconic Bay, and into the basin at New Suffolk.

"The boys were much put out," observed Morris, when they learned that the folk in this sleepy little town saw a chance to make some quick money by raising the rates for room and board.

There was much to do in preparation for another official trial before a new Naval Board of Inspection, a trial which the Company now confidently believed would lead to the purchase of the *Holland VI* under the Appropriation Act of 1896. The burden for these preparations at New Suffolk fell on the superintending engineer. A straight two-mile course in Little Peconic Bay was to be laid out by an authorized surveyor. Cable was to take the submarine into the Bay, submerge her, and swing her slowly through a series of headings as Morris carefully recorded the deviation of the compass. A new handle to operate the large breech block for the dynamite gun had to be designed and installed. A temporary tender had to be arranged to escort the *Holland VI*. Toward the end of June, Morris and Cable had the submarine in readiness for the arrival of Holland, F. W. Brady (the chief draftsman), and other employees of the Electric Boat Company who were now prepared to invade the quiet resort near the tip of Long Island. The naphtha launch *Sentinel* was dispatched from New York to New Suffolk to serve as tender.

On 29 June, the *Sentinel* was sent to Greenport to pick up John Holland and take him over to New Suffolk. The following day the *Holland VI* left the basin at the Goldsmith and Tuthill Yard and headed for the deep water beyond Robins Island. Frank Cable was at the controls in the conning tower, while Holland and Morris moved within the vessel as the new trial captain put the submarine through her paces. She dived three times, maintaining a "perfect" course; answered her helm as never before; and reportedly achieved a new speed record submerged.[15]

John Philip Holland returned to his room at the Wyandank Hotel in Greenport. The submarine's performance that day should have given him reason to rejoice; but he sensed a storm brewing on the not-too-distant horizon, a storm which threatened to relieve him of the command of his own creation. The warnings had been hoisted on his return from Europe; and, if their forecast proved correct, he had reason to be disturbed. The foreign patent affair was bad enough, but now Brady and his staff of draftsmen "knew it all" and ignored his advice. No one seemed to consult Holland any more, not even on technical matters. Soon he was to learn of Frost's order to Morris, the inventor's oldest associate in the submarine enterprise, that henceforth Morris was not to report to Holland, because "Holland forgets."[16] Frost's order might have ended the relationship between the professor and his engineer had it not been for the bonds of respect which had united them ever since the days of the *Fenian Ram*.

Perhaps the most difficult shift of responsibility which Holland was forced to accept was the appointment of Frank Cable as skipper of the submarine. There could be little consolation in the fact that he had trained the young electrician for this unique assignment. It was he, Holland, who had been among the first to pioneer underwater navigation; and now he was to be increasingly denied access to that new environment which he had so courageously penetrated.[17]

The next day the inventor, his mind still troubled, took the train from Greenport to the station at Cutchogue, where he disembarked to walk to the New Suffolk basin. When he failed to appear as scheduled, Morris sent a man in a carriage to look for him. He was found wandering in the wrong direction, obviously lost.

In early July, Frost, together with Isaac Rice and his family of five children with man and maid servants, arrived from New York, taking up lodgings in the Manhasset House on Shelter Island. The Electric Boat Company's steam yacht *Gleam* served as the ferry to New Suffolk for those who stayed on the island. Holland had found rooms for his own family in the Booth House, a modest residence behind Greenport on Stirling Basin, quite removed from all his associates.

The two-mile trial course, marked by flag buoys, was laid down and surveyed along a stretch of water in Little Peconic Bay running north to south parallel to Little Hog Neck and about a mile offshore. The bottom along the course provided level ground at nearly four fathoms throughout. When the *Holland VI* slid out of the basin destined for the training ground on the far side of Little Hog Neck, she was often accompanied by the *Sentinel* and the *Gleam* in something of a holiday atmosphere. Holland's children frequently joined Morris on board the *Sentinel,* while official guests of the Company were entertained on board the *Gleam*. The appearance of the *Holland VI* in the waters around eastern Long Island gave the townsfolk and oyster fishermen much to talk about.

On Sunday, 23 July 1899, under a leaden sky, the submarine made a surface excursion around to the former whaling port of Sag Harbor. Among the small group of people who came down to the waterfront to observe the *Holland VI* was Clara Barton, first president of the American Red Cross. In her diary of that date, the internationally renowned humanitarian, then a still vigorous seventy-seven years of age, wrote with an intense economy of words: "Go to see Torpedo Boat of inventor Holland, lying off Sag Harbor. Cold, rainy day. Cold as October. Couldn't recall all the people I met."[18] She was invited on board the submarine by Mr. Holland and she signed the guest log of the vessel.

If Frank Cable's account is correct, Miss Barton took a "dip" in the *Holland VI* and then chastised the inventor for developing a dreadful weapon of war. Holland received the verbal criticism calmly. He then explained his belief that the boats would actually demonstrate the futility of all wars, for submarines would serve as a powerful deterrent to international conflict.[19]

Perhaps with Miss Barton's words still heavy on his conscience, Holland wrote:

> No; as nearly as the human mind can discern now, the submarine is indeed a "sea-devil," against which no means that we possess at present can prevail. . . . It may be that the tacticians can solve the problem. To me it is the most profound puzzle. To me there seems but one solution, and that is too Utopian for serious consideration.

He then concentrated on the peaceful uses of the submarine in the remainder of the article he was writing for the *North American Review* (December, 1900).

In preparation for the next official trial of the *Holland VI*, Frost had been a very busy man. He had secured, through Senator William M. Stewart of Nevada, the passage of an amendment to the Act of 10 June 1896 providing that the naval appropriation set aside by that Act should now be designated for two boats "similar to the submarine boat *Holland*." When the time came to deliver a successful boat to the government, the *Holland VI* could be substituted for the *Plunger* under the existing contract. In a ten-minute test run of the steam plant on board the Baltimore boat the previous December, the temperature in the fireroom rose from eighty to one hundred and thirty-seven degrees Fahrenheit at two-thirds of the rated horsepower. "Had we been able to develop full power," Frost confessed to the Honorable John D. Long, Secretary of the Navy, "the temperature in the same position would probably have reached the boiling point, rendering it totally impossible for the men to work there."[20] If the bids to convert to diesel power were accepted, there would still be an eight months delay before the *Plunger* would be ready for trials. The *Holland VI* was a working boat, and the proverbial bird in the hand was worth two in the bush.

There were other matters calling for Frost's attention. He arranged that three regulation Whitehead torpedoes be set aside at the Bliss works in Brooklyn for the pending trials of the *Holland*. Then there were certain friends of the submarine in the Navy who had to be kept informed of progress on the boat, because of the possibility that they could be directed to serve on or to assist the next Board of Inspection. Would Creecy see that the orders assigning Lieutenant W. J. Sears to Manila were changed to an assignment on the Atlantic station? Could Captain John Lowe, who had survived the near collision of the *Holland VI* with the lumber schooner a year earlier, be given a leave of absence and assigned to New Suffolk? Through intrigue, both of these requests were fulfilled.[21]

Captain W. H. Jaques, former president of the Holland Torpedo Boat Company, failed to receive what he thought was his fair share of Electric Boat Company stock in surrender of his earlier holdings; and he threatened to expose the names of naval personnel for whom Frost held stock in trust. Jaques's "most impudent demand" called for all the legal counsel that Frost could muster to prevent an investigation of the alleged fraudulent activities.[22]

Frost knew that they needed all the friends they could get, and he was not averse to treading dangerous ground when he thought the end justified the means. The problem of persuading those in high public office of the merits of submarine warfare was a delicate business indeed.

As the summer drew to a close, the vacationing families of employers and employees alike returned to their homes, bringing a quieter but no less earnest routine to the docks and yard at the Goldsmith and Tuthill station. The *Holland VI* sailed to Greenport to be hauled on a marine railway for the repair of her main drive shaft and a fresh coat of paint. The long anticipated government inspection was now imminent.

The base at New Suffolk was expanded to include two large sheds. Meanwhile, tensions within the Company continued to mount as the organization grew more complex; newcomers jostled for position and prestige. Cable was saying that no one bothered to listen to John Holland any more, forcing him to make his own decisions in matters pertaining to the boat. On one occasion, Cable raised a fuss over Morris' refusal to let him take the *Sentinel* to Greenport so that he might be fitted to a uniform designed for his new post as captain of the trial crew. Brady would take orders from no one, and considered the drafting department his exclusive domain.

The payroll that year showed the weekly salaries of the three top men to be: Frost, $95.00; Holland, $75.00; Morris, $50.00. Cable received $40.00; and each member of the crew, $21.00.[23] The crew was now made up of Nathaniel Addison, Harry H. Morrell (Cable's cousin), William F. C. Nindemann, John Wilson, and Henry S. Lathrop. In June of 1899 salaries were raised. Holland's pay reached $80.00; and Morris', $70.00 Though these raises reflected the growing financial confidence of the Company under Electric Boat management, they did little to ease the internal power struggle. Twice Morris threatened to resign; twice it was Holland who persuaded him to stay on. Then, on 9 October, the superintending engineer submitted his letter of resignation.

Two days later, John Holland invited Morris to join him and his guests—Senators Stewart of Nevada and Marion Butler of South Carolina, and lawyers Charles E. Creecy and C. S. McNeir—on board the new tender-yacht *Josephine*, to watch, and to participate in, dives of the *Holland VI*. This was the superintending engineer's last dive in the underwater boat he knew so well.

Holland's party returned to the docks ahead of the submarine. As they stood there watching Cable bring the "sea-devil" in, they could hear his order to stop the gasoline engine and connect the electric motor. Since the Otto engine could not be reversed, this was the customary command when approaching a landing. At the time, Cable and two of the crew were standing on the deck of the submarine. The captain then gave the order to reverse the electric motor. Nothing happened. The submarine came plowing toward the narrow opening into the basin. The two crew men disappeared through the hatch. Still the boat advanced.

"Cut the motor," Cable shouted.

The order was not answered. Then it was the captain's turn to slip through the hatch. The motor stopped and the submarine glided into the basin.

The spectators waited for the crew to emerge from the conning tower, but no one appeared. As she came alongside, Morris and a dockhand slipped down onto the narrow deck of the submarine, hurled a line ashore, and rushed for the conning tower. A strong odor of gas struck their nostrils, telling them instantly of the trouble below. They descended into the bowels of the submarine. The crew lay collapsed on the deck below them. Cable had managed to reach the control panel aft and throw the main switch to the motor; but, in his effort to return to the conning tower, he too had been overcome by the fumes.

One by one the limp bodies of the unconscious crew members were passed through the hatch to hands on the deck, and each time the rescuers gasped for breath before returning to the hold. By the time a doctor had been summoned from the village, the five crew members had been revived by artificial respiration; and all, including Morris and his helper, were treated for gas inhalation.[24]

A gas leak in the exhaust system of underwater boats represented one of the more serious hazards in the early days of submarining and led to the introduction of the old mining technique of carrying a cage of mice on board. Recalling his own narrow escape, Cable succinctly appraised the effectiveness of this innovation: "When the mice died, it was time to go ashore."

Three days later, Morris returned from a shopping trip to Greenport to find a letter from Isaac Rice accepting "with regret" his resignation. His work on the *Holland VI* was over, but his friendship and association with the professor from Newark had not yet run its course.

On Sunday evening, 5 November, the lighthouse tender *Cactus* arrived at Greenport, bound in from New London, bearing the long-awaited Naval Board of Inspection and Survey: Rear Admiral Frederick Rodgers, president; Commander W. H. Emory; Commander C. R. Roelker; Naval Constructor W. L. Capps; and Lieutenant T. J. Henderson, recorder. Early Monday morning, John Holland joined the naval officers on board the *Cactus* for the trip over to the station in New Suffolk.

The morning was spent inspecting the *Holland VI* at dockside " . . . and the Board was impressed with the excellent condition of the boat and all its appliances," reported the admiral.[25]

After lunch, Captain John Lowe and Commander Emory boarded the *Holland VI* for the run out to the trial course in Little Peconic Bay. The remainder of the Board accompanied Holland, Frost, Rice, and others on the *Josephine*. The requirements for the exhibition were the same as those laid down in 1898 by Admiral Montgomery Sicard for the Naval Strategy Board.

In the laconic style of a ship's captain, the log of the *Holland VI* for that afternoon read, in part, as follows:

—Voltage at the start, 125.

12:45 P.M.—Start from wharf. Electric engine. Cruising trim. . . .
One torpedo in tube, one amidships, and one in starboard wing.

12:48 P.M.—Substituted gas engine. Making for course. Revolutions of the screw by gauge, 250. Pressure in all air tanks, 2,100 lbs. . . .

1:12 P.M.—Stopped and changed to electric engine.

1:14 P.M.—Closed conning tower.
[All the main tanks were then tested.]

1:30 P.M.—Dive. Revolutions 212.

1:37 P.M.—Rose to surface and blew out amidships tanks.

1:43 P.M.—Stopped. Turret open, awaiting arrival of consorts at course.

2:19 P.M.—Start for official run.

2:26 P.M.—Amidships tanks filled and conning tower closed, and ran awash.

2:28 P.M.—Dive. Revolutions 226.

2:35 P.M.—Got ready to fire torpedo.

2:41 P.M.—Rose to surface

2:42 P.M.—Fire torpedo.

2:43 P.M.—Dive. Vessel steered well in both vertical and horizontal plane.

2:56 P.M.—Rose to surface. Two of air tanks down to pressure of 1,300 lbs.
[Emory and one of the crew replaced by Constructor Capps and Lieutenant Commander Henderson.]

3:20 P.M.—Closed turret and went ahead awash.

3:35 P.M.—Dive. Ahead full speed, and fired torpedo at submergence of 5½ feet. [Voltage at the finish, 123.]

3:50 P.M.—Trial ended.

The *Holland VI* had successfully met all of the requirements stipulated by the Navy's Board of Construction. Therefore, on 23 November, Frost offered her for sale to the Navy for the sum of $160,000, suggesting that the *Plunger* be returned to the Company for completion. The offer seemed eminently fair, for it was estimated that the *Holland VI* had cost her owners $236,615.[26]

Back in New Suffolk, it had been decided that the submarine should be taken to Washington to "make her lobby for an appropriation." After a two-day passage under her own power, the *Holland VI* reached her old berth at the Atlantic Yacht Basin in Brooklyn, where she was hauled and painted on 29 November. In planning for the trip south, Frost learned that no insurance company would cover the risk of an outside passage from Sandy Hook to the Virginia Capes. Hence the route was changed to follow the inland waterway via the Raritan Canal to the Delaware River, down the Delaware Bay to the Chesapeake Canal and Elk River, into the Chesapeake Bay. After a stop at Annapolis, the submarine would proceed on to the Potomac.

Captain Cable has written a delightful account of the thirty-nine-day passage of the famous boat: how pontoons were attached to her sides to reduce her draft for the shallow waters of the Raritan Canal; how crowds gathered wherever she passed; and how crew members regaled the cadets at the U.S. Naval Academy with stories of their submarine ventures.[27]

By Christmas of 1899, the *Holland VI* lay quietly alongside her convoy, the *Josephine*, at the Washington Navy Yard, beyond the eyes of the curious. Her acceptance by the United States Navy now seemed assured. Twenty-five years of tireless experimentation had brought John Philip Holland to the pinnacle of his career on the very eve of the twentieth century.

CHAPTER NINE

THE NAVY'S FIRST SUBMARINES
1900-1904

No group of men could have been more sensitive to the subtle and prophetic dawn of the twentieth century than those naval officers and congressmen who witnessed the trial of the *Holland VI* on the Potomac River on 14 March 1900.

Admiral George Dewey testified to Congress on 23 April, "I saw the operation of the boat down off Mount Vernon the other day [14 March]." . . . "And I said it then, and I have said it since," asserted the hero of the American people, "that if they [Spanish Navy] had had two of those things in Manila, I never could have held it with the squadron I had . . . With two of these in Galveston, all the navies of the world could not blockade that place."[1]

Preparations for the trial, which the admiral was to attend, began the moment the ice started to melt in the river. A one-mile course was marked off near Sheridan Point between Fort Washington and Mount Vernon, where the four-hundred-yard-wide channel offered depths of five and six fathoms. Stakes, with white flags attached, were driven along the edges of the channel to indicate the outer margins of the mud shallows on either side. A shorter practice area was laid down off Alexandria some five miles upstream and closer to the Navy Yard.

Tests on the Alexandria course quickly revealed that in the fresh water of the Potomac the amount of ballast required in the tanks of the submarine was considerably less than that needed in the salt water off the Atlantic coast. To assure the requisite stability, blocks of cork coated with waterproof paint were carefully fitted into the ballast tanks in order to reduce their volume. Lead pigs were then taken on board to bring the boat to the desired trim.

At 10:30 A.M. on 14 March, the naval tug *Tecumseh* took the *Holland VI* in tow, moved into the Potomac, and headed south for the Mount Vernon course. The little convoy was soon followed by the government dispatch boat *Sylph* and the Holland Torpedo Boat Company's yacht *Josephine*. The two surface vessels transported some thirty official guests, including Admiral Dewey and his staff, Assistant Secretary of the

Navy Charles H. Allen, and members of both the House and Senate Committees on Naval Affairs.

The *Holland VI* carried a special guest that day—Admiral Dewey's personal aide, Lieutenant Harry H. Caldwell. The admiral had granted Caldwell's request to go down in the submarine as an observer. The lieutenant perched himself on a high seat just aft of the opening into the conning tower, a position that enabled him to read the needle on the depth gauge which was illuminated by a shielded light bulb. "I did nothing at all except to sit quietly on a stool and watch the manipulation of the boat. You can see it all, it is all open. You can see what every man is doing except the engineer who is a little hidden from this big room. It is a very good post of observation."[2]

When the *Tecumseh* reached the range, the submarine was cast adrift and moved away under her own power. She made a short practice dive, came to the surface, and waited for the arrival of the *Sylph* and the *Josephine*. Captain Cable listened for the signal to begin the run.

There were two blasts from the *Sylph*'s steam whistle, and the exhibition was under way. The *Holland VI* submerged with remarkable rapidity; only her jack and ensign were visible as she ran at six knots for ten minutes in a straight line. Then her turret broke water, and seconds later she disappeared again. Gunner Nindemann fired the torpedo which sped off in the direction of the landing at Mount Vernon. The two flagstaffs on the boat betrayed a sudden underwater maneuver, tracing a graceful one-hundred-and-eighty-degree turn as she headed back upstream. When she had retraced half her original run, the *Holland VI* surfaced. Captain Cable's head and shoulders appeared in the hatch. The *Sylph* blew her whistle three times; the trial was over.

Representative Amos J. Cummings of New York, who had watched the trial from the decks of the *Josephine*, asked Lieutenant Caldwell, "After the discharge [of the torpedo] did it affect the boat any?"

"Not in the least," replied the young officer. "There was a slight shock." Then he explained to the congressman how the submarine automatically took on board water ballast equal in weight to the loss of the eight-hundred-and-forty-pound torpedo.

Torpedoes were expensive, so two men had been stationed in a rowboat near the end of the course to retrieve the one expended during the test. Their vigilance, however, went unrewarded. Several days later a fisherman reported that he had found a strange object while dragging his nets. Elated at the discovery, the Electric Boat Company offered the fisherman fifty dollars for the torpedo's return, a fee which he begrudgingly accepted, as the torpedo was worth several thousand dollars.[8]

Additional trials of the *Holland VI* took place in the Potomac: one in March and three in April. The Holland Company distributed printed programs for these exhibitions, outlining the whistle signals to be used and the maneuvers to be performed. Appended was a description of the boat introduced in the best journalese of the day: "The Monster War Fish," "Uncle Sam's Devil of the Deep," and "The Naval 'Hell Diver'."[4]

On 11 April 1900, the *Holland VI* was purchased by the United States government under a contract drawn between the Secretary of the Navy, John D. Long, and the secretary of the Holland Torpedo Boat Company, Elihu B. Frost, for the sum of $150,000. Thus the United States became the second major power in history to adopt the submarine as a part of its naval force. Furthermore, the Navy clearly contemplated additional submarines, for not only did the Appropriation Act of 10 June 1896, as amended in 1899, provide for a second boat of the "Holland type" to replace the *Plunger,* but the Secretary also stipulated in the contract of 11 April that if new boats of the "improved Holland design" were accepted, such boats were in no event to exceed $170,000 each.[5]

This signal moment in the history of the United States Navy immediately led to interminable hearings before the Naval Committees of the Congress. Now that the government owned the submarine torpedo boat, what was to be done with it? How many should the government build? Could the United States control the type and design to the exclusion of all foreign powers? What role would the new vessel play, one of offense or one of defense?

Experts, and some who were not so expert, testified before the Congress: from admiral to lieutenant, from naval constructor to private shipbuilder, as well as the little Irish-born professor who had started it all by his dogged persistence.

Courteously introduced by the chairman of the House Committee on Naval Affairs, John Philip Holland modestly and succinctly told the quarter-century story of his experiments with underwater craft. "He is an admirable talker," observed a *Washington Star* reporter who had interviewed the inventor in January, "direct and to the point, and would be the delight of any stenographer on earth."[6] It was not easy to follow such witnesses as Admiral Dewey and Rear Admiral Philip Hichborn, but John Holland firmly answered the questions posed by Representative Amos Cummings.

"So it stands today as the Navy Department have reported that all the requirements have been fulfilled?" queried Cummings.

"Yes, sir."

"So that we will purchase this boat with the additional provision for building another of the same type?"

"Slightly altered," Holland corrected quietly. "We call this [referring to a model on the table before him] and the *Holland* the same type. This is the *Holland* with its defects eliminated. . . . The boat is a little longer, and she has much more power. She will have 180 horse power for surface running instead of 50, and 70 electric horse power for running submerged instead of only 50 now on the *Holland*."[7]

Blueprints of the improved boat had been completed and sent to the Navy on 23 November 1899, along with Frost's original offer to sell the *Holland VI*. A preliminary sketch, in Holland's own hand, also drawn in the fall of 1899, suggested the inventor's conception of the new type, its approximate dimensions, its rated horse power, and its powerful pneumatic dynamite gun.[8] A retractable slide on the forward superstructure would enable the twenty-two-foot gun to be pivoted forward of its center, the breech lowered from the horizontal position under the deck, and the muzzle raised twenty degrees above the plane of the water line. Since Holland held the patent on this improved dynamite gun, he was reluctant to give up a weapon which he considered an essential feature in the armament of his boats. One can be sure that he was overruled on this matter, for the accepted design, while otherwise nearly identical to his preliminary sketch, did not include the gun. The final plan utilized the space gained for an extra hatch to load torpedoes and for storage space for five "steel fish," instead of the three carried on board the *Holland VI*.

The question before Congress was: how many of these "improved boats" should the government build? House Resolution 6966, introduced by Representative Cummings, called for a submarine fleet of twenty boats, but the proposed bill did not pass. The Naval Appropriation Act of 7 June 1900, however, did provide for the construction of five boats of the improved *Holland* type. The contract for the original *Plunger* was canceled, and the $93,000 advanced by the government under that contract was returned by the Holland Company to the Treasury of the United States. "As though one *Holland* submarine boat were not enough," complained the *Buffalo Express*, "the Senate wants five. Has it a grudge against the Navy?"[9]

On 25 August, a contract was drawn for not five but six boats in addition to the *Holland*, the new submarines to be delivered in 1902 and early 1903. With the *Holland*, *Adder*, *Moccasin*, *Porpoise*, and *Shark* built at Lewis Nixon's Crescent Shipyard in Elizabethport, and with the *Grampus* and the *Pike* built at the Union Iron Works in San Francisco, for the Pacific Station, the Submarine Fleet of the United States Navy was born. Except for the *Holland*, but including a new *Plunger*, these underwater torpedo boats became known as the *Adder* class, or *A-1* through *A-7*.

The plans to inaugurate a submarine fleet did not silence the critics of the new weapon. However, if there were some officers of the United States Navy who still doubted the usefulness of the craft, and others who considered it as good as worthless, their views were largely offset by Admiral Dewey's testimony. Charles Creecy, who had suggested the exhibition on the Potomac, thought the admiral's declaration was "the greatest triumph in the history of the boat company," and that the Company's "years of patient toil, perseverance, disappointment, pecuniary loss, [and] everything else was solved that day and its success assured when the Admiral of the Navy said he could not have taken his fleet into Manila Bay if two of them had been there."

At the hearing in 1908 when Creecy made this statement, his interrogater asked: "That was when you began to go down hill?"

In answering this telling question, Creecy might have been speaking for John Philip Holland as well as for himself: "Well, I got buried then with glory."[10]

In June, 1900, within a month of the congressional hearings, and as if to note the passing of the high-water mark of his career, John Holland was presented with a five-year contract made retroactive to 1 April 1899. By the terms of this contract, he was demoted from general manager of the Holland Torpedo Boat Company to chief engineer.

Flushed with success, Isaac Rice and E. B. Frost, both practical men of affairs, began to turn against the one man whose dreams and perseverance had now brought them a handsome return on their investments. Let Holland be content with the image he has acquired in the public eye, they said, in effect; we now have need of technically trained constructors and engineers, not an untutored school teacher. And so Holland, too, was to be "buried then with glory." Well, perhaps not quite yet. He would make one more start. Creecy, Nixon, Morris, and Captain Kimball would stand behind him. He had plans, but they would have to wait for the right moment.

In the meantime, the *Holland VI* was temporarily assigned to Lieutenant Caldwell, pending his application for release from Admiral Dewey's staff; and the submarine was prepared for a voyage to the Naval Torpedo Station at Newport, Rhode Island. Under the terms of the agreement with the Navy, Captain Cable and three members of his crew were to remain with the vessel until naval men had been assigned to the submarine and properly trained for their duties.

On the trip north from Washington, the electric motor on board the *Holland* broke down. Whenever moisture managed to reach the copper bars under the windings in the motor, a ground was produced with the iron core, causing an arc to carbonize the insulation and burn out the armature. As a result of the breakdown, the submarine traveled but a short distance under her own power; for the remainder of the passage, she had to be towed by the escort tug *Osceola,* arriving at the Naval Torpedo Station on 24 June 1900.

It was a stroke of bad luck for the submarine to be hampered by burned out armatures during her first twelve months in the Navy. The precaution of running the motor daily to drive out any condensation proved but a temporary solution until such time as a new motor, incorporating an improved method of insulating the windings, could be installed.

By the end of August, Frank Cable decided that the Navy crew (Lieutenant Caldwell, Acting Gunner Owen Hill, and their men) was sufficiently trained to take over the submarine. "Had my heart been weak," Cable observed, "I may not have survived the experience." While he watched from the outside for the first time in more than two years, the veteran submarine navigator suffered the sensation of being unable to assist in case of an emergency. "Some error by the operator had caused the premature filling of the after tanks, and the stern consequently sank about fifteen feet. This meant a dangerous angle, with the bow still out of water. It looked to me as though she was going to stand upon her tail like a spar buoy and sink."[11] Lieutenant Caldwell grasped the predicament in time to fill the forward tanks and the little *Holland* settled down on an even keel. Cable sighed in relief. The new crew survived to prove itself highly competent in future experiments.

Then came the war games of the North Atlantic Squadron off Newport. The role played by the U. S. Torpedo Boat *Holland* captured the public's imagination, though it failed to win converts in the Navy Department.

At sundown on the second night of the maneuvers, USTB *Holland* slipped away from her dock at the Naval Torpedo Station and made her way through the passage east of Conanicut Island. Her course was set for a position east and south of Brenton Reef Lightship, from which point the search seaward began for the units of the blockading Red Squadron. It was one of those clear, cool nights when the sky is like velvet studded with brilliant stars, in marked contrast to the inky, undulating sea. The young lieutenant feared that under such atmospheric conditions the phosphorescent wake of his vessel might betray his presence. He brought her to a trim where only her turret and six inches of her hull remained above water. Somewhere in the darkness beyond lay the battleships *Kearsarge, Indiana,* and *Texas,* and the gunboats *Scorpion* and *Eagle.*

About 9:00 P.M., already seven miles at sea, a huge shadow loomed ahead. Caldwell aimed the bow of the submarine directly at the object, his "kill" or torpedo tube opening taking a deadly aim at the outline. He flashed his warning signal. There was no response. He brought the *Holland* in closer to the slowly moving shadow of a ship, and recognized her as Captain William M. Folger's flagship, the *Kearsarge*. At one hundred yards from his target, the young lieutenant showed his light and proudly shouted: "Hello, *Kearsarge!* You're blown to atoms. This is the submarine boat the *Holland*."[12]

When the umpire for the games added up the "casualties" among the ships of the blockading Red Squadron, there was some doubt about the *Holland's* score on the technical grounds that the *Kearsarge* had already been "knocked out" by the surface torpedo boats *Morris* and *Gwynn*, also units of the defending fleet. Caldwell reported that two other ships of the Red Squadron came within his range during the war games and that "the *Holland* could in all probability have torpedoed three blockading vessels without being discovered."

The technicality must have taken a little of the wind out of the officer's sails, but the testimonies which followed the official report could not have kept him long in the doldrums. Captain Folger himself declared: "It is clear that the *Holland* type will play a very serious part in future naval warfare. There is no doubt whatever that the vessel at Newport can approach a turret ship unseen, either by night or day." Then, speaking as if he had some clairvoyant grasp on future events, he added: "Her only danger is she may be run over herself by picket or larger vessel."

Rear Admiral Hichborn commented: "I place great importance upon what Captain Folger says. He used to be Chief of Ordnance in the Navy Department for many years. He is a pretty plain-spoken man and I must say that I was rather surprised to hear his statement. I was rather pleased, because it sustained my views."

Rear Admiral Norman H. Farquhar, who commanded the North Atlantic Squadron, observed that the technical hits of the surface torpedo boats probably had put the lookouts on the *Kearsarge* off guard. Nevertheless, he admitted that "The *Holland* impressed everyone with the idea that under ordinary circumstances she could always get in a torpedo, either day or night, without being discovered."[13]

Nathan Sargent captained the gunboat *Scorpion* of the Red Squadron on the second night of maneuvers in Narragansett Bay. The first naval officer sent to inspect the *Holland* in action, he had reason to be concerned upon finding himself on the possible receiving end of the submarine's potentially destructive power. In his report to the commander of the North Atlantic Squadron, he spoke of "the moral effect of an anticipated attack from the *Holland* submarine boat."[14]

Her mettle having been tested in "battle," the sixth submarine designed and perfected by John Philip Holland was, on 12 October 1900, appropriately commissioned the USS *Holland* (later designated SS-1) in ceremonies at Newport. Lieutenant Harry H. Caldwell became the first submarine captain in the United States Navy.

One of Caldwell's initial acts was to urge that the submarine be kept in commission throughout the approaching winter to avoid deterioration of her hull and machinery. The Bureau of Ordnance approved his suggestion; and, immediately following the commissioning, the naval tug *Leyden* was ordered to tow the USS *Holland* as far as Delaware City. There, the convoy was to be met by a gunboat that would take the submarine through the Chesapeake and Delaware Canal and on to her winter quarters at the U. S. Naval Academy in Annapolis.

Commander Richard Wainwright, formerly executive officer of the battleship *Maine*, famous for his command of the *Gloucester* in the Battle of Santiago Harbor, and now Superintendent of the Naval Academy, welcomed each member of the crew of the USS *Holland*. In addition to Captain Caldwell and Gunner Owen Hill, the crew then consisted of W. H. Reader, chief gunner's mate; B. Bowie, chief machinist's mate; O. Swanson, gunner's mate first class; H. Wahab, gunner's mate first class; A. Callahan, gunner's mate second class; A. Gumpert, gunner's mate second class; and W. Hall, electrician's mate second class—nine brave men in all. Other men who served in the *Holland* included Richard O. Williams, chief electrician, and Michael Malone, as well as Igoe, Kane, Simpson, and Rhinelander.

The Academy cadets were keenly interested in the $150,000 boat which could have blown up the $5,000,000 *Kearsarge* with a $3,000 torpedo. The presence of the *Holland* at Annapolis was, in part, contrived to win volunteers for the new service, men who would command the new A-boats after the shakedown trials. And in the best tradition of the Navy, volunteers were never wanting. Among the cadets who had the opportunity to examine the latest development in the science of naval warfare were First Classman Ernest J. King and Fourth Classman Chester W. Nimitz, both of whom later made major contributions to submarining, as well as to modern American naval history.

The Superintendent was as enthusiastic about the presence of the USS *Holland* as any cadet at the Academy, and Wainwright cruised in the submarine beneath the surface of Chesapeake Bay. "She will never revolutionize modern warfare, but then no vessel will do that," he asserted. "But for coast defense purposes she is of inestimable value as an addition to our Navy. Too much cannot be said in her praise."[15]

In November it was decided to sail the USS *Holland* down the Bay to the Navy Yard at Norfolk. Sixty miles from her destination, the armature again burned out, but the submarine made port under the power from her Otto engine. The skipper deemed it advisable to remain at Norfolk into the new year. Without an operating motor for backing down, it would be difficult and dangerous to bring her to a dock.

Meanwhile, at Lewis Nixon's yard in Elizabethport, work was resumed on submarines. Priority was given to an experimental boat designed to be a working model for the subsequent *Adder* class and christened the *Fulton* in honor of the famous progenitor of underwater vessels.

From the very inception of the renewed submarine work at the Crescent Shipyard, conflicts arose that were reminiscent of the interference Holland experienced with the *Plunger*. The government assigned Naval Constructor Lawrence Y. Spear to supervise the building of the submarines. He was an able technician, but his thorough, conservative, traditional way of doing things had so prolonged the production schedule of the surface torpedo boat *Rowan* at Seattle that she had been completed too late to serve in the conflict with Spain.[16] He was not familiar with submarines, in theory or in practice, and yet his will was felt even in the construction of the *Fulton*.

Frank Cable protested the costly changes and delay:

> The *Fulton's* construction was not troublesome in as far as it related to our contribution to her completion. The difficulty was that as a replica of the *Adder* class, built in advance of the others at the Nixon Shipyard, the boat in her fundamentals had to follow government specifications, and labored under the disadvantage of having technicians not of our choosing. She was not a naval vessel, but an experimental understudy intended for our operation, yet, as in the case of *Plunger*, she was not our own child in certain essential features.[17]

The former trial captain of the *Holland* had cause to be annoyed. The constructor's approval of the use of cast iron in certain key pieces of machinery was one example of the results stemming from the failure to heed the advice of experience. Shortly after the launching of the *Fulton*, when the engines were being tested, a tooth from the cast iron clutch broke away and flew into the face of the chief machinist seriously injuring him. Kingston valves, the main bodies of which were inside the boat, were cast of the same material; and Cable knew that a crack in their shells could spell disaster. Only by refusing to go down in a submarine that carried such valves could Cable force an agreement to replace the conventional castings with ones made of an improved metal.

To John Holland, these adverse developments had other meanings. As an engineer-director on the Board of the Holland Company, he was now a figurehead: a name to be exploited and remembered, but a voice to be ignored. A year later, in 1902, Lawrence Spear resigned from the Navy to accept E. B. Frost's lucrative offer to join the Electric Boat Company as vice president and naval architect. If a man with no experience in submarines were placed over Holland in the face of his objections, the

117

inventor knew that his days in the Company would be numbered. Along with Cable, he had labored under the constructor's costly decisions and had watched the modification of the basic principles for which he had so long fought. To modify a design is not to invent. Invention involves the introduction of new principles, forms, or methods—singly or in combination—by which a hitherto unrealized objective may be attained. At least from Holland's point of view, Spear was a modifier and not an inventor. Nor was the difference between the two men to be explained solely on the grounds of Holland's frustration.

The variations in design which Lawrence Spear began to introduce made a virtue of convention and moved the boats farther away from the type which Holland conceived. Addressing the Annual Meeting of the Society of Naval Architects and Marine Engineers less than four years after assuming his new post, Spear said:

> The surface buoyancy of the "submersible" has been materially decreased and that of the "submarine" slightly increased; and on the latter have been fitted raised bow superstructures, flying bridges, etc. in an attempt to increase habitability and comfort in cruising at sea. The means and methods of submerging remain identical as before. Trials having shown that the buoyancy of the latest French "submarine" is still insufficient for satisfactory cruising on the surface at sea, the two types in the future may be expected to merge into one, which will undoubtedly be termed a "submersible". . . . In passing, we may note that the "submersible" really originated in America, as the *Holland* was the first vessel built of the general type.[18]

It was this kind of analysis which provoked John Holland to angry words: "The Navy does not like submarines because there is no deck to strut on. . . . Sweep out all interesting but useless devices that encumber the present boats. . . . She cannot have a deck on which her men can enjoy sunlight."[19] His boat, a submersible? How dare the constructor!

And yet Holland sensed the losing battle. The merger prophesied by Lawrence Spear would soon occur; the dream of John Holland would have to wait the passing of two world wars before it could be realized.

Isaac Rice, in his testimony before a special committee of the House of Representatives, declared that what the Company needed was a naval constructor, not an inventor; and, he confessed, "this naturally did not please Mr. Holland."[20]

The pace of submarine activities quickened after the spring of 1901. The *Fulton* was launched on 12 June. In August, Mrs. Richard Wainwright came from Annapolis to christen the *Adder*; and, before the year was out, Mrs. Isaac Rice and Mrs. B. Frost performed similar ceremonies for the *Moccasin* and the *Porpoise*. Each completed boat was first assigned to Goldsmith and Tuthill Yard in New Suffolk to be readied for tests and trials. By fall, the Holland Torpedo Boat Company's station on

Cutchogue Bay looked the veritable submarine base that it was, the first of its kind in the United States.

In November, the crew of the *Fulton* surprised the world by spending fifteen hours on the floor of Peconic Bay, upsetting many a theory which maintained that such a feat was impossible. John Holland carefully computed the air supply available and advised Cable that there was a theoretic limit for seventy hours on the bottom, but one-fourth of that time, or about eighteen hours, would be "the probable duration of submergence of *Fulton* without suffocating the crew."[21] In this descent, Cable had with him, besides his faithful trial crew, Captain John Lowe and a young lieutenant by the name of Arthur MacArthur, Jr., who was later to become skipper of the *Pike* (*A-5*). During the test, those on board experienced an eerie sensation when they observed the depth gauge registering several feet more water than the known soundings for the position where they had submerged. Upon surfacing at the end of the test, they saw evidences of destruction in the bay area and at the docks in New Suffolk which told them that a severe storm, accompanied by unusually high tides, had passed over them without their knowledge.

The successful tests of the *Fulton* were followed shortly by two serious accidents. In December she sank at her dock in New Suffolk. In April, 1902, after a successful open run from Sandy Hook to the Delaware Breakwater, an explosion of battery gas injured three of her crew and damaged the interior of the boat.

Early in the winter of 1901-2, Frank Cable went to Barrow-in-Furness, England, to train the crew of the British *A-1*, built by Messrs. Vickers, Sons and Maxim from the "improved Holland" plans submitted under a contract which Isaac Rice had negotiated with the Admiralty. The mossbacks in America who thought little of the submarine's future were no match for the old guard of His Majesty's Navy. A century earlier Lord St. Vincent had condemned Pitt as "the greatest fool who ever existed" for encouraging Robert Fulton's submarine schemes. He had declared that underwater boats were for the weaker nations only, and his judgment was heard again in Parliament in 1901. But even the Admiralty was jolted from its complacency when the French *Gustave Zédé* struck the great battleship *Jauréquiberry* with a dummy torpedo as the pride of the French Fleet moved out the roads of Ajaccio.[22]

It was perhaps inevitable that John Holland's name should be linked to the early failures and tragic accidents which befell Britain's first submarines. Captain R. H. S. Bacon, Royal Navy, firmly believed that the plans submitted by the Electric Boat Company were not only unusual in many details, but also in places obviously in error. Furthermore, the major accidents that struck the British *A-1*, *A-4*, *A-5*, and *A-8*

119

boats, with a loss of some thirty lives, all occurred in the first four years of operation. But when John Devoy imputed these catastrophes to John Holland's early Irish loyalties, claiming that the expatriate had opposed the sale of his boats to England, had been overruled by his Company, and so had altered the drawings which the British used, then Devoy was carrying patriotism too far. It was very unlikely that Holland had the opportunity to tamper with standardized prints; and there is no reason to suppose that he was so inclined.[23]

The year following Cable's return from England, the busy trial captain received orders to report to the Union Iron Works in San Francisco for the shakedown cruises of the *Grampus* and the *Pike*. He took with him an experienced crew of submariners —William F. C. Nindemann, Harry H. Morrell, Henry S. Lathrop, and Herman W. Noblett. Lawrence Spear and Gunner Owen Hill, U. S. Navy, arrived from the East in time for the official trials in March and April, 1903. The runs before the Naval Board went off to everyone's satisfaction. The *Pike* exceeded the eight-knot surface speed required by the government. No incidents marred the tests. In fact, inspections and government trials were becoming "old hat" for Cable and his crew.

Back in New Suffolk, the Goldsmith and Tuthill Basin was now crowded with the five boats of the *Adder* class, the *Fulton*, and the original *Plunger*, an obsolete hulk towed up from the Triggs Iron Works in Richmond where an effort had been made to complete her. The tender *Kelpie*, the yacht-tender *Mindora*, and the torpedo boat *Craven* were also there. Then, one by one, the A-boats left the station to become units in the Submarine Flotilla of the North Atlantic Squadron of the United States Navy.

Unobtrusively, John Holland went about whatever jobs came his way; but in his mind he was still keenly critical of all that transpired around him. He followed with interest the rise of Simon Lake, reading whatever he could about Lake's *Protector*, which had been launched in 1902 as a direct challenge to the Electric Boat Company "lobby." The legal antics of the two competing companies, the charges and countercharges, must have both amused and disturbed Holland. He knew that Lake was determined to break the monopolistic hold which Electric Boat seemed to have over officials in Washington. Intentionally or unintentionally, John Holland was about to assist Simon Lake's cause.

With increased time on his hands, Holland turned to his drawing board to draft a new submarine which would preserve the essential features of his earlier boats. Once confident that he had found a solution to the problem of increased tonnage with higher speeds submerged, he discussed with Creecy, Nixon, and Morris his proposal to build privately the new boat. Assured of their moral and material support, and with his contract about to expire, he decided that the time had come to resign from the Holland Torpedo Boat Company. His brief letter to Isaac Rice, dated 28 March 1904, closed with a masterful stroke of irony:

Dear Mr. Rice:—

As my contract with the company expires on the 31st inst., and as it is proper that I should then withdraw from my directorship, I beg to offer my resignation.

The success of your company can never be as great as what I ardently desired for it.

Yours, very sincerely,
John P. Holland.[24]

CHAPTER TEN

THE PASSING OF A PROPHET
1904-1914

At the age of sixty-three, John Philip Holland had severed his connections with Isaac Rice and E. B. Frost—with the Company which had nurtured him—"traded on his matchless genius," as John Devoy put it—and then brushed him aside. For thirty-five years he had followed the dream of mastering submarine navigation, from the embryonic insights at Dundalk through the crowning achievement of the *Holland VI*. Now his mature vision of the submarine of the future appeared to be a reality just short of his grasp. It was too early to admit defeat; it was too late to rest content. He would attempt to capitalize on whatever remained rightfully his, searching the ever-widening horizons of mechanical innovations.

Holland had amassed no personal fortune. His highest salary before 1900, under the Rice regime, never exceeded $90.00 per week, a fact which his former employers were too embarrassed to reveal when questioned by an investigating committee of Congress.[1] By his own reckoning, he held no more than one-half of one per cent of the stock of the parent organization. His stock was valued at perhaps $50,000, inadequate capital with which to launch a company of his own.[2] Not only had his lawyer friends managed to gain control of the foreign rights of his inventions, but also they had arranged to have twenty major domestic patents assigned to the Electric Boat Company.

In spite of the limited resources at his command in 1904, John Holland continued to possess certain invaluable assets: a circle of loyal friends, a number of minor but unassigned patents, and the exclusive rights to his "new type, high speed submarine boat designed for coast defense and for work on the high seas."[3] These assets constituted the bases for his confidence and were possible ingredients for success, notwithstanding the doubts which assailed him as he undertook the risks of independent action.

The first step was to build a scale model of the high-speed boat. With the permission of the Secretary of the Navy, and under the watchful eyes of the naval officers in charge, Holland tested his model in the experimental tank at the Washington Navy

Yard with encouraging results. If the French engine which Lewis Nixon had acquired could generate its indicated horsepower, such an engine installed in a full-scale, ninety-six-foot vessel of the same hull lines ought to attain the startling surface speed of twenty-two knots, or six knots faster than the swiftest battleship.

Charles Creecy, who had resigned from the Electric Boat Company in 1903 because of the unfriendly relations which had grown up between Frost and himself, interceded with the Navy Department on Holland's behalf. Creecy requested that the inventor be given the chance to present his plans before a special Naval Board. After a full day of examining the blueprints of the latest Holland proposal, the Board concluded that while the inventor unquestionably could achieve the speeds he claimed for his boat, the dangers inherent in such a swift craft were too great to accept; further, the speed of a vessel running submerged should never exceed six knots because of the difficulties of navigating underwater.

Holland had much to think about when he returned to his home at 38 Newton Street in Newark. The usual objections from high places were becoming somewhat monotonous. Previous tank tests had convinced him that the A-boats already in commission did not represent his best work. Besides, there had been too many interferences, too many alterations in the basic design. He observed: "The young lawyer who had acted as engineer of the Holland company, acting upon advice of some misguided naval officer, who knew even less of submarines than he did, insisted upon using the plans I had condemned, and the so-called Holland boat of today is the result."[4] Whether or not this criticism was fully justified, there is little doubt that Holland wished to hold the design of the new, high-speed submarine for the exclusive use of the United States government.

In the meantime, foreign interests beat a path to his door. He had work to do. The little shop behind his home became the subject of gossip in the neighborhood. Japanese men were seen to come and go in clandestine fashion, generating what some called "a cloak and dagger atmosphere." In fact, John Holland was instructing Kojiro Matsukata, director of the Kawasaki Dockyard at Kobe, in the construction details for two moderate-sized, medium-speed submarines, the plans for which had been purchased by the Emperor's government. Construction engineer Mason S. Chace studied with the Japanese in anticipation of his assignment to Kobe to supervise the building of the boats. Nathaniel Addison of the old *Holland VI* crew would accompany Chace to Japan. From time to time, others visited the little shop, including Holland's old acquaintance, Lieutenant Kenji Ide, naval attaché at the Japanese Embassy in Washington. Ide had been among those who had submerged in the Potomac on board the *Holland* in April, 1900.

Japan's interest in John Holland's submarines dated back to the days at Nixon's Yard subsequent to the launching of the *Holland VI* in 1897. Later that summer, in sweltering July heat, two of the Emperor's high ranking officers stripped to the waist to explore the interior of the submarine. Then on 29 September 1898, Count Kosuke Kizaki visited Holland and Morris to discuss the war potential of submarines and inspect the famous craft that then stood on the ways at the Atlantic Yacht Basin in Brooklyn. Less than a month later, on 21 October, Count Takashi Sasaki descended in the boat during trials in the Narrows of New York Harbor, thus preceding the feat of Lieutenant Ide.

In 1904, Takata and Company of New York represented the Japanese government in the negotiations which led to the purchase of the plans for the two Holland submarines. The indications are that this order was placed within a month following the signing of a contract 14 June 1904 with Electric Boat Company for the purchase of five boats of the A-class to be built at the Fore River Yard in Massachusetts. These boats were to be dismantled and shipped to the Gokaska Docks at Yokosuka on Tokyo Bay for reassembly by Arthur Busch. The outbreak of hostilities between Russia and Japan, in February of 1904, served as the catalyst to stepped-up Japanese submarine activity; and security seemed to reside in the magic name of "Holland."

In 1905, while Frank Cable was in Japan training the crews of the five A-boats, the two Holland submarines were being completed at Kobe. Cable sought permission from the host government to inspect the rival craft at the Kawasaki works. "I was anxious to see these boats," he admitted, "but despite my acquaintance with Lieutenant Ide, the Japanese officer in charge of the work for his government, red tape barred me from access to the Kobe yard."[5]

Well might Cable wish to see the latest Holland boats. They were, by all accounts, faster than any previously devised, being capable of sixteen knots submerged and developing three hundred horsepower on the surface. One was seventy-five feet in length; and the other, eighty-seven feet. By comparison, the A-boats were twenty feet shorter; they barely exceeded an underwater speed of eight knots; and their Otto engines generated one hundred and sixty horsepower. Furthermore, Holland claimed that his special Japanese boats would not be dependent upon the coast nor be confined to harbor defense, but could operate in sorties against the enemy in distant waters.[6]

The two Holland submarines were duly commissioned in the Japanese Navy, along with the five A-boats which Busch finished assembling in July. But five weeks earlier, Vice Admiral Heihachiro Togo had virtually wiped out the Baltic Fleet under Vice Admiral Zinovi Rozhdestvenski in the decisive Battle of Tsushima Strait. As was the case in the Spanish-American War, the submarine lost its chance to demonstrate its war potential, all newspaper stories to the contrary. Togo's victory convinced the great naval powers, if they needed convincing, that heavily armored battleships should be given priority in all programs of naval construction. Undaunted, John Holland continued to be the prophet for the submarine. His faith in his Japanese boats contained the usual unheeded admonitions:

> Japan has incomparably superior war men than we have. Mr. Matsukata, her national engineer, spent a year with me, daily learning the devices and secrets of the *Holland*. He returned to his country when no breath of hostility stirred the air. Unlike most people, the Japs work independently and indefatigably. They are building boats designed and fitted to accompany a fleet in any kind of weather for any distance and at any speed. Think of that! Admiral [Robley] Evans' vast fleet would be blown from the seas with such submarine craft against him.
>
> Our boats cannot travel with a fleet, and they cannot venture far from port. Japan's boats work; they don't do stunts. Our submarines, I am sorry to say, are now a joke. My patterns have been subjected to the treatment of young, inexperienced engineers who professed to know more about problems I had battled with for years, and ruined.
>
> It is amazing how the United States can spend millions for submarines and then get really nothing compared to what skillful Japanese engineers are building for their country.[7]

There was a tragic sequel for one Kobe-built boat. Five years after her commissioning, she went to the bottom, in Hiroshima Bay, with all hands. When the vessel was raised from her ten-fathom grave, salvage men found the log of Captain Sakuma. In words of courageous restraint, the lieutenant depicted the final two hours and forty minutes of the terrible ordeal which he and his men suffered before death overtook them. "Words of apology fail me for having sunk His Majesty's Submarine No. 6," wrote the doomed skipper. "My subordinates are killed by my fault, but it is with pride that I inform you that the crew to a man have discharged their duties as sailors should with the utmost coolness until their dying moments." The log then expressed the fear that the incident might affect adversely the development of submarines. Sakuma begged the Emperor to continue the search for the perfect underwater vessel, asserting, "We can then die without regret." As the spreading gases poisoned the oxygen supply, the skipper penned farewells to his relatives and colleagues, including Captain Kenji Ide. "My breathing is so difficult and painful." Then the log closed: "It is now 12:40 P.M."[8]

It must not be presumed that Russia had overlooked the war potential of the submarine. She had experimented for years with underwater boats and had built the surprisingly effective *Le Diable Marin* of 1855 for the determined Austrian cavalry officer, Wilhelm Bauer. Russia had also financed the production of four boats—between 1877 and 1886—for her own engineer, Drzewiecki. These efforts were followed by designs and trials of boats of lesser importance. Then, in 1902, Captain M. Beklemishev and Naval Architect Bubonoff launched the *Delfin*. But if the Czar's Imperial Navy were to add submarines to its Asiatic Squadron at Vladivostok for the purpose of securing Russia's "window" on the Pacific, then completed boats were urgently needed. Intelligence reports received from Russia's embassies abroad indicated that only in the United States were such vessels ready for delivery.[9]

In 1904, open submarine competition in the United States finally became an established fact despite the legal gambits devised by Isaac Rice to checkmate each insurgent rival of the Holland Torpedo Boat dynasty. Thomas J. Moriarty's little one-man boat posed no serious threat, even though it was available to the highest bidder. The dissident inventor of the Holland boats, already a contender in the Japanese market, was rumored to be organizing a company of his own. Simon Lake had formed the Lake Torpedo Boat Company of Bridgeport, Connecticut, and had secured an amendment to the Naval Appropriation Act of 3 March 1903 that compelled the Navy to hold competitive trials for all completed submarine boats offered to the government, whether these boats competed against themselves or against the best in the government-owned flotilla. Lake then finished the privately built submersible, *Protector*, to challenge the Electric Boat "monopoly." Turned down by the Navy Department, but given a nod of approval as a mine layer and destroyer by a United States Army Board composed of artillery officers meeting at Newport in January, 1904, the *Protector* was scheduled for comparative trials with the experimental Holland-type *Fulton* when the Russian government suddenly purchased the Lake craft.

The *Protector* was Simon Lake's third underwater vessel. The primitive wooden box, called the *Argonaut Junior*, had been completed in 1894. The *Argonaut I* had been built at the Columbian Iron Works in Baltimore alongside Holland's *Plunger* and had been launched in the same year, 1897. The *Argonaut II* was simply the Baltimore boat lengthened and remodeled in 1899 at the dry dock of John N. Robbins in the Erie Basin, Brooklyn. These submersibles were designed for underwater exploration. Though they included the kinds of innovations later promoted by Lake, they remained sufficiently crude so as to offer no challenge to the supremacy of the sophisticated *Holland*. With the *Protector*, however, this inventor initiated a whole new breed of underwater boats.

Simon Lake's third boat was sixty-five feet long and displaced one hundred and thirty tons. She exhibited the marine engineer's fondness for wheels to guide the vessel over the ocean floor. On the *Protector*, Lake mounted his first rather cumbersome hydroplanes just fore and aft of the circular conning tower, reintroducing the level-keel principle of submergence formerly employed by Garrett and Nordenfeldt. A small gun bristled in the little observation dome which bulged out of the conning tower forward of the main hatch. Low in her bow, under the interior decking and separated from the living compartment by an air lock, she contained a diver's chamber similar to those on the *Argonauts*, but designed for the more hostile purpose of laying mines or grappling for mine cables. Out of her commodious conning tower rose the "Omniscope" tube, bearing the optical eyes of the submersible, a Lake-patented device of 1903, which the inventor claimed was superior to the deficient periscopes of the day. A man who could produce a craft such as the *Protector* would indeed bear watching.

Shipping the *Protector* to Russia involved the touchy problem of circumventing the neutrality laws of the United States. To create a legal fiction, her batteries were removed to make her inoperative as a submersible in the event she was intercepted and inspected during her hopefully secretive passage from Bridgeport to New York. Early one rainy Sunday morning she rendezvoused in Princess Bay with the Russian-hired collier *Fortuna*. The strange cargo was hoisted on board the collier, lowered into a prearranged cradle on deck, lashed down, and covered with tarpaulins. Before dawn broke over the Atlantic, the steamer was outside the three-mile limit, bound east for Kronstadt, Russia.

Simon Lake and his Bridgeport crew tested the *Protector* under the eyes of curious officers of Vice Admiral Rozhdestvenski's Baltic Fleet which was outfitting for its voyage to the Orient via the Cape of Good Hope. Shortly after their arrival, the *Delfin* sank in the Neva River with a loss of twenty-one lives. Undeterred by this careless and tragic accident, the Imperial Navy approved the *Protector*, renamed her the *Oestr*, and prepared her for the strangest trip of all. Lashed across two specially built flat cars with trucks of sixteen wheels each to distribute her one hundred and thirty tons evenly on the light rails, the vessel began a six-thousand-mile overland journey on the trans-Siberian railroad—destination, the Port of Vladivostok. But as in the case of the Japanese boats, hostilities ceased before the *Oestr* could be tried in combat. Pursuant to their purchase agreement with Lake, the Russians ordered five additional boats of the *Protector* class, which were later built at the Newport News Shipbuilding Company.[10]

Wars evoke a ruthless competition in armaments, exciting what John Holland called "the strangely unpatriotic heart which beats in the breast of a corporation." The Electric Boat Company had been willing to serve both combatants in the Russo-Japanese War, first the Czar and then the Emperor. Shortly after the *Protector* affair, and with similar subterfuge, the A-boat *Fulton* was loaded on board the English freighter *Menantic* in Gardiners Bay, inside Montauk Point, on the morning of 25 June 1904. The *Fulton* followed the *Protector* to Russia, Frank Cable followed Simon Lake, the competitors passed each other off Björkö in the Gulf of Finland, and both boats ended up in Vladivostok.

In the United States, the highly competitive war for submarine contracts mounted to a new climax. On 18 May 1905, John P. Holland's Submarine Boat Company, 751 Broad Street, Newark, was formally incorporated for the purpose of privately building the twenty-two-knot submarine of Holland design. The coolness of the Navy Department, after the tank tests of the model in Washington, forced the inventor into the contradictory position of seeking a foreign market. Letters went out to England, Holland, and Germany offering to enter into negotiations either for the patents or the boat herself. Holland's indomitable faith in his own inventive skill blinded him to the inevitable. The replies from English and Dutch shipyards expressed their understanding that the sales of his patent rights to Messrs. Vickers, Sons and Maxim, and to De Schelde and Fiume, were absolute sales of right and would in all probability legally bar them from further investigations into Holland's offer.

The decisive blow to John Holland's efforts to strike out anew in the submarine business came with the public notice of the incorporation of his firm. This reversal is told in his own appeal to the Honorable C. E. Foss, chairman of the House Committee on Naval Affairs, dated 8 February 1906, and reads in part:

> ... the Electric Boat Company filed a suit against me in the Court of Chancery of New Jersey, applying for an injunction, and claiming substantially that I had agreed to assign to them all my inventions and patents during the term of my natural life. Two other suits have been started, one against my new company in the United States Circuit Court to enjoin the use of the name "Holland"; the other against me personally, alleging a verbal contract never to compete with the Electric Boat Company, was commenced in the New Jersey Court of Chancery. My contract with the Electric Boat to act as their engineer, and to give them my patents and inventions, was for the five years during which I acted as engineer, and no longer, and expired April 1, 1904, as stated above.[11]

In a sworn affidavit filed with the courts, Isaac Rice alleged that the Electric Boat Company had once threatened to discharge Holland, and that Holland had then agreed never in his lifetime to use his talents in competition to the Company. "This allegation is absolutely false," Holland sharply retorted. He further claimed that the fictitious agreement was never reduced to writing, parrying that this was a surprising oversight for such astute lawyers as Rice and Frost. But the square deal he begged the Congress to grant him never materialized. The law suits pending in the courts frightened away Holland's capital and brought to a standstill all thought of construction of the new, high-speed submarine. The courts dismissed the suits, but by then the damage had been done.

It is unlikely that John Holland would have accepted the Foss document as his swan song in his active work on submarines. But that is what it was—a brave, last fight; restrained but terse; in part prophetic and in part confident. His friends rallied around him in a final effort to pick up the pieces of his shattered plans. Lewis Nixon arranged for meetings with a Boston capitalist. Charles Morris sought support from his many business acquaintances, and he also warned Holland of a man who was close to Rice whose pretended interest in the new company was simply a disguise to find out what Holland was doing.[12] Charles Creecy wrote to Holland that he would take care of matters in Washington and would gladly advise his old friend on the reputation of those who had expressed a willingness to invest in the company. He added: "It is likely that Nixon can be of service to us in the Department. I know he is sore at Frost for taking away from him the building of the Electric Co.'s boats."[13]

Lewis Nixon's yard had been bypassed in favor of the Fore River Shipbuilding Company at Quincy, Massachusetts, beginning with the assignment of contracts for the five Japanese boats and for the U. S. Navy's three B-class submarines, plus the *Octopus*. In November, 1903, Admiral Francis T. Bowles retired from the Navy to head the Quincy yard. A few months later contracts for the nine boats were consummated. There was a bit of irony in the choice of the firm headed by Bowles, for in 1901 the admiral, then Chief of the Bureau of Construction and Repair, complained in testimony of the unreasonable price of the A-boats that put a "handsome profit" into the pockets of the Electric Boat Company. In 1908, when questioned by the special committee hearing the Lilley Resolution, the admiral struggled to adjust his earlier calculations of submarine costs per ton of construction, admitting that he had been in error. Nevertheless, his Fore River yard built the next eleven Holland boats for the Navy (SS-9 through SS-19) and four boats for foreign countries.[14]

Back at his home in Newark, John Holland fired his final salvos at the naval authorities in Washington. In September, 1906, he wrote Secretary of the Navy Charles J. Bonaparte pleading again for the chance to have the Department review his high-speed submarine.[15] He warned the Secretary that if the Department insisted on requiring that submarines be lengthened in proportion to their diameter, he could not then achieve "two to three times more speed submerged than any other submarine in use." It is clear from this letter that he had not forsaken the insights of the dynamic hull lines so beautifully built into both the *Fenian Ram* and the *Holland VI*, though at this very time Lawrence Spear was inaugurating the lengthened and flattened hull shape that would throw the submarine back into the category of the submersible.

In the first of two documents on the ninety-six-foot "New Type, High Speed Submarine Boat," Holland suggested a speed on the surface of twenty-two knots to overtake the enemy's ship, and then a submerged run-in for the attack at eight and one-half knots. Following his correspondence with the Secretary, on 8 October he addressed a twenty-three-page communication to Lieutenant Commander W. Strother Smith, senior member of the Board on Submarines. In this second document, Holland promised to attain an underwater speed of twenty-two knots. "The ideal submarine," Holland wrote, "is the smallest boat that can carry a sufficient armament at the highest speed to the largest radius, even across the Atlantic, with ample accommodations for its small crew." The boat described is identical to that given in the earlier paper. Her computed radius of action was to be far beyond the vision of many a competent engineer of his day: 814 miles at maximum speed or 8,490 miles surface cruising at ten knots. This was no harbor defense boat, as he planned it, but an ocean-going craft capable of prowling the seven seas. Holland dared prophesy in 1906 that "Submerged speed equivalent to the torpedo is not beyond reach."[16] It is interesting to speculate that these plans and specifications may well have passed into the hands of Germany through the offices of a Captain H. G. Hebbinghaus who had been in touch with Holland and Nixon from the very founding of Holland's new company in 1905.[17]

The prospectus sent to the Board on Submarines contained some of Holland's most significant statements.[18] He discussed his views on the accidents of the British boats *A-1*, *A-5*, and *A-8*, and gave his thoughts on how the loss of the French *Farfedet* might have been avoided. He explained his own safety device for controlling the diving depth of a submarine, a sophisticated mechanism involving a special twelve-hundred-pound water reservoir that would be blown automatically by a pressure regulator whenever a preset depth was reached. Prior to the historic descent of President Theodore Roosevelt in the *Plunger* (*A-1*) off his home at Sagamore Hill on Oyster Bay, Long Island, 25 August 1905, Lieutenant Charles P. Nelson installed Holland's depth regulator which had been omitted in the construction of the A-boats.[19] This invention was a far cry from the crude drop-keel device first suggested by David Bushnell and employed by Lake on the *Protector*.

But the fruits of Holland's toil withered under the indifference of officialdom and the stifling effect of the legal tactics initiated by Rice and his associates. One by one investors withdrew their support, canceled appointments to meet with the inventor and Nixon, and altogether retreated during the financial panic of 1907. The long game was over.

While perhaps still hoping for some rumble out of Washington, Holland occupied himself with certain "Sketches and Calculations" (1907). Among these papers was a plan for a thirty-foot, ten-ton, forty-passenger submarine "for amusement at seaside resorts." The sides of the vessel were to be lined with large, circular ports for viewing the underwater world. He noted, with his usual care and optimism, that such a vessel would ensure its investors a daily income of $200 from the sale of tickets. This scheme was reminiscent of an earlier plan for a submarine service between England and France. "The Channel," Holland observed, "was a body of water on which the most hardened traveler becomes seasick," but a submarine passage would provide no such discomfort. In the article containing this proposal, written for the *North American Review*, the inventor explored the peacetime uses of the submarine and discussed its potential role in scientific research. But he would not live long enough to see these prophecies come true.

Quietly John Holland withdrew from public life. For several years he had felt the slow and painful encroachment of rheumatism. His once firm and legible handwriting now sped hurriedly across the page as if the task of writing were too much and he would have done with it. In 1907, he moved his family out to 11 William Street in East Orange, New Jersey, but within a year they were back at the old home in Newark. Frank Cable wrote a touching description of the man who had put him on the road to fame, a description that was accurate save for its setting in East Orange instead of Newark:

> Unknown to his neighbors as a man of any note, he lived in East Orange, New Jersey, his small frame stooping, his gait awkward, his manner nervous, due to his near-sightedness which increased with the years, yet keen-brained, studious, and ambitious to the last spending much of his time at the rear of his home, where he had a workshop sealed with various locks.[20]

The problems of flight may have served as a diversion for the failing inventor; at any rate he continued to labor with his dreams. His work on the submarine now belonged to the past, but not so his visions of its potential. Those who berated him by declaring that "the Holland submarine had far outgrown the conceptions of its inventor" spoke either from an exaggerated view of their own contributions to the science or from a calculated refusal to recognize the greatness of his vision.

It was natural that the public would not leave Holland alone entirely; and, when asked to comment on submarine developments or disasters, his answers now often came as bitter denunciations of old acquaintances and of events that were irretrievably relegated to history. "I did not graduate from Annapolis," he irritably commented in 1909, "I am not disloyal or without patriotism, but I am ashamed of the boasted efficiency of our bureaus of construction. . . . When I review the supposed improvements in submarine work by our youthful naval architects, graduates of Annapolis, I am severely arraigned by these selfsame youngsters. They presume to know more about submarines than I do. They favor nothing but what comes from England. Uncle Sam will have nothing to do with me, and I am sure I have as little respect for English Naval constructors as they have for me."[21]

Such unhappy utterances brought upon him the censure of indiscretion. Yet only lesser men would try to imply that these comments were basic to his character when, in fact, they were but the impatient outbursts of a tired man who had left behind a far greater legacy than his critics supposed. His chief competitor in the United States, Simon Lake, writing to Holland's son some time after his father's death, observed: "Replying to your favor of February 11th [1916], I can sympathize with your feelings regarding getting something out of the submarine boat business, as I know something of the treatment which was accorded your father and which is common to the lot of most inventors." Indeed, Lake generously acknowledged the genius of Holland in later recollections.[22]

Two rumors persist that are extremely difficult to document, but are nonetheless both intriguing and possible. First, it is said that the Emperor of Japan conferred on John Holland the Order of the Rising Sun, 29 February 1908, in honor of Holland's contributions to submarine development. It was not the Emperor's answer to the final plea, in 1910, of the dying Lieutenant Sakuma. The second story is that Holland wished to go to England in the closing days of his life to warn the British Admiralty of the submarine menace should England be drawn into conflict with Germany. Ill health, supposedly, prevented the aged inventor from making the journey.

It remained for Holland to seek the comfort of his family—his wife, Margaret, and his children, John, Jr., Robert Charles, Joseph Francis, Julia, and Marguerite. His bachelor brother, Alfred, lived in nearby Elizabeth. His younger brother, Michael, married Mary Anne Fennon of Boston. Michael alone of all his family would carry on the Holland line through a son who bore the name of his famous uncle.[23]

Community life also occupied John Holland's attention. He founded the Entre Nous Club of Newark, taught Sunday School in the local parish, and supported a dramatic society of which he was an original director. There is also evidence that he resumed his interests in Irish independence and the whole movement of the Gaelic revival, for he became a member of the American Irish Historical Society.

Unhappily, Holland was not to be spared additional sorrow. His friend, William Nindemann, died following the loss of his only child. Then, in November, 1913, Holland was stunned by the death of his nineteen-year-old daughter, Julia. These events were enough to shock the old man into complete resignation, but he lived on into the new year. Within less than three months, on 8 March 1914, he also lost his old friend, Charles Morris, whose loyalty had not faltered since the days of Holland's second submarine, the *Fenian Ram*.

By late summer, the inventor himself lay ill at his home in Newark. And there, on 12 August, John Philip Holland, aged seventy-three, succumbed to pneumonia.

At St. Joseph's Church, the Reverend Andrew L. Clark celebrated a Requiem High Mass for John Holland before a large congregation of friends and admirers. From the choir loft came the contralto voice of Holland's cousin, Clara Scanlon, singing "Flee as a bird to the mountain." The Teachers Association of Paterson, the Sinn Fein Club and Clan-na-Gael of Newark, came in groups to pay their last respects and to solace his widow and four surviving children. The Irish-born American school teacher and inventor was buried in the Holy Sepulchre Cemetery in Paterson not far from the spot where he had first dared to submerge in a craft of his own creation. "He was a fair fighter, a most interesting and amusing companion, the staunchest of friends," declared Rear Admiral William W. Kimball. "God rest his soul."[24]

Seventeen years before—on 17 May 1897—the late edition of *The New York Times* had carried a cautiously expressed account of a ship launching earlier that day:

> ... the *Holland*, the little cigar-shaped vessel owned by her inventor, which may or may not play an important part in the navies of the world in the years to come, was launched from Lewis Nixon's shipyard this morning.

Forty days after Holland died, the German Navy's *U-9* torpedoed the British cruisers *Aboukir*, *Cressy*, and *Hogue* off the Dutch coast. A submarine of only four hundred and fifty tons, manned by twenty-six men, had sunk thirty-six thousand tons of the enemy's ships and had sent some fourteen hundred men to their death in the waters of the North Sea.

By September, 1914, there was no longer any doubt about the part which the submarine would play "in the navies of the world."

A SUPPLEMENT

Ever since its first appearance in 1966, this biography of John Philip Holland has been cited, summarized, abridged, praised, quoted, criticized, and discussed by authorities on the history of submarine navigation in England, Ireland, and the United States.[1] But, as the preface to this edition points out, this book makes no claim to be a definitive biography of Holland's mechanical genius. Whatever is here added to this work, the focus remains on the man himself—John Philip Holland.

The thirty-two years that Holland lived in Ireland are now somewhat clearer. After attending Saint Macreechy National School in Liscannor, County Clare, where he first learned to speak and write in English, young Holland is said to have walked daily five-and-one-half-miles inland from the coast to attend the partially national-subsidized school of the Irish Christian Brothers in Ennistymon before the family moved to Limerick upon the death of John Sr., in 1853. Widow Mary Scanlon Holland, John's mother, no doubt received a small pension from the English government for her husband's service in the Coast Guard, but the effects of the Great Famine were still being felt. The times remained troublesome for the family.

At the school on Sexton Street, Limerick, John Holland found a stimulating curriculum. When he learned that his nearsightedness would likely bar him from a career at sea, he accepted an offer to join the Irish Christian Brothers as one of their teachers. Taking his vows in the Order at the age of seventeen, 15 June 1858, as recorded in the Novitiate Records at the North Richmond Street Headquarters in Dublin, Holland was provided with clothing, room and board, and transportation as needed, if nothing else. Such security meant he would no longer be a burden on his mother.

There are conflicting reports about his success as a teacher. The Order, founded by Edmund Rice in 1802, kept meticulous records. In its annual *Vows Scrutiny Book*, Brother Phillip, as Holland was known to the congregation, did not fare well. Evaluations dubbed him opinionated, unable to maintain classroom discipline, and as one who would rather dream of mechanical things than get down to the business of teaching the three "R"s. Furthermore, he exhibited resentment at directives requiring the routine drilling of students, who, in turn, were relieved of such practices in his classroom.

On the other hand, several of his immediate superiors, men like Brother James Dominic Burke of the North Monastery in Cork and Brother Aloysius Yorke in Dundalk, held him in high esteem. They became lifelong friends with the errant Philip. As the Order spread missions as far away as India, Australia, and South America to teach children of the poor, and as Brother Philip became famous in the United States, correspondence from his former colleagues increased, and Holland never failed to respond. These exchanges continued well into the twentieth century.

Perhaps Holland's happiest years as a Christian Brother were those he experienced in Dundalk under Brother Yorke whom he greatly admired. Here, as pointed out earlier, Holland first gave serious thought to the possibility of underwater boats.[2] It is possible that he recalled the "submerged experiments" with explosives performed by Dominic Burke back in Cork, but this rumor cannot be substantiated. Yet, as Henry Adams observed, "A teacher affects eternity; he can never tell where his influence stops." In any case, at Dundalk, Brother Philip's musical talents came to the fore. He organized a boy's choir, which gained an enviable reputation. Years later, after some fame, fortune, and recognition in the world press had attended him, he wrote Brother Yorke:

> There is far more pleasure in the remembrance of what I helped to do for that choir than in all that may be hoped for from submarines.[3]

As late as 1906, Brother Thomas Hughes wrote to Holland from Buenos Aires vividly describing his efforts to establish an Irish Christian Brothers' school in Argentina.[4] Holland had not been forgotten by his Brothers, and he readily contributed moral support and money to their cause, whether it was to erect a memorial or support a new school.

Back in the Old Country, his aging former students were eager to associate themselves with their now famous pedagogue, and, with the usual Irish gift of gab, volunteered many a forgotten anecdote about their earlier mentor: his mechanical duck that waddled about the monastery garden, his wooden model of the Rock of Cashel, his hand-carved wooden crucifix, his sundial, the telescope he shared with his pupils to view the heavens, and his clock-driven *sous marin,* which he demonstrated in a tub of water. Holland could not have been the hopeless teacher his superiors sometimes reported, nor did he deserve the epithet Cable was later to try to impose upon him.[5]

After arriving in Boston, where he rejoined his mother, brothers Alfred and young Fenian activist Michael, he received an invitation to resume teaching as a lay member of the staff at St. John's Parochial School in Paterson, New Jersey. The school was run by the Christian Brothers of the Order founded by Jean Baptiste de la Salle in France in 1648. Again, John could not resist the temptation to explore with his students things mechanical. A historically accurate mural in the Paterson Museum depicts the Irishman at his blackboard explaining mechanical flight with goose feathers attached to a broomstick and a drawing on the board of a one-man submarine—the two dreams that obsessed him.

Holland soon found a champion for his cause in William H. Dunkerly, who operated a family business that manufactured spindles for the cotton and silk mills in the highly industrialized city. Dunkerly played a major role in the school teacher's first real experiments with a full-scale underwater craft.

But money was necessary to build the boat, and here Michael came into the picture. It was he, by his own account, who introduced his older brother to John Devoy and John J. Breslin. This pivotal meeting for Holland has already been recorded.[6]

Breslin, the hero of the rescue of James Stephen from Richmond Prison and the mastermind of the *Catalpa* affair, wrote to John Holland in June 1877:

> Dear Sir:
>
> I laid your plans and proposal before the parties concerned [the trustees of O'Donavan Rosa's Skirmishing Fund] with the following results:
>
> They are in favor of voting the necessary amount for the trial construction on the condition that you give them a half interest in all the patents necessary for the effective working of the boat, also inserting a clause binding both parties to the contract not to sell to any third party without the consent of the other; they are willing to give you $2,000 per annum for the use of your invention or pay you a royalty on every boat constructed.
>
> If these terms meet your ideas let me know at what time it will be most convenient for you to explain your plans to an expert and I will arrange for the interview.
>
> Ever Sincerely Yours,
John J. Breslin[7]

The letter is signed with a flourish, and it may be the key that turned John Holland's life completely around, ended his teaching career, and put him on the road to success. It also dismisses the claim of revisionists who would insist that Holland's financial connections with the Fenians began with the much publicized *Fenian Ram*.

On 27 May 1878, Breslin informed Holland that "under the circumstances" he would not be present at the test trial of Boat No. I in the waters of the Upper Passaic River. There was no flourish under the signature this time. Breslin was careful to maintain secrecy about what Dr. Carroll had called "the saltwater enterprise." He shared with Holland concern about the inefficient Brayton petroleum engine and urged the ex-schoolteacher to attempt to improve it. Three years later, when the Fenians endorsed the building of a second Holland boat, Breslin expressed his regrets for allowing himself to ever have become involved with Brayton.[8]

The *Ram*, of course, followed. Its remarkable performance attracted worldwide attention. Holland, elated by this success, immediately set about exploring new ideas, which he incorporated in a third boat that was also built with money from the Skirmishing Fund. When the two boats were stolen and Boat III was lost in tow (as recounted in Chapter Four, pp. 46–47), Holland became irate. He wrote to Devoy, "I was not informed of the financial difficulties in the Skirmishing Fund."[9]

Bitter about the unexpected turn of events, Holland followed through with a caustic reply to the Fenian leadership, listing ten points to protect himself against Breslin's declaration that he owned the boats. Point eight is worth citing: "Doing all that was possible to secure another Irish scandal by removing the creditors' security [i.e., the boats] out of state . . ." Breslin hoped to avoid a temporary settlement.[10]

Reynolds, in New Haven, to which port the *Ram* had been towed, may have tried to solve the debt problem among the Fenians by calling for a meeting with Devoy, Breslin, and Holland. But Holland would have nothing to do with their bickering. "Devoy and Reynolds agree on nothing but their absurdity," he wrote, ". . . disregarding the name of Nationalists by laying themselves open to charges of stupid mismanagement, theft and swindling."[11]

General Bourke, a trustee, refused to get in touch with Dr. Carroll but agreed to answer Reynolds; however, nothing came of these efforts at reconciliation.[12]

At the height of this divarication, Holland received an invitation from Lieutenant William W. Kimball to have lunch with him aboard the USS *Tennessee,* which was tied up at the Brooklyn Navy Yard. Neither man could have foreseen the strong friendship that would develop and last from that day to Holland's death. The young lieutenant found Holland to be a quiet, modest, informed, and straightforward conversationalist. The meeting lasted far beyond the lunch hour.

Kimball not only became the Navy's chief and tireless advocate of submarines as an important arm of the naval fleet of the United States, but he recognized in Holland the genius that could bring about such an innovation. Further, he was later, and prophetically, to spend hours encouraging the Irish-American inventor to perfect his ideas of a flying machine—long before the success of the Wright Brothers—convinced that both the submarine and the aeroplane would drastically alter the nature of warfare. Holland's naive dream was that both machines would terminate all future conflicts among nations.[13]

So Holland was determined to let the trustees of the Skirmishing Fund resolve their difficulties and let the *Fenian Ram* "rot on their hands." The new design, Boat III, lost off Whitestone Point, "would be as useless to them as the one now in New Haven."[14]

Holland was again his own free agent and now a citizen of the United States. While the "Old Sod" held his heart, his new country held his mind; his patriotic loyalties had shifted.

Kimball introduced Holland to Army Lieutenant Edmund Zalinski, who then hired Holland as a draftsman in his Pneumatic Gun Company. Together, the Army ordinance officer and Holland founded the Nautilus Submarine Boat Company and began to build Holland's fourth submarine, the fifty-foot, so-called *Zalinski Boat*. They chose the parade grounds behind the walls at Fort Hamilton as the site to build on, in order to avoid snooping reporters who, as Holland put it, "are worse than sore corns and blisters." Upon launching, the spindle-shaped, wood-on-steel-frames craft was seriously damaged when the tallowed wooden railway collapsed under the submarine's weight. As for power, Holland protested against the use of steam as a source for propulsion. The plant would require too much space and absorb too much displacement. "I have always been compelled to build the cheapest boat possible . . . My designs do not face the vital quality lacking in the Nordenfeldts, the power to dive quickly."[15]

In the meantime, John Holland had been courting Margaret Foley, making unannounced trips back and forth from Brooklyn to Paterson. He is reported to have been attracted to her when he was directing the boy's choir at St. John's Parochial School and was so taken by her singing voice that he made an exception to the rules and allowed her to participate in the choir.[16] When they married in Brooklyn on 17 January 1887, he was forty-six and she but twenty-five, but the marriage lasted twenty-seven years, until John passed away in 1914. Margaret Foley Holland lived on for another five years and nine months. It appears that their sons John, Jr., Robert, and Joseph attended Manhattan College, Riverdale, N.Y., the college that in 1905 bestowed upon their famous father the degree of Hon. Master of Science at ceremonies held in Carnegie Hall.[17]

The Hollands had seven children in all, two of whom died in infancy. Marguerite, their youngest, was the last to survive; she died in 1960.

After "the lean years," during which the inventor returned to his interest in flying machines and produced the remarkable document on "The Practicality of Mechanical Flight" (1891), the government again expressed interest in submarines. Holland was ready. Then came the inevitable bureaucratic shifts and delays until finally a contract was signed to build the *Plunger*, his fifth boat. That story has been told (chapter six), but one aside is worth exploring.

On 12 August 1896, Holland wrote directly to Secretary of the Navy John P. Long requesting that the *camera lucida* installed in the *Plunger* be removed.[18] He had used such an instrument on the *Zalinski Boat* and found it useless. So he became surprisingly cautious on the whole subject of how a commander of an underwater craft should best secure visibility when submerged or running awash. The *camera obscura*, which could project an image on a maneuvering table below, had some advantages, but even that did not satisfy him. Normal vision, direction, and range concerned him. For the time being, he preferred the deadlights surrounding the conning tower which alone could give the helmsman the 360° vision he needed. He wanted nothing above the turret that would reveal his boat's presence to the "enemy." And so it would be for the *Holland VI*. He had also followed the French experience with periscopes aboard submarines. Then he modestly concluded, ". . . even though I know very little about optics our friends' preference for that type of instrument compels me to consider its possibilities."[19]

Rightly or wrongly, he blamed the accidents involving the sinking of the Royal Navy's A-1 and the French *Faradet* on misreading distances through their periscopes. That seems clearly to have been the case with the French boat, which failed to estimate the distance to a stone jetty in its path. In both cases, the loss of lives shocked the respective navies.

All the foregoing is not to say that the Irish-American inventor did not keep abreast of the major innovations which eventually led to a satisfactory periscope—far from it. In 1904 he wrote a paper on the subject. He knew of Simon Lake's patented omniscope—"though I have never seen one."[20] He was quite aware of the work of Dublin's astronomical instrument maker, Sir Howard Grubb, and of his hydroscope. This latter instrument he favored, though he pointed out that when the tube was turned 90° to port or starboard, the horizon tilted. An improved Grubb version, called the telops, allowed the commander a view astern and could be used at normal vision or as a telescope of three power. The upper tube was hermetically sealed to prevent fogging, and, if spray distorted the outer lens, it could be dried off with a burst of air from inside the vessel. But what may have most attracted Holland to the telops was the fact that the viewing screen contained on its upper edge a scale calibrated to measure the distance away of an object of known size.[21]

Holland's success in Japan is a matter of record, from the first five A-Boats which Arthur L. Busch assembled in Tokyo to the two built in Kobe.[22] For a long time it was rumored that Emperor Hirohito conferred on the "professor" from Paterson the Order of the Rising Sun. Now the story can be told.

The award presented to Holland through the Japanese legation in Washington read as follows:

ORDER OF MERIT
RISING SUN RIBBON TO JOHN P. HOLLAND
   The Emperor of Japan has maintained the unbroken Imperial line by Divine aid. Here, by presentation of the Meiji decoration 4th Class, Order of Merit Rising Sun Ribbon to John P. Holland, United States of America, I express the tenderness from the throne of the Emperor.
   Junmu's 2,568 years, Meiji 41 (1908) February 29 at Tokyo Palace.[23]

It is stamped with the Seal of Japan, Meiji 41, and the signature of Count Otamo Ko (and his seal). The certificate numbered 3499 "has been investigated and recorded on the Order of Merit Book" and duly signed and sealed by two secretaries of the Medal and Decoration Department.

After his resignation from Electric Boat Company, on 28 March 1904, Holland's fortunes began to decline. The use of his name in the new company he tried to establish was forbidden by injunctions secured by Isaac Rice and E. B. Frost; his patents, both domestic and foreign, were controlled by "my ancient friends."

In spite of these legal setbacks, Holland went ahead with a new design for a high-speed submarine. Model tests in the towing tank at the Washington Navy Yard substantiated his claim that a submarine built to his specifications could attain the astonishing speed of twenty-two knots *submerged*—three times the underwater speed of the fleet in service. His Japanese friends Matsukata and Kenji Ide were interested. Lewis Nixon would build the boat if he had a new yard. Kimball, a master for details, sensed that Holland was right. A French shipbuilder of torpedo boats in Le Havre worried about foreign patent rights. Charles Schwab of Bethlehem Steel was interested, but shied off for fear of legal entanglements with Electric Boat.[24] Simon Lake, though acting independently and having his own boat ready, backed the Rice-Frost lobby in Congress to see that any government competition for submarines be held within three months. Holland's friends could not meet such a deadline—and the lobbyists knew it. Creecy, still loyal, represented Holland in Washington; instead of the twelve months the Newark inventor requested, he had to settle for nine.[25] But that was still impossible. Potential investors needed to produce the high-speed design faded away. Holland's "ancient friends" had won the battle.

Holland's name was still prominent in many circles, and he was in demand as a speaker at universities and professional societies in the East. He was overwhelmed by requests from legitimate inventors and numerous cranks seeking his advice on how to secure patents for sundry devices—from amphibious vehicles and kites, to sprinkling systems and massage machines. None were shy about asking him to invest money in their dreams. Yet few of these entrepreneurs ever fully understood his financial circumstances.

Kenji Ide, now a commander in the Imperial Navy, was finally assigned to oversee the completion of the two Holland boats at Kobe's Kawasaki Dockyard. Neither Holland nor Ide were pleased with the progress, both criticizing Constructor Mason Chase and Matsu-kata. Holland wanted to remove some defects he had spotted in his design, but the Takata Company would not release the plans for his inspection. Nothing further "from me would be either desirable or welcome," he wrote to Ide.[26]

Two months later, the Japanese commander answered that it was too late to make any changes to the arrangements within the boats, but he wanted Holland's appraisal of the new and improved double-action, four-cycle, multiple-cylinder Riotte engines, said to be able to develop 600 to 800 hoursepower.[27] Smaller Riotte engines were installed in the Kobe boats.

Another three months passed, and Ide wrote to now Captain William W. Kimball:

> Now the terms of peace have been settled and I think they may be signed by the Emperors of Russia and Japan very soon. Then we may be able to talk over whatever we were doing during the war. [He expected the Kobe boats to be launched by the 1st of October—1905, and added:] I am very sorry to know that Mr. Holland has been sued by HTBCO [Holland Torpedo Boat Co., then a subsidiary of Electric Boat]. Yes; it is too bad to have such [an] event. My sympathy is with Mr. Holland, and I hope it can be settled without any disastre [sic.] to Mr. Holland.[28]

In the years that immediately followed, John Holland's health began to deteriorate with the advance of rheumatism. He spent a summer with his family at his house on Fleets Point in Cutchogue, Long Island, a few miles from the country's first submarine base in New Suffolk. It was familiar territory. He had hoped that the warm summer temperatures and salt air might revive him. Yet it was increasingly difficult for him to stand on his feet for any length of time, which annoyed him because he was building a flying machine in the barn behind the house and experimenting with a six-foot box kite which his children proceeded to destroy.

In May 1909, he wrote a letter to Ide announcing that his doctor informed him that he had suffered a stroke and paralysis. "My head was dazed. . . . they completely disabled me." He went on, nevertheless, discussing submarines and flying machines. "Regarding flying," he prophesied, "that's of incomparably more importance than boats or ships. A man can fly as long a time as he can walk . . ."[29] He then went into calculations of a pilot and a payload of 300 pounds, the kind of discussion that Kimball relished. The machine was about ready to fly, he told Ide, but he was rendered helpless and now it rests "neglected and rusting in my barn."

The extensive Kimball-Holland correspondence unveils the dreams, knowledge, determination, and friendship these two men shared; it reveals events in their lives that are not found elsewhere. There is humor and profundity, depression and exhilaration, touches of paranoia balanced with goodwill toward others, and a Weltanschauung tempered with parochial concerns. A few excerpts here must suffice.[30]

Kimball, now the captain of his own ship, the USS *New Jersey*, writes to Holland: "I wish the thing [the flyer] were finished so I could witness your triumph here next month—but I shall witness it, if not next month, next summer, next fall, next year."

Kimball sends Holland, 2 August 1904, a clipping from the *Washington Post* that poked fun at "the flyer." "This is no more jocose than the newspaper's witticism's about the submarine."

Holland to Kimball, 11 February 1905: "The flyer's wings are folded. . . . Old Charon has his oars shipped ready to put me over the River Styx." Holland survived, but "Charon has looked my way invitingly once or twice since. But I fancy he must wait a little longer."

Kimball to Holland, 13 October 1905: "If you can't use your name without a long law suit [vs. EBCO], then call it [the new company] the real or true or Anti-Humbug or Blue Water Submarine Boat Co., it won't matter."

Kimball to Holland, 21 August 1906, from aboard the *New Jersey*: "Oh, yes, within three months of the time the flyer flies you will have the backing for the [high speed] boat. That is axiomatic."

The inventor's brother Alfred had moved from Elizabeth, New Jersey, to the West Coast where he had accepted a professorship in the Classics Department of St. Mary's College outside of Oakland, California, affectionately called "The Brickpile." That the two brothers corresponded with each other is certain, though the letters are lost. Alfred made what seems to be rather exaggerated claims about how much his ideas influenced John's submarine designs. In 1903, however, John forwarded to Alfred an article entitled "Submarine Boats," which appeared in the first volume of the school's *The Collegian*. Alfred died in 1910.[31]

"The slings and arrows of outrageous fortune" caught up with John Holland. His daughter Julia died in 1913, striking Holland a severe blow. His close friend Charles A. Morris went out to Palo Alto for his health and never returned. Holland's own health rapidly deteriorated and Old Charon got across the Styx to carry him home, though he had time to complain that, while he didn't mind being buried six feet under, he was afraid it would not be in the right sod.[32]

The "Inventor of the Modern Submarine" belonged to the age of Alva Edison, Alexander Graham Bell, Octave Chanute, Samuel P. Langley, Simon Lake, the Wright brothers, Henry Ford, and a host of others. Holland's place among these creative giants is high and secure. He lived in the day when the inventor was the scientist; he did not live to see the day when the scientist became the inventor.

ILLUSTRATIONS

1 John Philip Holland, in 1876, at age thirty-five.
2 Mrs. John Philip Holland, about 1895, with John, Jr., and Julia.
3 Holland's birthplace on Castle Street in Liscannor, County Clare.

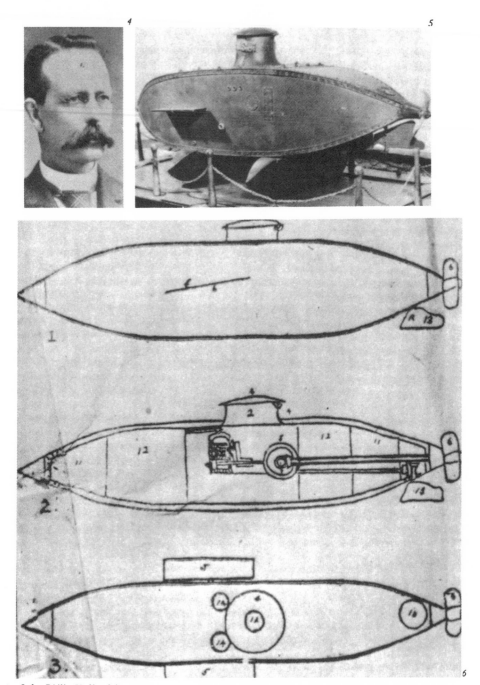

4 *John Philip Holland in 1895.*
5 *Scale model of the* Holland No. 1 *in the Paterson Museum, Paterson, New Jersey.*
6 *The* Holland No. 1 *as drawn by William Dunkerley in 1916 for a Paterson newspaper.*

7

8

7 *Memorial tablet presented to the City of Paterson, with the hull of the* Fenian Ram, *by Edward A. Browne in 1927.*

8 *The hull of the* Fenian Ram *on the grounds of the New York State Marine School at Clason Point, between 1916 and 1927.*

9

9   *The* Zalinski Boat *as drawn by an artist of the* Scientific American, 7 *August 1886.*

10 Interior of the Holland VI, *looking aft, during construction of the submarine in 1896.*
11 *Christening of the* Holland VI. *Mrs. Lewis Nixon and E. B. Frost on the staging at the ceremony.*
12 *Launching of the* Holland VI *at Lewis Nixon's Crescent Shipyard in Elizabethport, New Jersey.*

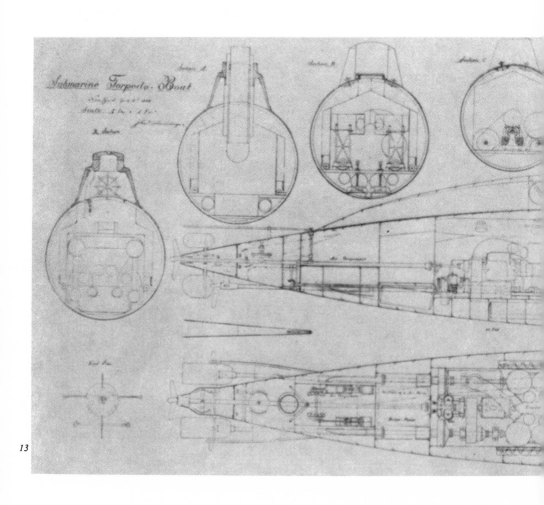

13

13   *Drawings for the Submarine Torpedo Boat* Plunger, *launched at Baltimore, Maryland, in 1897.*

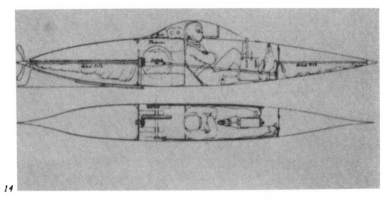

14

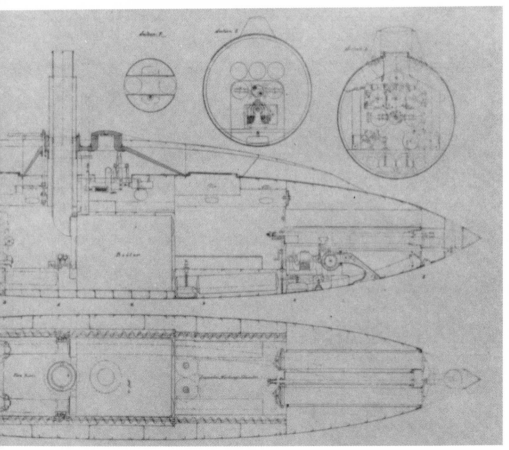

14   Drawing from printed copy of Lieutenant F. M. Barber's lecture at the Naval Torpedo Station
in 1875.

STEEL FISH WITH REVOLVING TAIL THAT WILL PROTECT OUR HARBOR AGAINST ANY FLEET

The Holland Submarine Terror, the Newest Wonder of Naval Science, Which Dives and Swims Under Water and Noiselessly and Unseen Creeps Up Under a Enemy's Side, Hurling Into It Thunderbolts of Dynamite from Its Torpedo Guns

15

15   A schematic drawing of the Holland VI *by an artist of the* New York Herald, *15 April 1898.*

16   John P. Holland in the conning tower of his submarine, April, 1898, Perth Amboy, New Jersey.

17   *The* Holland VI *prior to her trial before the U. S. Navy's Board of Inspection on 20 April 1898.*

18

18   *The* Holland VI *and the* George P. Roe *off Old Orchard Shoal Light in Raritan Bay during the trial on 20 April 1898.*

19

19   *Officials and guests of the John P. Holland Torpedo Boat Company on board a tug, with the* Holland
    VI *alongside, at the trial run on 20 April 1898.*

20

20   *The* Holland VI *before the trial dive on 20 April 1898.*

21 At the Raritan Dry Dock on the day of the trial, 20 April 1898, left to right, *Walter Thompson*,
   superintendent of the Raritan Dry Dock; Charles A. Morris, superintending engineer of the John P.
   Holland Torpedo Boat Company; John P. Holland, inventor of the Holland VI; *and Mr. Mat-*
   thews, a stockholder in the John P. Holland Torpedo Boat Company.
22 *The* Holland VI *surfacing after a dive of one hour's duration, 20 April 1898.*

23   *Following the trial on 20 April 1898, the* Holland VI *is awaiting a tow back to Perth Amboy.*

24

25

24 *The* Holland VI *in the Erie Basin Dry Dock, Brooklyn, New York, 26 May–1 June 1898. The positioning of the propeller and rudder are clearly shown.*

25 *The little* Holland VI, *forerunner of the technological developments of the twentieth century, is dwarfed here by the towering masts of a brig whose era was waning.*

26

27

26 The "cage," a torpedo loading device, at the Atlantic Yacht Basin, Brooklyn, New York, in the summer of 1898. Left to right, Frank T. Cable, John Wilson, and William F. C. Nindemann.

27 The Holland VI in the Morris Heights shipyard on the Harlem River in New York during the winter of 1898-99. William F. C. Nindemann, in the foreground.

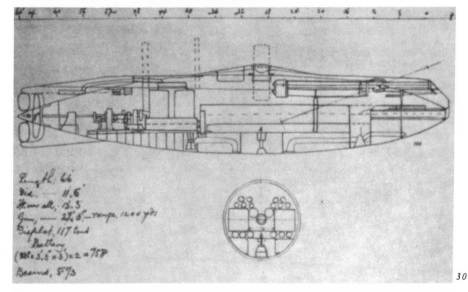

30

28 *Isaac L. Rice, founder and first president of the Electric Boat Company of which the Holland Torpedo Boat Company became the major subsidiary, 7 February 1899.*

29 *John P. Holland at the time of the acceptance of the* Holland VI *by the U. S. government, 1900.*

30 *Holland's conception of an improved* Holland VI *drawn in 1899. Note his patented 22-foot dynamite gun mounted to elevate 20 degrees above horizontal.*

31

31   *The* Holland VI *under tow in Gardiners Bay, Long Island, 1899.*

32

32   USS Holland *after her commissioning on 12 October 1900.*

33

33 *Captain and crew of the USS* Holland *in June, 1901.* Lower row, left to right: *William H.*
   Reader, chief gunner's mate; Augustus Gumpert, gunner's mate second class; Lieutenant Harry
   H. Caldwell, commanding; Arthur Callahan, gunner's mate second class; Barnett Bowie, chief
   machinist's mate. Upper row: *Harry Wahab, gunner's mate first class; O. Swanson, gunner's mate*
   first class; Gunner Owen Hill; W. Hall, electrician's mate second class.

34

34 The Fulton, *launched 12 June 1901, a working model for the later* Adder *class.*

35

36

35 *Launching of the USS* Porpoise (*later* A-6), *23 September 1901, at Nixon's Crescent Shipyard, Elizabethport, New Jersey.*

36 *The* Fulton *on the way to the trial ground, off Newport, Rhode Island, June, 1904.*

37

38

37   The Electric Boat Company's plant consisted of a machine shop, a drawing room, and docking
     facilities. This basin became the first submarine base in the United States after the launching of
     the A-boats in 1901.

38   Goldsmith and Tuthill Basin, New Suffolk, leased by the Electric Boat Company in 1899. In the
     foreground, the tender Kelpie and the Plunger; in the background, four A-boats.

39

39   *Workmen at the New Suffolk plant.* Standing, left to right: *Lawrence Sullivan, laborer; William Wood, machinist; Thomas Delaney, apprentice machinist; Ben Horton, laborer; Harry Morrill, chief electrician; Charles Lewis, laborer; Hugo Momm, machinist; Terrence Magee, apprentice machinist; Herman Noblett, electrician; Leroy Hammond, electrician; John Wilson, supervisory machinist; Patrick Glenn, captain of tender* Kelpie; *William Deslette, machinist.* Sitting: *Frank Acker, apprentice machinist; Charles Becktold, pipefitter; Peter Rehill, machinist; Harry Kirby, assistant supervisory machinist; John Sanders, machinist; Charles Berg, deckhand; Conrad Stick, machinist; Karl Kuester, machinist.*

40

40   *Electric Boat Company staff at the New Suffolk plant.* Seated in front, left to right: *Theodore Bailey, chief engineer; Lewis Eckert, chief hull draftsman.* Back row: *George Duncan, office boy; Grant Edgar, electrical draftsman; Arthur Newman, chief engineering draftsman; Paul Andrine, mechanical draftsman; William Curtiss, mechanical draftsman; Hugo Grieshaber, hull draftsman; Walter Leonard, mechanical draftsman.*

41

41   USS Moccasin *(later A-4) during trials in Little Peconic Bay, Long Island, summer of 1902.*

42

42 *New Suffolk Basin, 1902.* At left: *USS* Shark *(later* A-7*) and tender* Kelpie. Background: *USS*
Craven, *surface torpedo boat.* At right: *USS* Moccasin *and USS* Adder *(later* A-2*).*

43

43   *New Suffolk Basin, 1902. Outboard boats,* at left, *USS* Moccasin; at right, *USS* Shark.

44   *New Suffolk Basin, November, 1902.* In foreground, left to right: *USS* Fulton, *USS* Porpoise, *USS* Adder. In background: *USS* Shark *and USS* Moccasin.

45 USS Holland *at the U. S. Naval Academy, Annapolis, Maryland. Captain and crew,* left to right:
*Harry Wahab, chief gunner's mate; Kane; Richard O. Williams, chief electrician; Chief Gunner
Owen Hill, commanding; Igoe; Michael Malone; Barnett Bowie, chief machinist's mate; Simpson;
Rhinelander.* In the background, *a monitor of the* Arkansas *class,* at left, *and the USS* Terror, *a
pre-Spanish-American War monitor.*

46

46 *John P. Holland, in 1912, when he retired from public life. This is his last known portrait.*

MAPS

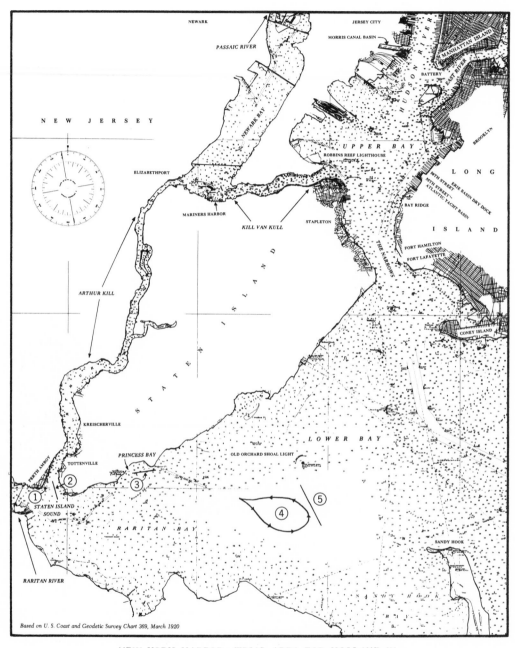

NEW YORK HARBOR—TRIAL AREA FOR *HOLLAND VI*

1 *Raritan Dry Dock Basin, first dockside submergence, 11 March 1898.*   **2** *First submerged run, 17 March 1898.*
3 *Testing grounds, April, 1898.* ' **4** *Trial run, 20 April 1898.* · **5** *Area of official Navy test, 12 November 1898.*

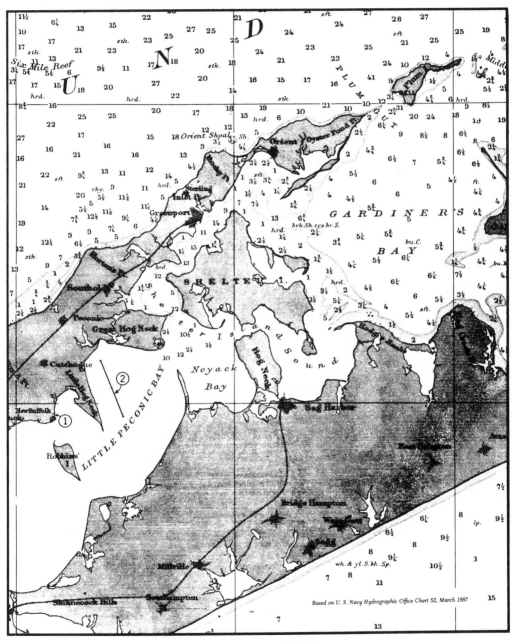

LITTLE PECONIC BAY

1 *Goldsmith and Tuthill Basin.*   2 *Two-mile trial course.*

HOLLAND'S MAJOR PREDECESSORS IN SUBMARINE DEVELOPMENT
1620-1870

CORNELIUS VAN DREBBEL, *Dutch*
No name for boat, *ca.* 1620
First practical effort at submarine navigation.

DAVID BUSHNELL, *American*
Turtle, 1775
Piston pumps to empty ballast tanks; minimum
reserve of positive buoyancy; stability of design; safety weight;
conning tower; fathometer; use of underwater
explosives; possible screw propeller; first submarine attack on
an enemy ship.

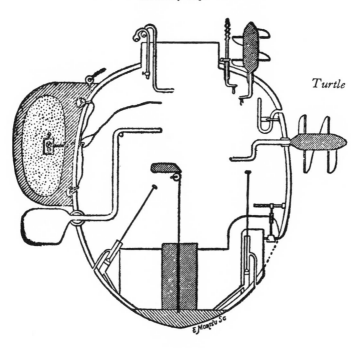

Turtle

ROBERT FULTON, *American*
Nautilus, 1800
First all-metal submarine; porpoise-shaped hull;
two independent means of propulsion; horizontal diving planes at
the stern, hence the diving-boat principle;
coined the word "torpedo."

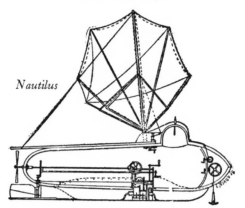

Nautilus

WILHELM BAUER, *German*
Le Diable Marin, 1855
Multiple ballast tanks with attention to trim;
demonstrated habitability of submarines; work on underwater
acoustics; longest record of submarine
experimentation before John P. Holland.

OLIVER RIOU, *French*
No name for boat, 1861
Two submarines: one driven by steam, the other by
electric motor.

JAMES McCLINTOCK and BAXTER WATSON, *American*
Hunley, 1863
First submarine to sink an enemy vessel, though
operating on the surface.

ALSTITT, *American*
Ram, 1863
A semisubmersible, but first to combine steam and
electricity as sources for propulsion; retractable smokestack.

CHARLES BRUN, *French*
Le Plongeur, 1863
Large submarine—140 feet; compressed air engine;
used compressed air to empty ballast tanks.

JOHN P. HOLLAND'S SIX SUBMARINES
1878-1900

Hull No. I

Name: *Holland No. 1*
Launched: *22 May 1878*
Place: *Paterson, N.J.*
Builder: *Handrin & Ripley, Albany Iron Works, New York, N.Y.*
Dimensions: *L 14.6' × B 3' × Ht. ?*
Tons[a]: *2.25*
Power[b]: *Brayton Petroleum Engine, 4 hp*
Armament[c]: *None*

Hull No. II

Name: *Fenian Ram*
Launched: *May, 1881*
Place: *New York, N.Y.*
Builder: *Delamater-Robinson, Delamater Iron Works, New York, N.Y.*
Dimensions: *L 31' × B 6' × Ht. 7.33'*
Tons[a]: *19*
Power[b]: *Brayton Engine, 15-17 hp*
Armament[c]: *One Pneumatic Bow Gun*

Hull No. III

Name: *Fenian Model*
Launched: *On Ways, November, 1883*
Place: *Jersey City, N.J.*
Builder: *Gannon & Cooper Shop, Jersey City, N.J.*
Dimensions: *L 16' × B 2' × Ht. ?*
Tons[a]: *1*
Power[b]: *"Explosive," probably Brayton*
Armament[c]: *None*

Hull No. IV

Name: *Zalinski Boat*
Launched: *4 September 1885*
Place: *Fort Lafayette, L.I., N.Y.*
Builder: *Cyrus Plant, Brooklyn, N.Y.*
Dimensions: *L 50' × B 8' × Ht. 10.6'*
Tons[a]: *?*
Power[b]: *Brayton Engine*
Armament[c]: *Zalinski Dynamite Gun*

Hull No. V

Name: *Plunger*
Launched: *7 August 1897*
Place: Baltimore, Md.
Builder: *William Malster's Columbian Iron Works, Baltimore, Md.*[d]
Dimensions: *L 85' × B 11.5' × Ht. 16'*
Tons[a]: *168*
Power[b]: *Twin Steam Triple Expansion, 1625 hp; Main Electric, 70 hp*
Armament[c]: *Two Torpedo Tubes; Five Torpedoes*

Hull No. VI

Name: *Holland VI.* Later: USS *Holland* (SS-1)
Launched: *17 May 1897*
Place: *Elizabethport, N.J.*
Builder: *Lewis Nixon's Crescent Shipyard, Elizabethport, N.J.*
Dimensions: *L 53.3' × B 10.3' × Ht. 11.6'*
Tons[a]: *63*
Power[b]: *Otto Gas Engine, 45 hp; Electric, 75 hp*
Armament[c]: *Originally Two Pneumatic Guns, One Torpedo Tube; Three Torpedoes, Six Projectiles.*

---

[a] Construction: *No. 1*, iron plating; *Ram*, 11/16" charcoal flange iron; *Zalinski Boat*, wood on iron frames; *Plunger* and *Holland VI*, ½" oil-tempered steel. Submerged tonnage listed, except in *Holland VI*, for which light tonnage is given.

[b] Main propeller originally aft of rudder in all boats, excepting the *Zalinski Boat*.

[c] *Camera lucida* used on *Zalinski Boat* and *Plunger* only.

[d] *Plunger* completed at Triggs Iron Works, Richmond, Va.

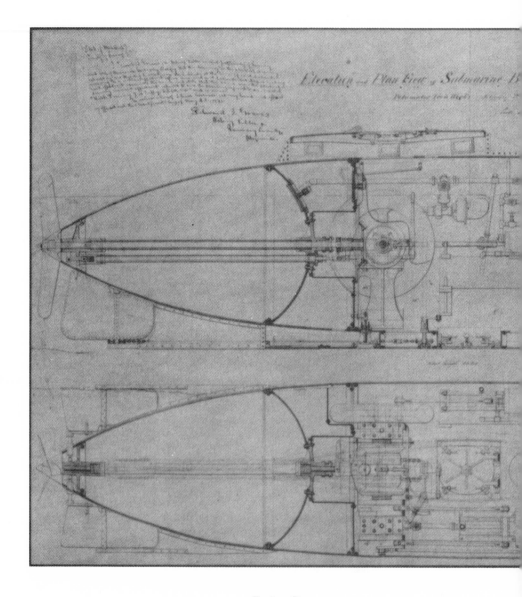

Fenian Ram

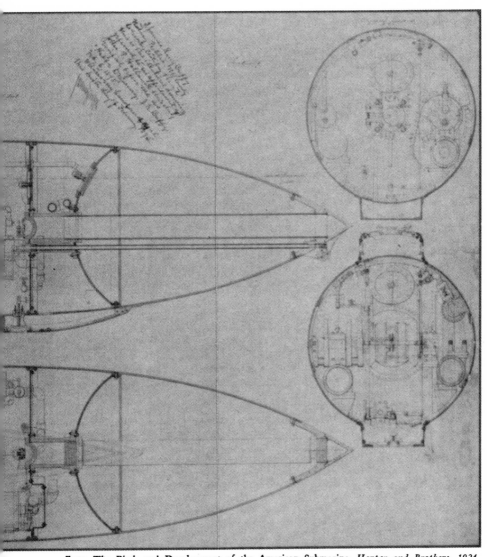

From The Birth and Development of the American Submarine, *Harper and Brothers, 1924.*

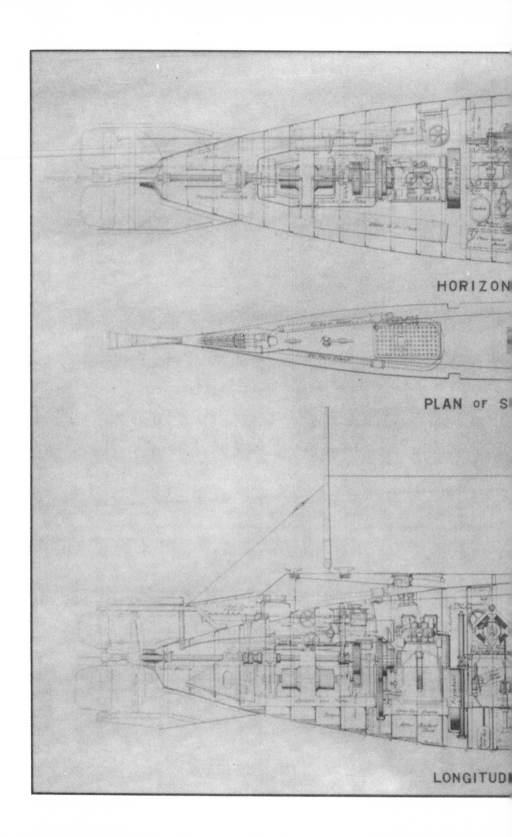

HORIZON

PLAN OF S

LONGITUDE

SECTION.

STRUCTURE.

SECTION.

HULL - 6
"THE HOLLAND"

6
H
1

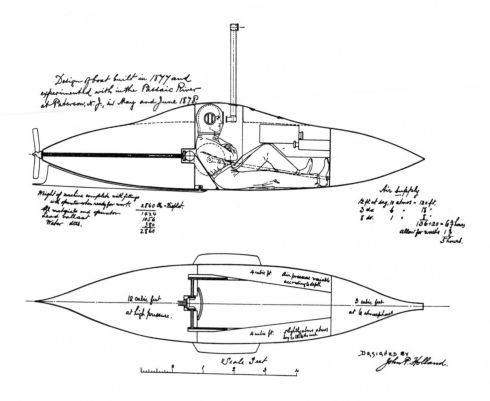

Holland's idealized drawing of his first submarine.

DESCRIPTIVE SPECIFICATION AND DRAWINGS OF THE SUBMARINE *HOLLAND VI*

(From the original description written in 1899.*)

She is 53.3 feet overall, largest diameter is 10.3 feet; draft in cruising position, 8.5 feet; draft in a diving position, 11.5 feet; 63 tons light displacement and 75 tons submerged. Her speed varies from 6 to 10 knots according to power used. The radius of action with gasoline alone is 1300 knots, with gasoline and electricity, 1330 knots, allowing 30 knots for electricity. The air reservoirs contain 30 cu. ft. of air at 2000 lbs. per square inch.

The hull is parabolic, spindle-shaped. It is constructed of steel plating; the frames are of angle iron which are all perfect circles, the largest being 10.25 feet placed a little forward of amidships, tapering to both ends and all set up from a center line through the ship. This construction will resist a pressure of 35 lbs. per square inch, which is sufficient to allow her to dive to a depth of 75 feet.

She is fitted with 5 tanks placed along her bottom, the fuel tank having a capacity of 1000 gallons, the sinking and trimming tanks 10.5 tons capacity.

The boat has a 45 H.P. Otto Gas Engine connected so as to drive the propeller or dynamotor for charging the batteries. The dynamotor can also be connected to drive the propeller. These connections are made by friction clutches. The dynamotor is connected to run at any speed or power from 10 H.P. to 150 H.P.

The batteries are placed amidship, occupying a space of 15 ft. long by 6.25 ft. wide and 3 feet deep, have 60 cells and a capacity of 1500 ampere hours. There is an extra 10-horse electric motor which operates the bilge pump and air compressor. The bilge pump is piped so as to empty or fill all tanks independently, or to pump out the bilge. The compressor is capable of compressing 50 cu. ft. at 2000 lbs. pressure per hour. There is also ⅛ H.P. electric motor for ventilating and operating an exhaust pump for exhausting the air from the vessel when making long submerged runs, atmospheric pressure being maintained within the vessel by this pump together with a special valve which admits air into the vessel from receivers when pressure falls below atmosphere. The air is stored in three pairs of reservoirs at 2000 per sq. in. and by pressure regulating valve is reduced to 50 lbs., then another pressure regulating valve reduces to 10 lbs. pressure to the square inch, from which the atmospheric valve operates. The 50-lb. tank supplies the expulsion tube, steering gear, whistle, and trimming tank; the

---

* The original is in the handwriting of Engineer Charles A. Morris and is edited here only as needed for clarity. From the Morris Collection, Submarine Library, U. S. Naval Submarine Base, New London, Conn.

10-lb. tank operates the sinking tanks and atmospheric valve. The steering engine is controlled by hand from the turret or automatically by a vane placed aft over the rudder; it is connected by a rod running aft through a stuffing-box to the rudder which is balanced and placed above and below the propeller, a second rod connects the vane to a valve on the steering engine.

The diving engine is controlled by hand from the turret or automatically by diaphragms operated by the water pressure together with the pendulum and springs connected by a rod through a stuffing-box to two diving rudders placed on either side of the propeller at right angles to the steering rudder.

A regulation Whitehead torpedo tube is fitted in her bow at the centre and is discharged by air through a special valve for the purpose. The Whitehead torpedoes are shipped through the tube into the boat; i.e., the outer door is opened, the torpedo inserted into the tube from the outside, the door is then closed, the water discharged from the tube, the inner door opened, and the torpedo hauled in and placed into a rack. Provision for two of these torpedoes has been made in the boat and one may be left in the tube, making three in all. A special crate or cage has been designed for loading the torpedoes, which eliminates all risk, making it possible to supply the "Holland" from a tender in any harbor.

Directly above this expulsion tube is placed the Holland Pneumatic Dynamite Gun of 8.425 inches bore, having a fixed elevation of 15 degrees, but by filling or emptying the trim tanks this can be increased or decreased. The muzzle of gun is fitted with a water-tight cap. It will discharge a projectile of 222 lbs. weight, charged with from 50 to 80 lbs. gun cotton, giving a range in the air of 1000 yards or 30 yards when fired under water. It is operated by air and gun-powder and is quickly handled. Six or more of these projectiles can be carried. [Formerly, "Holland" had two such guns, but the after gun was removed.]

She is fitted with a sounding apparatus, speed indicator, and all necessary gauges, controllers and regulators; is completely lighted by electricity; has a water-closet; and a crew of 6 men can comfortably live aboard for 40 hours.

The turret is where the commander or operator is located; it is fitted with a hinged manhole cover 24-inches in diameter, through which entrance to the boat is obtained. The turret is fitted with thick plate glass windows 3 inches long by ¾-in. high, arranged all round so that the commander has an all around view.

There is a spirit compass, a pressure gauge, which indicates the exact depth at which boat is traveling; bell pulls for starting and stopping; two speaking tubes; whistle pull; indicators for showing position of both rudders, together with two controllers for the steering engine. Gauges, compass and indicators are lighted by covered electric lights. Three glass windows 1-inch in diameter are fitted in the cover to turret; these are used to indicate when passing under a vessel.

The crew consists of a commander, assistant-commander, electrician, engineer, gunner, and machinist who acts as assistant-gunner.

NOTES

INTRODUCTION

1. For further reading about nuclear submarines, see Clay Blair, *The Atomic Submarine and Admiral Rickover* (New York: Henry Holt, 1954); Norman Polmar, *Atomic Submarines* (Princeton: D. Van Nostrand Co., Inc., 1963); and W. R. Anderson, with Clay Blair, *Nautilus 90 North* (Cleveland: The World Publishing Co., 1959).

CHAPTER ONE
The Launching
1897

1. *The New York Times*, 17 May 1897. See also *New York Herald*, 18 May 1897.
2. The launching flag, an oversized ensign, was later used on the tug which accompanied the *Holland* during the official trials of the submarine. The flag is now in the Submarine Library, Gilmore Hall, U. S. Naval Submarine Base, New London, Conn. One may still make out the names of "L. Nixon" and "C. A. Morris" written in indelible ink on the hem.
3. See Courtlandt Canby and Richard K. Morris, "The Father of the Modern Submarine," *American Heritage*, XII (1961), No. 2, p. 35.
4. *Ibid.*, p. 96.
5. W. W. Kimball, in the Supplementary Chapter, Frank T. Cable, *The Birth and Development of the American Submarine* (New York: Harper and Brothers, 1924), p. 336.
6. John P. Holland, "Submarine Navigation," *Cassier's Magazine*, The Marine Number (1897), pp. 541-60.
7. *Ibid.*, p. 551.
8. *Ibid.*, p. 541.
9. See Chapter Four, The *Fenian Ram*, 1879-1883.
10. See J. Niven, *et al.* (eds.), *Dynamic America* (New York: General Dynamics Corp. and Doubleday & Co., Inc., n.d. [1960]), p. 51, caption for picture No. 122. For Lake's admission of the influence of Jules Verne on his own thinking, see Simon Lake, *Submarine, An Autobiography* (New York: D. Appleton-Century, 1938), p. 10: "Jules Verne was in a sense the Director General of my life." This may help to explain Lake's early concern with underwater craft for marine archaeology and salvage, the commodius accommodations he designed for his early boats, and his fondness for wheels to move the craft along the ocean floor. Cf. Simon Lake, *The Submarine in War and Peace* (Philadelphia: J. P. Lippincott Co., 1918), p. 119.
11. John P. Holland, "Sketches and Calculations." (Submarine Library, Gilmore Hall, U. S. Naval Submarine Base, New London, Conn. Hereafter cited as Submarine Library.)
12. *Cassier's Magazine*, The Marine Number, p. 544. See also the excellent description of the *Holland* by W. W. Kimball in "Submarine Torpedo-Boats," *Harper's Monthly*, CI (September, 1900), 557-69.

13. The only exception to this pattern was the Hellmuth Walter hydrogen-peroxide engine used in some German U-boats during World War II.

14. "Letters of the Holland Torpedo Boat Company" (Submarine Library), 25 May 1899, p. 261. See Holland's own sketch of a diesel, dated 10 February 1900 and reproduced in Niven, *op. cit.*, p. 102.

15. W. H. Jaques, a news release, 24 April 1898, Morris Collection (Submarine Library), Vol. I, p. 32. See also the statements on this subject by W. W. Kimball in Cable, *op. cit.*, pp. 324-25.

16. See Chapter Seven, The *Holland VI*, 1896-1898.

17. Cf. Norman Polmar, *Atomic Submarines* (Princeton: D. Van Nostrand Co., Inc., 1963), pp. 140-43; and Wilbur Cross, *Challengers of the Deep* (New York: William Sloane Associates, 1959), pp. 247-48.

18. Holland's discussion of the submarine as a torpedo guided by human intelligence bespeaks his concern for the submarine proper and her potency as a weapon of war. *Cassier's Magazine*, The Marine Number, p. 558.

19. The joy stick may be seen clearly in a faithful drawing by a staff artist of the *New York Journal*, Sunday, 6 March 1898. This drawing also shows the propeller aft of the rudders as it originally appeared on the *Holland*. A similar joy stick device was used on the *Zalinski Boat* (1885), for which see, "A New Submarine Torpedo Boat," *Scientific American*, 7 August 1886.

20. Howard I. Chapelle, *The History of the American Sailing Navy* (New York: W. W. Norton & Co., Inc., 1949), pp. xv-xvi.

CHAPTER TWO
The Irish Years
1841-1873

1. In various sources, references to the day of the month on which Holland was born include the 24th, 26th, and 29th of February, while the years mentioned range from 1840 through 1844.

2. Quoted in a letter from Edward M. Graf, Paterson, N.J., and taken from papers in Mr. Graf's collection of Holland memorabilia. Some of the Graf papers are unquestionably those which John, Jr., once loaned to Simon Lake and which Lake quoted in *The Submarine in War and Peace*, pp. 84-113. Lake states emphatically that Holland was born on 24 February 1841. Holland himself has elsewhere indicated that he was born in 1841. In "The Submarine Boat and its Future," *North American Review*, December, 1900, he says, ". . . though I am 59 years old." It is reasonable to suppose that he wrote these words within the calendar year of 1900, after his birthday and before December. The date must, in any event, be prior to 1842, for thereafter parish records were available. As for obituary notices which state that he died on 12 August 1914 in his 73rd year, these might suggest 1842 on one interpretation, but if they meant he had passed his 73rd birthday, then they may be said to confirm 1841. In any case, it is impossible to derive the date of 29 February 1840 assigned by his daughter, Marguerite, in conversations recorded at the dedication of the Submarine Library, Electric Boat Company, Groton, Conn., 11 April 1955.

3. "Griffith's Valuation," begun in 1855, is a list of all tenants in County Clare. The Holland family is not listed as living in Liscannor. It is therefore clear that they had moved from the cottage on Castle Street prior to 1855.

4. Simon Lake, *The Submarine in War and Peace* (Philadelphia: J. P. Lippincott Co., 1918), pp. 86-87.

5. Quoted in Frank T. Cable, *The Birth and Development of the American Submarine* (New York: Harper and Brothers, 1924), p. 24.

6. J. P. Holland, Jr., as told to Simon Lake, *op. cit.*, p. 86.

7. John P. Holland, "Submarine Navigation," *Cassier's Magazine,* The Marine Number (1897).
8. John P. Holland, "The Submarine Boat and its Future," *North American Review,* December, 1900, p. 54.
9. John P. Holland, "How to Fly as a Bird" (Newark: Gasser Print Shop, n.d. [ca. 1906]).
10. *Ibid.,* p. 2.
11. Cable, *op. cit.,* p. 28.
12. T. P. O'Connor, "An Anglo-Irish Tragi-Comedy," *T.P.'s and Cassell's Weekly,* Vol. 4, No. 80, 2 May 1925. The use of "brother" in this account is confusing, but since John Holland was not to emigrate to the United States for another five years, and Michael was obviously in the United States by April, 1869, the "editor of a little weekly in Dublin" must have been brother Alfred.
13. From notes supplied through the kindness of the Reverend Father Martin Coen, St. Mary's College, Galway.
14. Holland, "Submarine Navigation," *Cassier's Magazine,* The Marine Number.
15. Father Martin Coen to Richard K. Morris, 10 September 1960. One undocumented account, Frank Morriss, *Submarine Pioneer: John P. Holland* (Milwaukee: Bruce Publishing Co., 1961), says that Holland sailed on board the steam packet *Essex* and disembarked at New York. It, of course, implies arrival in the winter of 1872. Startling, too, is the suggestion that Holland first met his friend, William Kimball, during this passage, while Kimball was an Annapolis midshipman returning from a vacation in Europe. This would date the remarkable friendship between these two men from the beginning of Holland's residence in America. However, no sources are given to support this claim, and it is in direct contradiction to the rear admiral's own recollection of his first meeting with Holland in 1883. (See Chapter Five).

The date of the severance of Holland from the congregation at Dundalk, 26 May 1873, does not agree with all previously published chronologies, but it is unlikely that the record at Dundalk is in error. The new date used in this work has the merit of removing certain improbabilities regarding the order of subsequent events in America, improbabilities that arise in all accounts which date Holland's arrival in America as 1872. As for the chronology of Holland's teaching assignments in Ireland, these follow the correspondence of E. G. Clancy, of the Dublin Headquarters of the Irish Christian Brothers, to the Reverend Father Martin Coen, 2 February 1960.
16. From an interview in the *Washington Star,* 6 January 1900. Also quoted by Cable, *op. cit.,* p. 38.
17. E.g., see Cable, *op. cit.,* p. 27.

CHAPTER THREE
The First Submarine
1873-1879

1. *Washington Star,* 6 January 1900.
2. It is possible that Father Patrick Whelan, later Monsignor Whelan, was among the first of Holland's American friends, and that it was he who invited Holland to rejoin the Christian Brothers as a lay instructor in Paterson when the boys' division of St. John's Parochial School passed from the control of the Sisters of Charity to the Brotherhood.
3. From notes in the Paterson Museum, Paterson, N.J. These notes appear to be a copy from the fragmentary "Memoir" which John P. Holland began but never completed. The original is presumably in the collection of Edward M. Graf, of Paterson, who was given custody of certain papers which John P. Holland, Jr., originally assigned to The Stevens Institute at Hoboken. Simon Lake presumably quotes the entire manuscript in his account of Holland in *The Submarine in War and Peace* (Philadelphia: J. P. Lippincott Co., 1918), pp. 85-111.
4. Correspondence in the Paterson Museum.

5. William O'Brien and Desmond Ryan, *Devoy's Post Bag*, Vol. I, p. 3. The two volumes of *Devoy's Post Bag* constitute the best source of material on Fenianism in America and Holland's relation to the Fenian Movement. They were much used in the preparation of the present work.

6. This information is based on a copy of a letter of warrant from the collection of Edward M. Graf, Paterson, N.J. In 1869, O'Donovan Rossa was himself serving a life term in prison, but was to return to the United States as one of the "Cuban Five" following the Amnesty of 1871. The letter of warrant reads, in part:

Erin Go Bragh   *Fenian Brotherhood*

Know all members of the Fenian Brotherhood that MICHAEL J. HOLLAND who is described on the endorsement of this letter, has been duly initiated by the Centre of Circle No. 159 on the _____ day of April 1869. . . .

Now, therefore, I, JOHN SAVAGE, Chief Executive of the Fenian Brotherhood, do by these Presents call upon and command all to whom this Letter shall come to receive the said MICHAEL J. HOLLAND, if known to be in good standing, with true fraternal kindness and confidence. And for so doing this shall be your warrant.

JOHN SAVAGE
Chief Executive, F.B.

New York, July 9, 1869

The endorsement on the back of the warrant gives Michael's address as 12 Genesee St., Boston; age 22 [actually not quite 21]; height 5'9"; eyes dark blue; complexion dark and "slightly Pockmarked."

7. *Devoy's Post Bag*, Vol. II, p. 515, Michael J. Holland to John Devoy, 1916.

8. Original letter in Paterson Museum, Paterson, N.J. The Mr. Collins to whom this letter is addressed could not be the alias for John J. Breslin, later appointed by the Trustees of the Skirmishing Fund to oversee the development of Holland's submarine, for Breslin did not arrive in New York until the middle of August on board the *Catalpa*, bound in from Australia. Mr. Collins is unquestionably Jerome Collins, science reporter for the *New York Herald*, who in 1879 joined the tragic De Long polar expedition as chief scientific observer and weather forecaster. After the ice-locked *Jeannette* was abandoned off the Siberian coast, Collins reached the Lena Delta only to perish there on 30 October 1881. One of the few seamen to survive the arctic ordeal was W. F. C. Nindemann, who later became a member of the trial crew of the *Holland VI*. (See Chapter Eight).

9. There is an excellent account of the *Catalpa* affair in W. J. Laubenstein, *The Emerald Whaler* (New York: The Bobbs-Merrill Co., Inc., 1960).

10. John Devoy in the *New York Gaelic American*, July, 1927. Retold by Major D. J. Doyle, "The Holland Submarine," *An Cosantóir* (The Defender), Special Naval No., June, 1947.

11. *Ibid.*

12. Issue of 20 August 1916.

13. *Devoy's Post Bag*, Vol. I, p. 230.

14. *Daily Guardian* (Paterson, N.J.), 24 May 1878; *Daily Press* (Paterson, N.J.), 23 May, 7 June, and 15 June 1878. These accounts are the basis for the eyewitness reports.

15. *Devoy's Post Bag*, Vol. II, p. 46 ff. LeCaron wrote his own account of his astute informing in the service of England and Canada, *Twenty-Five Years in the Secret Service*. It is perfectly clear that he was fully aware of the submarine activity of John Holland.

16. John P. Holland, "Notes on *Fenian Ram*," from the fragmentary "Memoir," Paterson Museum, p. 3.

17. Quoted by H. Stacy in "The First Holland Submarine" (MS in Paterson Museum, Paterson, N.J., 1959).
18. Two interesting accounts of the *Holland No. 1* are to be found among the papers in the Paterson Museum: H. Stacy's unpublished manuscript, "The First Holland Submarine," and a clipping from the *Sunday Chronicle* (Paterson), 20 August 1916, which contains the recollections of William H. Dunkerley and Joseph Risk. The *Chronicle*'s spelling of Dunkerley has been used in this book, although Lake (see note 3) and others drop the second "e".
19. Holland, "Notes on *Fenian Ram*," *op. cit.*, p. 2.
20. *Devoy's Post Bag*, Vol. I, pp. 358-59.
21. *Ibid.*, Vol. II, p. 515.
22. Holland was affiliated with the Christian Brothers for twenty years, 1858-78, but he was absent from teaching for reasons of health for more than two years (December 1861 to September 1862 and May 1873 to September 1874). During the second period of absence, he emigrated to the United States. Most sources, however, refer to his "sixteen years" as a teacher.

CHAPTER FÒUR
The Fenian Ram
1879-1883

1. *Devoy's Post Bag*, Vol. I, p. 302, John Devoy to James Reynolds, 6 February 1878.
2. Many sources state that the submarine was built in a yard on the East River, while they give West 13th Street as the site. This is but one example of many where succeeding authors have perpetuated an earlier error, leaving the subject of submarine history in hopeless confusion. Holland, himself, has clearly stated that the boat was launched on the Hudson River side of Manhattan. See *Cassier's Magazine*, The Marine Number (1897), p. 553. This is confirmed by John Devoy in the *New York Gaelic American*, July, 1927.
3. Quoted in Simon Lake, *The Submarine in War and Peace* (Philadelphia: J. P. Lippincott Co., 1918), p. 97.
4. *Ibid.*
5. *Devoy's Post Bag*, Vol. I, p. 323. See also pp. 315-22.
6. John Devoy in the *New York Gaelic American*, Vol. XI (22 August 1914), pp. 1 and 3.
7. This figure includes submarines No. 1, No. 2, and No. 3. The third boat was Holland's 16-foot working model. See *Devoy's Post Bag*, Vol. I, p. 471, and Vol. II, p. 515. Rossa's estimates ran as high as $90,000.
8. From 1877 to 1888, the Russian engineer, Drzewiecki, developed five submarine models. These were small boats, and only the fourth and fifth broke from foot-treadle power to electric motors. Thereafter, Drzewiecki designed a submersible (1896). His persistent efforts, though unsuccessful, rivaled those of Bauer and Holland. The Russian inventor is credited with being the first to use the optical tube, forerunner of the periscope. See Alan Burgoyne, *Submarine Navigation, Past and Present* (London: Grant Richards, 1903), Vol. I, p. 100. See also note 16, Chapter Five, of this biography.
9. The location of these operations is clearly ascertained from papers which Holland left with his son, John, Jr., and which were loaned to Simon Lake. Lake, *op. cit.*, p. 98.
10. John P. Holland, "Notes on *Fenian Ram*" ("Memoir," MS in Paterson Museum), p. 10.
11. *Ibid.*, p. 11. Identical passages appear in Edward M. Graf's "The Fenian Ram, First Successful Submarine," *Passaic County Historical Bulletin*, Vol. III, No. 6, December, 1944. Frank Cable's description is also in accord; see *The Birth and Development of the American Submarine* (New York: Harper and Brothers, 1924), p. 78.

12. Holland, "Notes on *Fenian Ram*," p. 7 It was rumored that Goubet's little boat, launched in 1883, lost its longitudinal stability whenever the operator thrust his arm forward. Nordenfeldt later experienced the same instability in his Turkish boats.

13. These descriptions are based on the Delamater Iron Works' final drawings of the *Fenian Ram*, dated 7 February 1880 (General Dynamics Corporation, Electric Boat Division, Groton, Conn., Negative No. 1513), and on Holland's notes.

14. Papers of John P. Holland, Jr., loaned to Simon Lake, in Lake, *op. cit.*, pp. 98-99.

15. Holland, "Notes on *Fenian Ram*," pp. 5-6.

16. *Ibid.*

17. For the early history of the Whitehead torpedo, see C. Sleeman, *Torpedoes and Torpedo Warfare* (Portsmouth: Griffen and Co., 1889), pp. 171-203.

18. These are Holland's figures for the flight of the projectile. Cable's account does not agree. See Cable, *op. cit.*, p. 78.

19. Based on a report in the *New York Daily Tribune*, 26 December 1881, and John Devoy's memorandum in the *Irish World* libel action of 1923 (*Devoy's Post Bag*, Vol. II, p. 514). For the subsequent discussion of depths achieved in the *Ram*, compare Holland, "Notes on *Fenian Ram*," p. 11, with quotation in Lake, *op. cit.*, p. 107.

20. *Devoy's Post Bag*, Vol. II, p. 189.

21. *New York Gaelic American*, Vol. XI, No. 34, 22 August 1914.

22. *Devoy's Post Bag*, Vol. II, p. 213.

23. Writers do not agree on the location of the *Ram* when she was stolen. This account follows Holland's own recollection as revealed in the papers loaned to Lake, *op. cit.*, p. 108.

24. The 16-foot model submarine still lies under 110 feet of water in the East River off Whitestone Point.

25. Letter of John P. Holland to John Devoy in the Graf Collection, Paterson, N.J.

26. Lake, *op. cit.*, pp. 107-8.

27. Cable, *op. cit.*, p. 90; Colby Rucker, "The Fenian Ram," *United States Naval Institute Proceedings*, Vol. No. 61 (August, 1935), p. 1136; J. Niven, *et al.* (eds.), *Dynamic America* (New York: General Dynamics Corp. and Doubleday & Co., Inc., n.d. [1960]), p. 63.

28. *Devoy's Post Bag*, Vol. II, p. 306.

29. *Ibid.*, pp. 515-16.

30. Cable, *op. cit.*, p. 88.

31. Quoted in Burgoyne, *op. cit.*, Vol. II, p. 3, and repeated by other writers.

CHAPTER FIVE
The Lean Years
1883-1893

1. See W. W. Kimball's Supplementary Chapter to Frank T. Cable, *The Birth and Development of the American Submarine* (New York: Harper and Brothers, 1924), pp. 314-37.

2. Holland's repeated declaration on this point may be found in his article, "Submarine Navigation," *Cassier's Magazine*, The Marine Number (1897), p. 554.

3. Kimball in Cable, *op. cit.*, p. 316.

4. *Ibid.*, p. 318.

5. Holland, *Cassier's Magazine*, The Marine Number, p. 553.

6. See C. W. Hovgaard, *Submarine Boats* (London: E. & F. N. Spon, 1887), p. 51, and Edmund L. Zalinski, "Submarine Navigation," *The Forum*, II (January, 1887), 470-83.

7. Descriptions of the *Zalinski Boat* are based on reports in *Harper's Weekly*, 12 September 1885, p. 599, and in *Scientific American*, 7 August 1886, in addition to other sources already cited.

8. Kimball in Cable, *op. cit.*, p. 319.

9. As told by Simon Lake, *The Submarine in War and Peace* (Philadelphia: J. P. Lippincott Co., 1918), p. 109.

10. See *Scientific American*, 7 August 1886.

11. Information about John P. Holland's wife, Margaret, is scarce. The main sources used here are the research of Father Martin Coen and notes based on a conversation with Holland's daughter, Marguerite, recorded at the dedication of the Submarine Library, Electric Boat Company, Groton, Conn., 11 April 1955.

12. See Alan Burgoyne, *Submarine Navigation, Past and Present* (London: Grant Richards, 1903), Vol. I, pp. 113-15, and C. W. Hovgaard, *op. cit.*, pp. 38-39.

13. Holland, *Cassier's Magazine*, The Marine Number, pp. 556-58.

14. W. W. Kimball, "Submarine Torpedo-Boats," *Harper's Monthly*, CI (September, 1900), 565.

15. See W. B. Parsons, *Robert Fulton and the Submarine* (New York: Columbia University Press, 1922), p. 90, and Burgoyne, *op. cit.*, Vol. II, p. 252.

16. Some sources claim that fifty Goubet boats were built in Paris and delivered to Russia in 1883, but there is no evidence for this claim. Early boats using only electric power included Drzewiecki IV (1884), Campbell and Ash (1884), and Waddington (1885). Alstitt had used a primitive electric drive in association with steam as early as 1863. See note 8, Chapter Four.

17. A lengthy account of *Goubet II* is found in Burgoyne, *op. cit.*, Vol. I, pp. 274-81.

18. From the papers of John P. Holland, Jr., as reproduced in Lake, *op. cit.*, p. 110.

19. Other than the excerpt given in Lake, *op. cit.*, nothing has been found of this article by Holland.

20. "Circular: Showing the General Requirements Desired to be Fulfilled in Design and Trial of a Steel Submarine Torpedo Boat for the U. S. Navy," 20 August 1888 (Submarine Library).

21. *Ibid.*

22. "Submarine Boats of Many Nations," *New York Herald*, 27 March 1898.

23. Kimball in Cable, *op. cit.*, p. 322.

24. C. A. Morris, "Diaries," 1889 through 1907 (Submarine Library). The library also has one of two original copies in Holland's own hand of the document on "The Practicality of Mechanical Flight." The other copy is in the Library of Congress, Washington, D.C.

25. "Submergible Torpedo Boat," U. S. Patent No. 472,670 (12 April 1892). That this is the boat referred to is clear from the correspondence between Kimball and Frost on 2 December 1893 and found in the bound "Letters of the John P. Holland Torpedo Boat Company, 1893" (Submarine Library).

26. Told by F. Bishop in *The Story of the Submarine* (New York: D. Appleton-Century, 1943), p. 75, and repeated by W. J. Abbott in *Aircraft and Submarines* (New York: G. P. Putnam's Sons, 1918), pp. 276-77. The original edition of Bishop was 1916.

27. "The submergible torpedo boat" (see note 25, above) was a huge steam-driven ship with retractable smokestack and was designed for brief runs totally submerged. "The Submarine Gun" patent (No. 491,051) was issued 31 January 1893. A "Steering apparatus for Submarine Vessels" incorporated the results of experiments with an automatic pilot vane on the 16-foot Fenian boat and its patent (No. 492,960) was issued 7 March 1893. On 23 May 1892, Holland applied for another patent on an improved "Submarine Torpedo Boat," and this was granted in 1894.

CHAPTER SIX
The Government Contract
1893-1896

1. Simon Lake in *The Submarine in War and Peace* (Philadelphia: J. P. Lippincott Co., 1918), p. 120, simply refers to that "appointed day in June, 1893." The precise date is taken from the bound volume of "Letters of the John P. Holland Torpedo Boat Company, 1893" (Submarine Library), p. 25.

2. Lake, *op. cit.*, pp. 120-21. In a later version of this story in *Submarine, An Autobiography* (New York: D. Appleton-Century, 1938) p. 39, he reports saying to himself, "Lakey, the church is right, but you're in the wrong pew."

3. "Letters of the John P. Holland Torpedo Boat Company, 1893," John P. Holland to Mr. Alger, 31 July 1893.

4. *Ibid.*, John P. Holland to Lieutenant Commander C. S. Sperry, 8 September 1893.

5. *Ibid.*, E. B. Frost to Hon. Hilary A. Herbert, 13 September 1893.

6. *Ibid.*, E. B. Frost to C. E. Creecy, 14 November 1893.

7. *Ibid.*, E. B. Frost to General C. M. Shelley, 19 and 21 October 1893.

8. *Ibid.*, John P. Holland to Hon. Hilary A. Herbert, 12 December 1893.

9. *Ibid.*, John P. Holland to Mr. MacNair, 13 November 1893.

10. *Ibid.*, E. B. Frost to Richard Deming, 2 December 1893.

11. *Ibid.*, quoted in John P. Holland's letter to C. E. Creecy, 2 December 1893. The "submerger" referred to Holland's patent for a huge gunboat that could be made to disappear beneath the surface of the sea, apparently a brief concession which Holland made to those who favored the submersible over the submarine proper and who claimed the former to be a more versatile naval vessel.

12. On the whole matter of foreign patents and agencies abroad, see the bound volume, "Letters of the John P. Holland Torpedo Boat Company, 1895," pp. 22, 43, 44, 57, 101, 102, 160, 218, and 278.

13. For the complete testimony, see the House of Representatives, United States, House Committee on Naval Affairs, *Hearings on House Bill 6966*, 23 April 1900, (Washington: Government Printing Office, 1900). Note that the words "The John P." had been dropped from the company's official title prior to 1900. See also Alan Burgoyne, *Submarine Navigation, Past and Present* (London: Grant Richards, 1903), Vol. II, pp. 63-126.

14. C. A. Morris, "Diaries," 1895 (Submarine Library) and "Letters of the John P. Holland Torpedo Boat Company, 1895," John P. Holland to Messrs. Brown and Miller, 15 March 1895.

15. *Ibid.*, John P. Holland to Mrs. George Brayton, 4 April 1895.

16. *Ibid.*, E. B. Frost to C. E. Creecy, 17 April 1895.

17. *Ibid.*, E. B. Frost to J. A. Scott, 17 August 1895. For the subsequent discussion of the increased control by the company over the ideas, patents, and life of inventor Holland, see letters on pp. 106-7, 140-41, 175, and 220.

18. James B. Conant, *On Understanding Science* (New Haven: Yale University Press, 1947), p. 114.

19. "Letters of the John P. Holland Torpedo Boat Company, 1895," E. B. Frost to C. E. Creecy, 28 October 1895.

20. From clippings in the Morris Collection, Vol. I (Submarine Library).

21. C. A. Morris, "Diaries," 1896, entry for 8 December 1896.

22. See Chapter One, p. 5, of this text, and cf. Burgoyne, *op. cit.*, Vol. I, pp. 27, 33-34.

23. *Ibid.*, Vol. II, pp. 98-99.

CHAPTER SEVEN
The Holland VI
1896-1898

1. Alan Burgoyne, *Submarine Navigation, Past and Present* (London: Grant Richards, 1903), Vol. II, p. 9.
2. *New York Herald*, 20 March 1897.
3. For the details of the launching, see Chapter One. For a complete description and drawing of the *Holland VI*, see Appendix D.
4. Frank T. Cable, *The Birth and Development of the American Submarine* (New York: Harper and Brothers, 1924), p. 109.
5. *Ibid.*, p. 108.
6. Frank T. Cable to Charles A. Morris, 25 February 1898, in the Morris Collection (Submarine Library).
7. *New York Herald*, 17 March 1898.
8. See note 8, Chapter Three, regarding Jerome Collins.
9. Quoted in Cable, *op. cit.*, p. 122.
10. See J. Niven, *et al.* (eds.), *Dynamic America* (New York: General Dynamics Corp. and Doubleday & Co., Inc., n.d. [1960]), p. 69 for photocopy of the Roosevelt letter.
11. Quoted in Cable, *op. cit.*, p. 105.
12. *New York Sun*, 27 May 1898.
13. The original McAllister cartoon is in The Mariners Museum, Newport News, Virginia.
14. See Chapter Four.
15. *New York Herald*, 19 June 1898.
16. *Ibid.*, 20 July 1898.
17. Told by Cable, *op. cit.*, p. 122.
18. A complete list of the trial runs of *Holland VI* for 1898, and a list of all those who went down in her, was compiled by C. A. Morris in his own handwriting. Typed copies of the same were also kept. Morris Collection (Submarine Library).
19. Based on the lists cited in note 18.
20. For an account of Rice's business ventures, see Niven, *op. cit.*, pp. 26, 70-73, and 78.
21. Frank T. Cable to Charles A. Morris, 8 August 1898, Morris Collection (Submarine Library).
22. For a complete report of the Board of Inspection and Survey, 13 November 1898, see Burgoyne, *op. cit.*, Vol. II, pp. 36-41. The Board included, in addition to Chairman Rodgers, Chief Engineer Cipriano Andrade, Captain Robley Evans, Commander W. H. Emory, and Lieutenant Nathan Sargent.
23. Cable, *op. cit.*, pp. 125-26, but see C. A. Morris, "Diaries," 1898-1899, and other documents in the Morris Collection.

CHAPTER EIGHT
The Two Years of Decision
1898-1900

1. "Letters of the John P. Holland Torpedo Boat Company, 1899" (Submarine Library), E. B. Frost to R. McA. Lloyd, 28 March 1899.
2. *Ibid.*, E. B. Frost to Captain F. M. Barber, 13 March 1899.
3. *Ibid.*, E. B. Frost to Captain A. Tromp, 15 March 1899.
4. C. A. Morris, "Diaries," 1899 (Submarine Library). Morris and Cable saw Holland off for Europe.

5. Brother Fintan E. Eagan, as told to Peter E. Kilroy, *Dublin Standard*, 3 September 1951.

6. Frank T. Cable, *The Birth and Development of the American Submarine* (New York: Harper and Brothers, 1924), p. 191. Cable states that while Holland was so occupied, he, Cable, was "demonstrating in American waters the practicality of each boat we produced." The dates, the fact that there was only one boat, and Cable's minor role at this time, all indicate that this statement is a serious exaggeration of the facts.

7. John P. Holland to Captain A. Tromp, (?) June 1899, a private letter in the Holland file (Submarine Library). The accident on board the *Etruria* occurred on 4 May 1899.

8. "Letters of the John P. Holland Torpedo Boat Company, 1899," E. B. Frost to Lieutenant Commander W. W. Kimball, 19 April 1899.

9. Morris, "Diaries," 13 May 1899.

10. John P. Holland to Captain A. Tromp, (?) June 1899, private letter.

11. See "Letters of the John P. Holland Torpedo Boat Company," 18 March 1899, pp. 89 and 102, and Morris, "Diaries," entries for 18 and 25 March 1899.

12. House of Representatives, Report No. 1727, 60th Congress, 1st Session, *Hearings*, Vol. II, p. 458, 9 March 1908 (Washington: Government Printing Office, 1908).

13. "Letters of the John P. Holland Torpedo Boat Company," C. A. Morris to Goldsmith and Tuthill, 27 and 31 May 1899.

14. *Ibid.*, E. B. Frost to McAllister Brothers, 14 June 1899.

15. For newspaper accounts, see Morris Collection, Vol. I, p. 38 (Submarine Library).

16. Morris, "Diaries," entry for 6 September 1899.

17. Frost's decision to relieve Holland of command of his submarine was dictated by the refusal of insurance companies to issue policies on the inventor's life that would cover his activities submerged, and by Holland's tendency to be distracted by details within the boat, leaving his piloting position in the conning tower to investigate some internal machinery.

18. Clara Barton, "Diary" (Submarine Library).

19. Cable, *op. cit.*, pp. 132-33. By all accounts, Miss Barton was the first woman to go down in a submarine.

20. "Letters of the John P. Holland Torpedo Boat Company," E. B. Frost to Hon. J. D. Long, Secretary of the Navy, 27 June 1899.

21. *Ibid.*, E. B. Frost to C. E. Creecy, 15 June 1899, pp. 321-24, and E. B. Frost to Captain John Lowe, 24 June 1899, p. 353.

22. *Ibid.*, letters of 7 April 1899, p. 156, and 1 July 1899, pp. 386-87.

23. These were the salaries as of 10 March 1899.

24. For accounts of this near tragedy, see Cable, *op. cit.*, pp. 133-35; Morris, "Diaries," entry of 11 October 1899; and newspaper clippings in Vol. I of the Morris Collection.

25. For a complete report of the Board of Inspection and Survey, and for Engineer Lowe's supporting document, see Alan Burgoyne, *Submarine Navigation, Past and Present* (London: Grant Richards, 1903), Vol. II, pp. 43-56.

26. See Courtlandt Canby and Richard K. Morris, "The Father of the Modern Submarine," *American Heritage*, XII (1961), No. 2, p. 98. The figure given in Burgoyne, *op. cit.*, Vol. II, p. 120, appears to be in error in the placing of the decimal point. Other sources give various figures, but the amount shown is based on Frost's own figure. The Navy actually paid $150,000 for the *Holland VI*.

27. Cable, *op. cit.*, pp. 141-46.

CHAPTER NINE
The Navy's First Submarines
1900-1904

1. U. S. Congress (56:1), House Committee on Naval Affairs, *Hearings on H.B. 6966*, 23 April 1900 (Washington: Government Printing Office, 1900).

2. *Ibid.*

3. The cost of an 18-inch diameter, regulation Whitehead torpedo in 1900 was about $2,500. Frank Cable uses the figure $5,000, but he must have had in mind the cost of a "fish" at a later date.

4. "Program for Exhibition Run of *Holland*, 31 March and 3 April 1900" (Submarine Library).

5. U. S. Congress (56:1), *Senate Document No. 321* (Washington: Government Printing Office, 1900). The 11th of April, now designated as "Submarine Day," was first observed by a directive issued by Secretary of the Navy James Forrestal on the 47th anniversary of the purchase of the *Holland*, April, 1947.

6. "An Inventor's Story," *Washington Star*, 6 January 1900.

7. *Hearings on H.B. 6966*, 23 April 1900. See also U. S. Congress (60:1), House Select Committee Under House Resolution 288, *Hearings beginning 9 March 1908* (Washington: Government Printing Office, 1908), Vol. I, p. 176. The model referred to by Holland is the one shown in Alan Burgoyne, *Submarine Navigation, Past and Present* (London: Grant Richards, 1903), Vol. II, p. 20, and erroneously labeled Boat No. 10.

8. The original sketch by John P. Holland is in the Paterson Museum, Paterson, N.J.

9. *Buffalo Express*, 5 May 1900.

10. *Hearings beginning 9 March 1908*, Vol. I, pp. 98-99.

11. Frank T. Cable, *The Birth and Development of the American Submarine* (New York: Harper and Brothers, 1924), p. 166. Cable places the date of this event in September, but Lieutenant Caldwell's official report shows it to be 30 August 1900.

12. For accounts of the role of the *Holland* in the war games, see "Navy Chief Praises *Holland* for Grand Work at Newport," *New York Journal*, 27 September 1900; J. Niven, *et al.* (eds.), *Dynamic America* (New York: General Dynamics Corp. and Doubleday & Co., Inc., n.d. [1960]), pp. 72-73; and Lieutenant Caldwell's own story, quoted in Burgoyne, *op. cit.*, Vol. II, p. 114.

13. These testimonials are taken from the records of the Bureau of Navigation, "Concerning the USTB *Holland*," and reproduced in Burgoyne, *op. cit.*, Vol. II, pp. 111 and 139-40.

14. See Chapter Seven, p. 85, with regard to Nathan Sargent.

15. *Daily Times* (Troy, N.Y.), 22 December 1900.

16. Lawrence Y. Spear, "Correspondence" (Submarine Library). See letters in 1897-1899.

17. Cable, *op. cit.*, p. 174. Cable does not mention Spear by name. He simply speaks of "the chief engineer," a government man.

18. Lawrence Y. Spear, "The Development of Submarines," *Papers*, 14th Annual Meeting, Society of Naval Architects and Marine Engineers, New York, 22 and 23 November 1906.

19. See Chapter One.

20. *Hearings beginning 9 March 1908*, Vol. I, p. 458.

21. For Holland's notes and calculations, see Niven, *op. cit.*, p. 75.

22. See Cable, *op. cit.*, pp. 190-204; W. B. Parsons, *Robert Fulton and the Submarine* (New York: Columbia University Press, 1922), *passim*; F. W. Lipscomb, *The British Submarine* (London:

A. & C. Black, 1954), pp. 63-69; and P. K. Kemp, *H. M. Submarines* (London: Jenkins, 1952), pp. 28-31.

23. John Devoy, "Holland Obituary," *New York Gaelic American*, XI (22 August 1914) 1 and 3.

24. A photostat of Holland's letter of resignation, taken from the files of the Electro Dynamic Division of the General Dynamics Corporation, appears in Niven, *op. cit.*, p. 78, ill. 191.

CHAPTER TEN

The Passing of a Prophet

1904-1914

1. The testimony of Isaac Rice: U. S. Congress (60:1), House Select Committee Under House Resolution 288, *Hearings beginning 9 March 1908* (Washington: Government Printing Office, 1908), Vol. I, p. 485. From June, 1900, his contract called for an annual salary of $10,000, still a small income for the millions his patents reaped.

2. From an interview in the *New York World* (*ca.* 1906) and reprinted in U. S. Congress (60:1), *Hearings beginning 9 March 1908*, Vol. I, p. 359.

3. Document, n.d., but after 1905, 11 pp. Folder II, Marguerite Holland Papers (Submarine Library).

4. "American Shipbuilder," an undated clipping in the Holland File (Submarine Library).

5. Frank T. Cable, *The Birth and Development of the American Submarine* (New York: Harper and Brothers, 1924), p. 251.

6. Sources: Letter, John P. Holland to Kagiro Matsukata, 10 November 1906, Holland File (Submarine Library); E. M. Graf, "J. P. Holland's Submarines Built for Russia and Japan," *Paterson Morning Call*, 26 April 1923; two unidentified clippings in the Holland File (Submarine Library).

7. *New York World* (*ca.* 1906), reprinted in U. S. Congress (60:1), *Hearings beginning 9 March 1908*, Vol. I, p. 359.

8. The complete log of this event may be found in *The New York Times*, 19 May 1910, and in Cable, *op. cit.*, pp. 251-53.

9. Regarding Bauer's *Le Diable Marin*, see Alan Burgoyne, *Submarine Navigation, Past and Present* (London: Grant Richards, 1903), Vol. I, pp. 27-34; for Drzewiecki, see *ibid.*, Vol. I, pp. 76-78, 84-85, 99-100. For the fate of *Delfin*, see *New York Evening Mail*, 29 June 1904, and Simon Lake, *The Submarine in War and Peace* (Philadelphia: J. P. Lippincott Co., 1918), pp. 65-66. Cf. Chapter One, *supra*. Other references could be included, but these may be sufficient to lead the reader to the other sources used.

10. See Lake, *op. cit.*, pp. 62-67, 209-16; and Simon Lake, *Submarine, An Autobiography* (New York: D. Appleton-Century, 1938), pp. 164-75. Also, for the *Protector*, see Lake Torpedo Boat Company, *The Submarine versus the Submersible* (Bridgeport, Conn., 1906), pp. 19-22, 56, 68, 72-73. For Lake boats in general, see H. O. Hopkins, "Simon Lake and His Submarines," *United States Naval Institute Proceedings*, Vol. No. 83 (March, 1957), pp. 324-29.

11. The Foss document may be found in its entirety in Simon Lake, *The Submarine in War and Peace*, pp. 114-18, as taken from the papers of John P. Holland, Jr. A cartoon in the *Newark Evening News* of 3 May 1906, entitled "Drawn from Surface Indications," shows John Holland shot from the torpedo tube of a submarine labeled "House Committee on Naval Affairs" into the jaws of a shark labeled "Electric Boat Company Monopoly."

12. Letter, Charles A. Morris to John P. Holland, 8 June 1905, Morris Collection (Submarine Library).

13. Letter, Charles E. Creecy to John P. Holland, 23 February 1906, Holland File (Submarine Library).
14. See U. S. Congress (60:1), *Hearings beginning 9 March 1908*, Vol. II, pp. 1732-37. See the General Dynamics Corporation, Electric Boat Division, list of Holland-type boats constructed in the United States and abroad under license from a memorandum compiled 16 May 1923; see also "United States Submarine Data Book," 1961 ed.
15. Letter, John P. Holland to Hon. Charles J. Bonaparte, (?) September 1906, Morris Collection (Submarine Library).
16. Letter-document, John P. Holland to Lieutenant Commander W. Strother Smith, 8 October 1906, 23 pp., Folder II, Marguerite Holland Papers (Submarine Library). Cf. also the prophetic insights of Holland found in Chapter One, *supra*.
17. Letter, John P. Holland to Captain H. G. Hebbinghaus, 16 February 1907. Folders I and VII, Marguerite Holland Papers (Submarine Library).
18. Cf. Chapter One, *supra*.
19. See H. Hagedorn, *The Roosevelt Family of Sagamore Hill* (New York: The Macmillan Co., 1954), pp. 226-29; *New York World*, 26 August 1905, and *New York Herald*, 27 August 1905. After his trip on board the *Plunger*, the President issued a directive that changed the pay of submariners from a shore-duty to a sea-duty rate.
20. Cable, *op. cit.*, p. 290.
21. This quotation has been repeated by several writers, chiefly using Cable, *op. cit.*, p. 288.
22. Letter, Simon Lake to John P. Holland, Jr., 15 February 1916, Folder VII, Marguerite Holland Papers (Submarine Library). For Lake's appraisal of Holland, the inventor, see *The Submarine in War and Peace*, p. 118, and *Submarine, An Autobiography*, p. 225.
23. The known facts of the Holland family may be outlined as follows:

John Holland (died *ca.* 1853) m. 1. Anne (1810-1835)
                              2. Mary Scanlon

  I. Alfred Holland (183–-1910)—a teacher
  II. John Philip Holland (1841-1914) m. Margaret T. Foley (1862-1923)
      1. John P., Jr. (died in infancy, 1888)
      2. John P., Jr. (1890-*ca.* 1917)
      3. Robert Charles (*ca.* 1891-19—)
      4. Julia (1894-1913)
      5. Joseph Francis (died 1942)—a lawyer
      6. Mary Josephine (died in infancy)
      7. Marguerite (*ca.* 1897-1960)
  III. Robert Holland (1845-1847)
  IV. Michael Joseph Holland (1848-19—) m. Mary Anne Fennon
      1. Patrick
      2. Frederick
      3. Mary
      4. Alfred
      5. John P. Holland m. (?)
         two children

24. See John Devoy, *New York Gaelic American*, XI (22 August 1914) 1-3, and two obituary notices from local Newark papers preserved in the Morris Collection (Submarine Library). The words of Kimball are found in the Supplementary Chapter of Cable, *op. cit.*, p. 337.

A Supplement

1. See, for example, John de Courcy Ireland, "John P. Holland, 1841–1914." *The Irish Sword*, Vol. VIII, No. 31, 1967; Rev. Martin Coen, "Pioneer of the Submarine." *The Irish Times*, 12 August 1964, and Coen, "Father of the Submarine." *The Mantle*, Vol. III, No. 2, Summer 1960; P. Richard Compton-Hall, *Submarine Boats: The Beginning of Underwater Warfare* (London: Conway Maritime Press, 1983), and "Holland's *Hollands*." USNI (United States Naval Institute) *Proceedings*, Vol. 117, No. 2, February 1991; and Captain Donald McIntyre, RN (ret.), "Comment and Discussion." USNI *Proceedings*, Vol. 93, No. 12, 1967, pp. 105–107.

2. See Chapter Two, p.19, *supra*.

3. Letter, John P. Holland to Aloysius Yorke, 22 June 1898 (Christian Brother's Generalate Archives, the Vatican, Rome).

4. Letter, Brother Thomas Hughes to John Holland, 1904. (Graf Collection, Paterson Museum, hereinafter cited as GC, PM).

5. See Chapter Two, p. 20, *supra*.

6. For details, see Chapter Three, p. 25, *supra*.

7. Letter, J. J. Breslin to John P. Holland, 12 June 1877 (GC, PM), File No. 33.01.

8. Letter, J. J. Breslin to J. P. Holland (GC, PM) File No. 35.06.

9. Letter, John P. Holland to John Devoy, 14 Oct. 1883 (GC, PM), File No. 33–2.06.

10. Holland note, 1883 (GC, PM), File No. 33.

11. Letter, Holland to Captain Simon, master of the tug that towed the two Fenian boats into Long Island Sound, 27 August 1883 (GC, PM) File No. 33.

12. See *ibid.*

13. The voluminous correspondence between these two men can be found in the Paterson Museum. Kimball-Holland Correspondence (GC, PM) File 25:1.01–44.

14. Letter, n.d. (GC, PM) File 33.

15. Letter, Holland to Edmund Zalinski, 4 Oct. 1884 (GC, PM), File No. 35.

16. As told to *Paterson Evening News*, 24 April 1954 quoting Marguerite Holland. Courtesy of Edward Smyk, Passaic County Historian in "John Philip Holland: Submarine Pioneer." Special supplement, p.7.

17. *Ibid.*, n.51.

18. Letter, John P. Holland to Secretary of the Navy J. P. Long, 12 August 1896 (GC, PM), File No. 28.06.

19. John P. Holland paper (GC, PM), pp.5–6, File No. 35.25.

20. John P. Holland on periscopes, 1904 (GC, PM), File No. 34.19.

21. Cf. John de Courcy Ireland, "John P. Holland: Pioneer of Submarine Navigation." *Journal of the North Munster Archaeological Society* (1967), p. 212.

22. John P. Holland to Atty. F. P. S. Sands, re: patents filed before his resignation from Electric Boat Co. Mentions Busch and the first five Japanese submarines (GC, PM), File No. 35.30.

23. Letter, John H. Yauch, Esq. to R. K. Morris, with photograph of the original parchment, 25 March 1967 (trans. M. Michigama for the author). Medal and ribbon now in Paterson Museum.

24. Letter, John P. Holland to Charles Schwab, 15 December 1904 (CG, PM), File No. 35.23.

25. Letter, Charles E. Creecy to Holland (GC, PM) miscellaneous.

26. Letter, John P. Holland to Kenji Ide, 17 April 1905, p.3 (GC, PM), File No. 34.25.

27. Letter, Kenji Ide to J. P. Holland, 17 June 1905 (GC, PM), 34.27.

28. Letter, Kenji Ide to W. W. Kimball, 17 September 1906 (GC, PM), File No. 34.28.

29. Letter, J. P. Holland to Kenji Ide, 21 May 1909 (GC, PM), File No. 34.39.

30. Kimball-Holland Letters. (GC, PM) File No. 25.00–25.44

31. Letter, Brother Cormac Murphy, F. S. C. (St. Mary's, California) to Frank Uhlig, USNI, 23 September 1970, with enclosed material forwarded to R. K. Morris.

32. John Philip Holland is buried in the Totowa (New Jersey) Cemetery. His grave is marked by a monument with bas-relief circle showing Holland emerging, with his familiar bowler, from the turret of the *Holland VI*—a trademark of the man. The monument was dedicated 10 October 1975 and made possible through the efforts of Chief Raymond J. Guernic USN (ret.), and the veterans of the Silent Service. A smaller marker was removed and shipped to Holland's native Liscannor, County Clare, Ireland, where it stands today on Main Street, a few yards from the Coast Guard cottage on Castle street where Holland is said to have been born.

BIBLIOGRAPHY

COLLECTIONS

Cable, F. T. "Notebooks." Submarine Library, U. S. Naval Submarine Base, New London, Conn. This is primarily a collection of newspaper clippings covering the period of Frank Cable's ascendancy in the employ of the Electric Boat Company, 1901-11. It includes some rare and excellent photographs of the *Fulton*, the government's A-boats, and the submarine base at New Suffolk, Long Island. The emphasis is on Cable.

Holland, J. P. "Memorabilia, Notes, etc." Paterson Museum, Paterson, N.J. A small but key catalogue of miscellany pertaining to Holland's early years in America: letters, documents, unfinished memoirs, and unpublished manuscripts. The Museum also houses the original hull of submarine *Boat No. 1*, recovered from the Passaic River in 1927.

Holland Torpedo Boat Company. "Letters." Bound volumes for 1893, 1895, and 1899. Submarine Library, U. S. Naval Submarine Base, New London, Conn. In spite of the gaps in this correspondence (the years 1894 and 1896 through 1898 are missing), these volumes contain significant details hitherto ignored by writers on the subject of the early Holland submarines. Hundreds of letters enable one to correct numerous past errors in the chronology of events and to explore the complicated transactions which eventually enabled others to exploit Holland's mechanical genius.

Holland, Marguerite. "Papers." Seven Folders. Submarine Library, U. S. Naval Submarine Base, New London, Conn. These papers, originally housed in the Paterson Museum, were transferred to the Submarine Library at the request of the late Marguerite Holland, daughter of the inventor. Here is much of the source material for John Holland's declining years, 1905-14: letters, sketches, calculations, patents, and family records through 1917.

Morris, R. K. "Morris Collection." Six bound volumes, newspaper clippings, photographs, diaries (1889-1904), etc. Submarine Library, U. S. Naval Submarine Base, New London, Conn. A unique and extensive collection of Holland memorabilia, covering the most productive years of the inventor's life, 1890-1904. It includes, in addition to the six bound volumes of photographs and clippings (completely indexed), sixteen diaries, notebooks, submarine plans, letters, expense accounts, documents, company circulars and contracts, and eighty-five original cut-film and gelatin plate negatives of the construction, repair, and trial runs of the *Holland VI*. These papers were kept by Holland's superintending engineer, Charles A. Morris.

Skerrett, R. G. "Skerrett Collection." Five bound volumes of articles, documents, and pamphlets on submarines (1869-1905). Submarine Library, U. S. Naval Submarine Base, New London, Conn. These volumes preserve a wealth of published technical material on early submarine construction, some from foreign journals. The selection tends to emphasize the theories and accomplishments of Simon Lake rather than those of John Holland. Skerrett was a journalist employed by Lake.

BOOKS

Abbott, H. L. *The Beginning of Modern Submarine Warfare (Under Bushnell, etc.)*. New York: Willets Pt. Engineering School of Application, 1881.

Abbott, W. J. *Aircraft and Submarines*. New York: G. P. Putnam's Sons, 1918.

Anderson, F. B. *Submarines, Submariners, Submarining*. A Bibliography. Hamden, Conn.: The Shoe String Press, Inc., 1963.

Anderson, W. R., with Clay Blair. *Nautilus 90 North*. Cleveland: The World Publishing Co., 1959.

Armstrong, G. E. *Torpedoes and Torpedo Vessels*. London: George Bell and Sons, 1896.

Bagenal, P. H. *The American Irish*. Boston: Robert Brothers, 1882.

Barnes, J. S. *Submarine Warfare*. New York: D. Van Nostrand Co., Inc., 1869. (Reputedly the first American book on submarines.)

Barnes, R. H. *U. S. Submarines*. New Haven: Morse Associates, 1944.

Bishop, F. *The Story of the Submarine*. New York: D. Appleton-Century, 1943. (First published by Century in 1916).

Blair, C. *The Atomic Submarine and Admiral Rickover*. New York: Henry Holt, 1954.

Burgoyne, A. H. *Submarine Navigation, Past and Present*. 2 vols. London: Grant Richards, 1903.

Busch, H. *U-Boats at War*. New York: Ballantine Books, Inc., 1955.

Cable, F. T. *The Birth and Development of the American Submarine*. New York: Harper and Brothers, 1924.

Chambliss, W. C. *The Silent Service*. New York: The New American Library (Signet), 1959.

Clerc-Rampal, G. *Les Sous-Marins*. Paris: Librarie Hachette, 1917.

Cope, H. F. *Serpent of the Seas*. New York: Funk & Wagnalls Co., Inc., 1942.

Corbin, T. W. *Romance of Submarine Engineering*. Philadelphia: J. P. Lippincott Co., 1913. (Same as Corbin, *Wonders of the Submarine*, 1918.)

Cross, W. *Challengers of the Deep*. New York: William Sloane Associates, 1959.

DeLatil, P., and Rivoire, J. *Man and the Underwater World*. New York: G. P. Putnam's Sons, 1956.

DeLong, G. W. *The Voyage of the* Jeannette. 2 vols. Boston: Houghton, Mifflin Co., 1883.

Delpeuch, Y. M. *Les Sous-Marins a Travers Les Siecles*. Paris: Société D'Edition et De Publications, 1907.

Dommett, W. E. *Submarine Vessels*. London: Whitaker, 1915.

Domville-Fife, C. W. *Submarines and Sea Power*. New York: The Macmillan Co., n.d.

————. *Submarines, Mines and Torpedoes in the War*. London: Hodder and Stoughton, 1914.

Felsen, H. G. *He's in the Submarines Now*. New York: McBride, 1942.

Field, C. *The Story of the Submarine*. Philadelphia: J. P. Lippincott Co., 1907.

Fisher, J. S. *A Short Treatise on Electricity and Management of Electric Torpedoes*. Landport, England: E. Annett, 1868. Private printing.

Foerster, O. G. *Wilhelm Bauers' Kampf um Das Erste Deutsche Tauchboot*. Berlin: Franz Schneider Verlag, 1937.

Forest, F., and Noalhat, L. *Les Bateaux Sous-Marins Historique*, 2 vols. Paris: C. Dunod, Ed., 1900.

Frank, W. *The Sea Wolves*. New York: Rinehart, 1955.

Fyfe, H. C. *Submarine Warfare, Past and Present* (2nd ed.). London: Grant Richards, 1907.

Hagedorn, H. *The Roosevelt Family of Sagamore Hill*. New York: The Macmillan Co., 1954.

Hall, C. *Modern Weapons of War*. London: Blackie & Son, 1915.

Hart, F. B. *A Fortnight in Ireland*. New York: G. P. Putnam's Sons, 1852.

Hay, M. F. *Secrets of the Submarine*. New York: Dodd, Mead & Co., 1917.

Herzog, B. *Die Deutschen U-Boote*. Munich: Lehmanns Verlag, 1959.

Hoar, A. *The Submarine Torpedo Boat*. New York: D. Van Nostrand Co., Inc., 1916.

Holbrook, S. H. *Lost Men of American History*. New York: The Macmillan Co., 1947.

Holland, J. P. "Can New York Be Bombarded?" Original lost. Reprinted in part in Lake, Simon. *The Submarine in War and Peace*. Philadelphia: J. P. Lippincott Co., 1918.

Hovgaard, G. W. *Submarine Boats*. London: E. & F. N. Spon, 1887.

Hull, S. *The Bountiful Sea*. Englewood, N.J.: Prentice-Hall, Inc., 1964.

Jackson, G. G. *The Romance of a Submarine*. London: Samson, Low, Marston & Co. Ltd., 1930.

James, Henry. *German U-Boats in Yankee Waters*. New York: Gotham House, 1940.

Jane, Fred T. *All the World's Fighting Ships*. London: Samson, Low, Marston & Co. Ltd., 1898, 1899, 1900, 1901, 1902.

Johnson, R. E. *Thence Round Cape Horn*. Annapolis: U. S. Naval Institute, 1963.

Kemp, P. K. *H. M. Submarines*. London: Jenkins, 1952.

Lake, S. *Submarine, An Autobiography*. New York: D. Appleton-Century, 1938.

———. *The Submarine in War and Peace*. Philadelphia: J. P. Lippincott Co., 1918.

Lake Torpedo Boat Company. *The Submarine versus the Submersible*. Bridgeport, Conn.: 1906.

Laubenstein, W. J. *The Emerald Whaler*. New York: The Bobbs-Merrill Co., Inc., 1960.

Lipscomb, F. W. *The British Submarine*. London: A. & C. Black, 1954.

Lott, A. S. *A Long Line of Ships*. Annapolis: U. S. Naval Institute, 1954.

Low, A. M. *The Submarine at War*. London: Hutchinson & Co. Ltd., 1941.

Newbolt, H. J. *Submarines and Anti-Submarines*. London: Longman, Green and Co., 1918.

Niven, J., *et al.* (eds.). *Dynamic America*. New York: General Dynamics Corp. and Doubleday & Co., Inc., n.d. [1960].

O'Brien, W., and Ryan, D. (eds.). *Devoy's Post Bag*. 2 vols. Dublin: C. J. Fallou Ltd., 1948 and 1953.

Parsons, W. B. *Robert Fulton and the Submarine*. New York: Columbia University Press, 1922.

Polmar, N. *Atomic Submarines*. Princeton, N.J.: D. Van Nostrand Co., Inc., 1963.

Porter, D. D. *Naval History of the Civil War*. New York: Sherman, 1866.

Robinson, W. M., Jr. *The Confederate Privateers*. New Haven: Yale University Press, 1928.

Roscoe, T. *United States Submarine Operations in World War II*. Annapolis: U. S. Naval Institute, 1949.

Rush, C. W., *et al. The Complete Book of Submarines*. Cleveland: The World Publishing Co., 1958.

Schaeffer, H. *U-Boat 977*. New York: W. W. Norton & Co., Inc., 1952.

Sleeman, C. *Torpedoes and Torpedo Warfare*. Portsmouth: Griffen and Co., 1889.

Talbot, F. A. A. *Submarines, Their Mechanism and Operation*. Philadelphia: J. P. Lippincott Co., 1915.

[Tomlinson, E.] *David Bushnell and His American Turtle*. New York: The Werner Co., *ca.* 1899. (The author is not listed on the title page, but the book is generally attributed to Tomlinson. It is a fictionalized biography.)

Verne, Jules. *Twenty Thousand Leagues Under the Sea*. New York: Heritage Press, 1956.

Woodbury, D. O. *What the Citizen Should Know About Submarine Warfare*. New York: W. W. Norton & Co., Inc., 1942.

PERIODICALS AND PAMPHLETS

Barnes, R. H. "Connecticut Submarines, John Holland, Pioneer," *Connecticut Circle* (April, 1942).

——. "Japan's First Submarines," *United States Naval Institute Proceedings*, Vol. No. 69 (February, 1943), 201-5.

Blair, C. H. "Submarines of the Confederate Navy," *United States Naval Institute Proceedings*, Vol. No. 78 (October, 1952), 1115-21.

Cable, F. T. "A Submarine Voyage in 1900," *The Military Engineer*, 26 (June, 1934), 191-92.

——. "History of the *Holland*," *The Military Engineer*, 24, 137 (September-October, 1932), 516-25.

——. "The Strange Cruise of the *Octopus*," *Cosmopolitan* (August, 1907), 410-17.

——. "The Submarine Torpedo Boat *Holland*," *United States Naval Institute Proceedings*, Vol. No. 69 (February, 1943), 173-80.

Canby, C., and Morris, R. K. "The Father of the Modern Submarine," *American Heritage*, XII, 2 (February, 1961), 34-39, 94-98.

Coen, M. "The Father of the Submarine," *The Mantle* (Galway, Ireland), 3, 2 (Summer, 1960), 21-24.

——. "In the Footsteps of John P. Holland," *The Mantle* (Galway, Ireland), 6, 2 (Summer, 1963), 8-12.

——. "Liscannor and Holland," *The Mantle* (Galway, Ireland), 7, 3 (Autumn, 1964), 5-7.

Daubin, F. A. "Cruise of the American *Underseeboot III*," *United States Naval Institute Proceedings*, Vol. No. 83 (March, 1957), 259-71.

DeFantes, Joao A. "Memoria Sabre o Submarino Fontes." Lisbon: Typographia Industrial Portugueza, 1902.

Devoy, J. "Holland Obituary," *The Gaelic American*, 11, 34 (22 August 1914), 1 and 3.

Fahey, J. C. "The Ships and Aircraft of the United States Fleet" (7th ed.). Falls Church, Va.: Ships and Aircraft, 1958.

Duboc, E. "Les Marines du Monde," *Le Yacht* (6 February 1897).

General Dynamics Corporation. "Little Known Facts About the Submarine." Groton, Conn.: Submarine Library, Electric Boat Division, n.d.

——. "Nuclear Powered Submarines of the U. S. Navy." Groton, Conn.: Electric Boat Division, January, 1964.

——. "Nuclear Powered Submarines of the U. S. Navy." Groton, Conn.: Electric Boat Division, 20 March 1965.

——. "The Submarine Library." Groton, Conn.: Electric Boat Division, n.d.

——. "United States Submarine Data Book." Groton, Conn.: Electric Boat Division, 1961.

Graf, E. M. "The Fenian Ram, First Successful Submarine," *Passaic County Historical Society Bulletin*, 3, 6 (December, 1944), 22-24.

Hendrick, B. J. "The Inventor of the Modern Submarine," *The World's Work Magazine*, 30, 3 (July, 1915), 284-94.

Hilton, C. H. "Isaac Peral and His Submarine," *United States Naval Institute Proceedings*, Vol. No. 82 (November, 1956), 1194-1202.

Holland, J. P. "How To Fly as a Bird." Newark, N.J.: Gasser Print Shop, n.d. [*ca.* 1906].

——. "The Submarine Boat and its Future," *North American Review*, December, 1900.

———. "Submarine Navigation," *Cassier's Magazine* (The Marine Number, 1897), 541-60.

Hopkins, H. O. "Simon Lake and His Early Submarines," *United States Naval Institute Proceedings*, Vol. No. 83 (March, 1957), 324-29.

Jameson, M. S. (compiler). "Submarines." Foreword by Simon Lake. A list of reprints in the New York City Public Library. New York, 1918.

Kelln, A. L. "Confederate Submarines," *The Virginia Magazine of History and Biography*, 60, 3 (July, 1955), 293-301.

Kimball, W. W. "Insurance of Property Against War Risks," *The Forum*, XIV (June, 1899).

———. "Submarine Torpedo-Boats," *Harper's Monthly*, 101 (September, 1900), 557-69.

Kissling, T. E. "Undersea Pioneer," *Columbia Magazine*, June, 1947. Reprinted in the *Catholic Digest*, August, 1947.

Lake, S. "Voyaging Under the Sea," *McClure's Magazine*, 12, 3 (January, 1899), 195-209.

McKee, A. I. "Recent Submarine Design Practices and Problems," *The Society of Naval Architects and Marine Engineers*, Monograph #11, 12-13 November 1959.

———. "Submarine Naval Architecture," *The Society of Naval Architects and Marine Engineers*, Address, N.E. Section of Annual Meeting, April, 1948.

Moore, S. T. "Fifteen Years Under the Sea" (The story of Frank T. Cable), *Popular Mechanics* (August, 1926), 228-33.

Morris, R. K. "The Story of the *Holland*," *United States Naval Institute Proceedings*, Vol. No. 86 (January, 1960), 78-89.

———. "Submarines," *The Dictionary of American History*. New York: Charles Scribner's Sons, 1961.

———. *See* Canby, C. "The Father of the Modern Submarine," *American Heritage*, XII, 2 (February, 1961), 34-39, 94-98.

Niblack, A. P. "Discussion of the Submarine Boat," *Marine Engineering*, 6 (December, 1898), 63-74.

O'Connor, T. P. "An Anglo-Irish Tragi-Comedy," *T.P.'s and Cassell's Weekly*, Vol. No. 80 (23 May 1925).

Rucker, C. "The *Fenian Ram*," *United States Naval Institute Proceedings*, Vol. No. 61 (August, 1935), 1136-39.

Sims, L. "The Submarine That Wouldn't Come Up," *American Heritage*, IX, 3 (April, 1958), 48-51, 107-11.

Skerrett, R. G. "The Invisible Navy," *Harper's Weekly* (April, 1908).

———. "The Relation of the Government to the Development of Submarines," *Scientific American Supplement*, 21 and 28 March 1908.

Scott, J. A. "The Submarine Torpedo Boat *Plunger*," *Journal of American Society of Naval Engineering*, 10, 2 (1897), 366-73.

Spear, L. Y. "The Development of Submarines," *Papers*, 14th Annual Meeting, Society of Naval Architects and Marine Engineers, New York, 22 and 23 November 1906.

Steele, G. P. "Killing Nuclear Submarines," *United States Naval Institute Proceedings*, Vol. No. 86 (November, 1960), 45-51.

Stevens, T. A. "Captain Ezra Lee of Old Lyme, Commander of America's First Submarine." Deep River, Conn.: Savings Bank Brochure, 1959.

Thomson, D. W. "David Bushnell and the First American Submarine," *United States Naval Institute Proceedings,* Vol. No. 68 (February, 1942), 176-86.

United States Naval Institute, "The First Fifty Years of U. S. Submarines," *United States Naval Institute Proceedings,* Vol. No. 82 (November, 1956), 1212-25.

von Kolnitz, H. "The Confederate Submarine," *United States Naval Institute Proceedings,* Vol. No. 63 (October, 1937), 1453-57.

Zalinski, E. L. "Submarine Navigation," *The Forum,* II (January, 1887), 470-83. *See also Harper's Weekly,* 599 (12 September 1885), and *Scientific American* (7 August 1886).

U. S. GOVERNMENT DOCUMENTS

Barber, F. M. "Lecture on Submarine Boats and their Application to Torpedo Operations." Newport, R.I.: U. S. Naval Torpedo Station, 1875.

Committee on Undersea Warfare. "Bibliographie NRC." Bulletin #307. Washington: Government Printing Office, n.d.

Federal Writers Project (WPA). "Holland Submarine." *Stories of New Jersey,* School Bulletin No. 37 (April, 1937).

House of Representatives. House Committee on Naval Affairs (56th Cong., 1st sess.). *Hearings on H.B. 6966,* 23 April 1900. Washington: Government Printing Office, 1900.

———. House Committee on Naval Affairs (57th Cong., 1st sess.). *Hearings . . . on Submarine boats.* Washington: Government Printing Office, 1902.

———. House Select Committee Under House Resolution 288 (60th Cong., 1st sess.). *Hearings beginning 9 March 1908.* 2 vols. Washington: Government Printing Office, 1908.

Navy Department, Bureau of Naval Personnel. "The Submarine." Washington: Government Printing Office, 1961.

———. Naval History Division. *Dictionary of American Naval Fighting Ships.* (Vol. I, App. II, "Submarines," 1893-1958, pp. 227-63). Washington: Government Printing Office, 1959.

———. Naval History Division. "The Submarine in the United States Navy." Washington: Government Printing Office, 1960.

———. Navpers 10011. "Submarine Recognition Manual." Rev. 1959. Washington: Government Printing Office, 1959.

Senate (56th Cong., 2d sess.). *Holland Submarine Torpedo Boat,* Doc. 115, Vol. II. Washington: Government Printing Office, 1901.

———. *Holland Submarine Boat,* Doc. 122, Vol. II. Washington: Government Printing Office, 1901.

MANUSCRIPTS

Holland, J. P. "Notes on *Fenian Ram.*" Typewritten manuscript, Paterson Museum, Paterson, N.J., n.d.

———. "Practicality of Mechanical Flight." Unpublished manuscript. 21 April 1891.

———. "Sketches and Calculations." Submarine Library, U. S. Naval Submarine Base, New London, Conn., n.d.

Stacy, H. "The First Holland Submarine." Unpublished manuscript, Rutgers University, 1959. Pp. 19. (Paterson Museum).

INDEX

Lister, John, boathouse operator, Paterson, N.J., 27, 28, 64

Little Peconic Bay, Long Island, N.Y., 100, 101, 102, 106, 119, *map* 181

Lois V. Chapele, lumber schooner, incident of, 91, 103

Long, John D., Secretary of the Navy, 87, 92, 103, 111, 139

Lowe, John T., naval officer, 91, 93, 103, 106, 119

MacArthur, Arthur, Jr., naval officer, 119

Mahan, Alfred Thayer, naval officer, 79

Maine, USS, battleship, 82, 116

Maneuverability, 10, 30, 41–42, 50, 53, 54, 84, 87–88, 110, 114–15

Maryborough (now Portlaoise), Queen's County, Ireland, 18

Massachusetts, USS, battleship, 3

Matsukata, Kogiro, Japanese naval engineer, 124, 126, 141

McClintock, James, submarine inventor, 5, 184

McKinley, William, President of the United States, 87

McNeir, C. S., Washington lawyer, 104

Menantic, English freighter, 128

Merrimack, CSS, ironclad, 17, 18

Meyers, Henry L., electrician, 83, 87

Mindora, yacht tender, 120

Mitchel, John, Irish journalist, 15, 23

Moccasin (USS *A-4*), 112, 118

Monitor, USS, ironclad, 17, 18, 42, 84

Moriarty, Thomas J., submarine inventor, 127

Morrell, Harry H., electrician, 104, 120

Morris, Charles A., inventor-engineer, 3, 49, 62, 63–64, 74, 76, 77, 79–81, 83, 85, 88, 90–91, 92, 93, 94, 95, 96, 98, 100–101, 102, 104, 105–6, 113, 120, 125, 130, 133–34, 143

Morris, USS, surface torpedo boat, 115

Morris and Cummings Dredging Company, 38, 41, 44, 46, 49, 62, 63

Motors. *See* Engines, electric

Mount Vernon, Va., 109, 110

Mulcahy, Dr. Dennis, Fenian leader, 35, 45–46, 47

Narkeeta, Navy tender, 82

Nautilus, Fulton's submarine, 6, 32, 184

Nautilus, submarine of Campbell and Ash, 58

Nautilus, USS (SSN-571), first nuclear submarine, 9

Nautilus Submarine Boat Company, 52–54, 55, 139

Naval Torpedo Station. *See* Newport, R.I.

Navigation, difficulties submerged, 22, 44, 52, 53, 62, 84, 87–88, 91, 102, 115

Navy Department, U.S., 51, 58–59, 61, 65, 69, 70, 72, 73–74, 84, 93, 111, 114, 124, 129, 130, 138

Nelson, Charles P., naval officer, 131

Newark, N.J., 49, 55, 61, 74, 78, 80, 98, 105, 124, 129, 130, 132, 133–34

New Haven, Conn., 46, 47, 68, 138

New London, Conn., 106

Newport, R.I., 21, 50, 70–71, 73, 96, 113–14, 115, 116, 127

Newport News Shipbuilding Company, Va., 128

New Suffolk, Long Island, N.Y., 100–102, 103, 104, 106, 107, 118–19, 120, *map* 181

New York Harbor, 5, 43, 46, 55, 56, 82, 89, 90–91, 93, 98, 125, *map* 180

Nimitz, Chester W., naval officer, 116

Nindemann, William F. C., gunner, 83, 85, 86, 87, 104, 110, 120, 133

Nixon, Lewis, naval officer and shipbuilder, 3–4, 74–75, 77, 79, 80, 89, 112, 113, 117, 120, 124, 125, 130, 131, 141

Noblett, Herman, electrician, 120

Nordenfeldt, submarine, 60, 139

Nordenfeldt, Thorsten, submarine inventor, 5, 8, 39, 56–57, 60, 61, 128

Norfolk Navy Yard, Norfolk, Va., 116

North Monastery, 136

Norway. *See* Strang, Georg

Octopus (USS *C-1*), 130

Oestr. See Lake's *Protector*

Old Orchard Shoal Light, Lower Bay, New York Harbor, 87, 93, *map* 180

Olympia, USS, Admiral Dewey's flagship, 89

Omniscope, Lake's device. *See* Periscope

Order of the Rising Sun, 140